Springer Business Cases

Editorial Board Members

Mehtap Aldogan Eklund, Department of CBA - Accountancy, University of Wisconsin–La Crosse, La Crosse, WI, USA

Karuna Jain, Shailesh J Mehta School of Management, Indian Institute of Technology Bombay, Mumbai, India

Dilip S. Mutum , School of Business, Monash University Malaysia, Subang Jaya, Malaysia

Henry Shi, Faculty of Arts, Business, Law and Economics, University of Adelaide, Adelaide, Australia

Marianna Sigala, Department of Business Administration, University of Piraeus, Athens, Greece

Springer Business Cases is a book series featuring the latest case studies in all areas of business, management, and finance, from around the world. The well-curated case collections in each of the books represent insights and lessons that can be used both in the classroom as well as in professional contexts. The books also place a focus on regional and topical diversity as well as encouraging alternative viewpoints which bring the knowledge forward. Both teaching cases as well as research cases are welcome.

Khaula Alkaabi • Veland Ramadani
Editors

Family Business Cases

Insights and Perspectives from the United Arab Emirates

Editors
Khaula Alkaabi
Geography and Urban Sustainability
Department
United Arab Emirates University
Al Ain City, United Arab Emirates

Veland Ramadani
Faculty of Business and Economics
South East European University
Tetovo, North Macedonia

ISSN 2662-5431　　　　　　　　ISSN 2662-544X　(electronic)
Springer Business Cases
ISBN 978-3-031-39251-1　　　　ISBN 978-3-031-39252-8　(eBook)
https://doi.org/10.1007/978-3-031-39252-8

© The Editor(s) (if applicable) and The Author(s), under exclusive license to Springer Nature Switzerland AG 2023

This work is subject to copyright. All rights are solely and exclusively licensed by the Publisher, whether the whole or part of the material is concerned, specifically the rights of translation, reprinting, reuse of illustrations, recitation, broadcasting, reproduction on microfilms or in any other physical way, and transmission or information storage and retrieval, electronic adaptation, computer software, or by similar or dissimilar methodology now known or hereafter developed.

The use of general descriptive names, registered names, trademarks, service marks, etc. in this publication does not imply, even in the absence of a specific statement, that such names are exempt from the relevant protective laws and regulations and therefore free for general use.

The publisher, the authors, and the editors are safe to assume that the advice and information in this book are believed to be true and accurate at the date of publication. Neither the publisher nor the authors or the editors give a warranty, expressed or implied, with respect to the material contained herein or for any errors or omissions that may have been made. The publisher remains neutral with regard to jurisdictional claims in published maps and institutional affiliations.

This Springer imprint is published by the registered company Springer Nature Switzerland AG
The registered company address is: Gewerbestrasse 11, 6330 Cham, Switzerland

To the Emirati families whose entrepreneurial spirit and dedication have shaped the landscape of business in the UAE. May your stories inspire future generations to continue your legacy and create a brighter future for all.

            Khaula Alkaabi

To my ancestors, Hajji Qazim, Hajji Ramadan, and Hajji Demirali for their entrepreneurial and philanthropic spirit, who decades ago had learned the business route to the Middle East, and back

            Veland Ramadani

Foreword

Family businesses are the backbone of many economies, especially in the United Arab Emirates (UAE). The UAE government gives special focus as they are considered vital for economic diversification and growth. These businesses create jobs, add economic value to countries, and are pioneers in entrepreneurship and innovation. Family firms are estimated to account for over 80 percent of the worldwide gross domestic product. According to Samara (2021), 90 percent of all businesses in the Arab Middle East are family firms, responsible for 80 percent of employment and 60 percent of Arab GDP. According to 2020 statistics, in the UAE alone, there were 350,000 Small and Medium Enterprises (SMEs) in the UAE. They represented over 94 percent of all companies operating in the country. They employed over 86 percent of the labor force in the private sector and made up over 60 percent of the GDP. Therefore, there is a need to be more scholarly case study literature on family-owned enterprises in the context of the UAE.

As a professor of entrepreneurship and family business at both the graduate and undergraduate levels, I find this book has been written with depth and understanding of the issues facing family businesses of UAE. It is an easy read, and family business students will find it enlightening. This book will help the reader get comprehensive and practical knowledge and the current status of family businesses in the UAE.

This book has fourteen chapters. The first chapter highlighted Al Masaood Group, a family-owned Emirati company, and summarized its business profile and market segments. The second chapter recognizes the importance of family businesses in UAE by covering deep insights into Barjeel Aerial Photography (BAPs). The third chapter explores Innovation Floor, its business profile, and services related to artificial intelligence, robotics applications, gaming & simulations for the education sector, GIS & Enterprise Solutions, smart devices, and a sample of its wearable technology incorporating augmented reality and virtual reality solutions. The fourth chapter explained the business plans of Securia Technologies through deep market analysis, the challenges in building the team, and financial and legal challenges. The fifth chapter covers an in-depth analysis of Safe City Group (SCG), uncovering its approaches and processes to deliver high-quality service packages to consumers across the Middle East. The sixth chapter focused on a tech start-up named MetaTouch. It explored its history, accomplishments, and challenges, emphasizing the essential roles of start-ups, academic institutions, and government support in fostering innovation and economic growth. In the seventh chapter, the authors introduced Nayel & Bin Harmal (NBH) Group, a family-owned construction company. They concentrated on their market segments, growth, sustainability efforts, and unwavering commitment to their morals, principles, and ethics. The eighth chapter provided a detailed overview of market segments and corporate social responsibility-related activities of DAMAC Group. The ninth chapter introduced a mobile cloud carwash services business, The Pronto Carwash Company, and its expansion plans. The tenth chapter concentrates on CADD Emirates Computers, a leading provider of CAD and engineering solutions, as well as ICT infrastructure, networking and security, hardware maintenance, and hospitality solutions. In chapter eleven, Nadheer et al. introduced and explained the extensive services of a notable commercial conglomerate, Bin Ham Group. The twelfth chapter describes ISpatial Tech, an AI company, and its information, leadership, business overview, products, projects, and rewards. Chapter 13 highlights the Juma Almajid Holding Group and its history, organizational structure, work culture, success factors, and significance in the Gulf region, while the last chapter discusses the history and achievements of M Glory Holding.

I look forward to making this book available to all my students as we continue to create an awareness of family businesses' vital role in the region's economy.

College of Business, Al Ain University Mosab I. Tabash Ph.D.
Al Ain, UAE

Reference

Samara, G. (2021). Family Businesses in the Arab Middle East: What do we know and where should we go? *Journal of Family Business Strategy, 12*(3), 100359.

Preface

The Importance of Family Business

Family businesses are an essential component of the global economy, contributing significantly to job creation, economic growth, and societal development. Family businesses are defined as companies in which a family holds a significant ownership stake and is actively involved in the management and decision-making process (Ramadani et al., 2023).

Family businesses account for a significant share of the global economy, with estimates suggesting that they contribute to more than 70% of the world's gross domestic product (GDP). In addition, family businesses are often long-standing and durable, with many of them being passed down through multiple generations. This longevity provides stability and continuity, which is crucial for economic growth and social development (Jahmurataj et al., 2023).

Family businesses have several advantages over non-family businesses. For instance, they tend to have a long-term perspective, which allows them to make strategic decisions that benefit the company and its stakeholders in the long run. They are also known for their commitment to their employees, customers, and communities, often being deeply rooted in the areas where they operate (Chang et al., 2022). In addition, family businesses tend to be more resilient during economic downturns, as they have a greater sense of responsibility to their stakeholders and are often better prepared for unexpected events (Alkaabi et al., 2023).

Family businesses face several unique challenges, such as managing family dynamics, succession planning, and balancing family interests with business objectives. However, with proper governance structures and planning, family businesses can overcome these challenges and achieve sustainable growth and success.

Structure of the Book

Family businesses play a significant role in the economy of the United Arab Emirates (UAE) and are a key contributor to the country's development and growth. They contribute to job creation, innovation, and societal development, while also representing the country's cultural and entrepreneurial spirit. They represent a unique feature of the UAE's business landscape, with a significant portion of the private sector consisting of family-owned and operated businesses.

This book, "Family Business Cases: Insights and Perspectives from the United Arab Emirates," brings together a collection of 14 case studies that showcase the diverse range of family businesses operating in the UAE. These cases provide insights into the challenges and opportunities faced by these businesses, their unique management practices, and their contribution to the development of the UAE's economy.

The case studies cover a diverse range of industries, from construction and technology to automobile manufacturing and smart city solutions. They also showcase the innovative and entrepreneurial spirit that characterizes the UAE's business landscape, particularly in the face of the COVID-19 pandemic.

Each chapter provides a unique perspective into the journey of a particular family business, offering readers an opportunity to understand the strategies, practices, and values that have contributed to their success. The authors provide a detailed analysis of the business models, the role of the family in decision-making, and the challenges faced by these businesses, making this book a valuable resource for business leaders, entrepreneurs, researchers, and students.

This book provides insights into the importance of family businesses in the UAE economy by highlighting fourteen cases of successful family-owned companies in various industries.

The *first chapter* is about the Al Masaood Group, which operates in 18 different market segments and is headquartered in Abu Dhabi. This chapter summarizes the company's business profile, market segments, geographical distribution, and diversification, as well as its initiatives related to women empowerment, CSR activities, and effective governance and leadership.

The *second chapter* is about Barjeel Aerial Photography (BAPs), a successful family-owned business in the photography industry. The chapter briefly describes BAPs' family dynamics, business overview, products, services, and projects completed, as well as its alignment with sustainable development goals.

The *third chapter* is about Innovation Floor, a technology-based company that offers services in artificial intelligence, gamification, GIS-based solutions development, and more. This chapter explores Innovation Floor's business profile, services, geographical distribution, and initiatives aligned with sustainable development goals.

The *fourth chapter* is about Securia Technologies, a family-owned business that focuses on implementing innovative technologies for smart and safe city development. This chapter discusses Securia's business plans, challenges, projects, and applications, as well as its initiatives related to sustainable development goals.

The *fifth chapter* involves Safe City Group (SCG), an Emirati family business that provides high-quality service packages to consumers across the Middle East. This chapter provides an in-depth analysis of SCG's approaches and processes, emphasizing SCG's business overview, geographic distribution, firm performance, and sustainable development initiatives. Start-ups play a crucial role in fueling innovation and economic growth by creating jobs and attracting investments.

The Emirati tech start-up MetaTouch is featured in the *sixth chapter* as an example of fruitful collaboration between academia, industry, and government support in fostering innovation and economic growth. This chapter explores MetaTouch's history, accomplishments, and challenges, highlighting the essential roles of start-ups, academic institutions, and government support in commercializing lab-developed products and services.

The *seventh chapter* addresses the Nayel & Bin Harmal (NBH) Group, a family-owned business in the UAE that has made significant contributions to the country's overall development. The chapter provides an overview of NBH's market segments and summarizes NBH's projects and activities aligned with the sustainable development goals (SDGs).

Chapter eight discusses DAMAC Group which is another well-known family-owned enterprise in the UAE that has grown into an excellent and diverse portfolio in a variety of industries. The chapter provides insights into the history of DAMAC Group since its inception, the locations of the spread of branches around the Emirates, and a detailed overview of its market segments and corporate social responsibility-related activities.

The *ninth chapter* discusses Pronto Carwash, a mobile carwash and cleaning service. The company offers car washing, waxing, and house cleaning services and has plans to expand by increasing the number of well-prepared vehicles.

The *tenth chapter* focuses on CADD Emirates Computers, a leading provider of CAD and engineering solutions, as well as ICT infrastructure, networking and security, hardware maintenance, and hospitality solutions. With a focus on innovation and strategic planning, CADD Emirates is well-positioned for continued success and utilizes location-based analytics tools to transport goods and services to its clients efficiently.

The *eleventh chapter* discusses the Bin Ham Group, a diversified commercial conglomerate in the UAE, highlighting its success and contributions to the UAE's economy and society. The company's focus on sustainable business practices and implementation of Sustainable Development Goals (SDGs) across its divisions is also discussed.

The *twelfth chapter* introduces ISpatial Tech, an AI company that provides solutions for smart cities. The study includes an overview of the company's history, leadership, products, projects, and rewards. This chapter emphasizes the benefits of using AI and machine learning in companies, such as increased efficiency and better decision-making.

Chapter *thirteenth* discusses Juma Almajid as a business that has played a significant role in the country's sustainable urban development by implementing state-of-the-art real estate projects. This chapter provides an overview of Juma Al Majid Holding group, its history, organizational structure, work culture, success factors, and significance in the Gulf region.

Chapter *fourteenth* highlights the accomplishments of Dr. Majida Alazazi, an Emirati businesswoman who founded and managed several factories, including the first gasoline and electric car factories in the UAE. This chapter also discusses M Glory Holding Group's organizational structure and plan to invest in a new assembly and production facility for electric vehicles, aligning with the UAE's national strategy for economic diversification and sustainability.

We would like to express our gratitude to the authors of each chapter who have contributed to this book and to the family businesses who have shared their insights and experiences with us. We hope that this book will serve as an inspiration to other family businesses and contribute to the continued growth and success of the UAE's economy.

Al Ain City, UAE   Khaula A. Alkaabi
Tetovo, North Macedonia   Veland Ramadani

References

Alkaabi, K., Ramadani, V., & Zeqiri, J. (2023). Universities, Entrepreneurial Ecosystem, and Family Business Performance: Evidence from the United Arab Emirates. *Journal of Knowledge Economy*. https://doi.org/10.1007/s13132-023-01384-9

Chang, E.P.C., Zare, S., & Ramadani, V. (2022). How a larger family business is different from a non-family one? *Journal of Business Research*, 139(1), 292-302

Jahmurataj, V., Ramadani, V., Bexheti, A., Rexhepi, G., Abazi-Alili, H., & Krasniqi, B. (2023). Unveiling the determining factors of family business longevity: Evidence from Kosovo. *Journal of Business Research*, 159 (April), 113745

Ramadani, V., Aloulou, W., & Zainal, M. (2023). *Family Business in Gulf Cooperation Council Countries*, Springer, Cham.

Acknowledgment

We would like to thank the respectable contributors of this volume to the upmost degree. The generosity and dedication shown through their experience, knowledge, and research were priceless. Without them, this book would never find its way to academic researchers, students, entrepreneurs, and policymakers.

To our colleague, a respectable researcher and good connoisseur of the Middle East business environment, Professor Mosab Tabash, we would like to extend a special acknowledgment for his appreciated foreword to this book. His remarkable ability to address readers with his thoughts and views provides justifiable proof of the significance of this pioneering book about informal ethnic entrepreneurship in an international context.

We are infinitely grateful to the owners and managers of family businesses, who agreed to offer their support, information, and views on the development of family businesses in the United Arab Emirates (UAE). A huge respect to the Emirati families, who have built successful businesses, generation after generation. Their unwavering dedication to hard work, innovation, and perseverance is a true inspiration to us all. Their commitment to family values and traditions, while also embracing modernity and progress, has made a significant contribution to the economic development of the UAE. Without them, the publication of this book would be impossible.

We owe a debt of gratitude to the United Arab Emirates University (UAEU) for the unreserved support of this research through its Research and Sponsored Projects Office (Grant No. G00003738).

To Springer's editors, Prashanth Mahagaonkar and Neelofar Yasmeen and their splendid team, we are grateful for their thoughtful suggestions, support, and encouragement that were offered and well received.

Finally, to our families, friends, and colleagues, we must express our affectionate thanks. They stood by us since the very first beginning when the idea of this book was launched. Their support and motivation are always irreplaceable and necessary for each of us. We dedicate our gratitude, appreciation, and love for them.

Khaula A. Alkaabi
Veland Ramadani

Contents

Al Masaood Group: Through Diversification and Geographical Expansion to Success 1
Khaula Alkaabi and Abdul Samad Farooq

Barjeel Aerial Photography Services: A Successful Geospatial Data Acquisition Company 23
Marwa Mohammed Al Suwaidi and Cristina I. Fernandes

Innovation Floor: 4.0 Technologies and Information Solutions 37
Khaled Khamis Al Arafati and Léo-Paul Dana

Secuira Technologies: Re-innovating Smart Technology 51
Abdulla Al Naqbi and Cristina Blanco González Tejero

Safe City Group: Enable Cities Safety 73
Aaesha Saif Ahmed Shehhi and Veland Ramadani

MetaTouch: A Case of Successful Transformation of a Research Idea into a Start-Up During the COVID-19 Pandemic 85
Fady Alnajjar and Yehya Al Marzooqi

Nayel & Bin Harmal Group: Integrated Services in the Construction Sector 97
Hessa Alkalbani, Eiman Almazrouei, and Veland Ramadani

DAMAC Group: Symbol of Successful Development 111
Sara Omar Aljaberi and Khaula Alkaabi

Pronto Carwash Company: Your Ride to the Mobility Car Wash 123
Asma Mohammed Al Madhaani and Mahra Al-Ali

CADD Emirates Computers: Providing Cutting-Edge Technology Solutions and Services for a Digital-First World 137
Mariam Slayem Alblooshi and Abeer Alyammahi

Bin Ham Group: Building a Legacy of Excellence in United Arab Emirates Investments 153
Aysha Nadheer, Fatima S. Alawani, and Ramo Palalić

iSpatial Tech: GEO-AI-Enabled Solutions for Smart Cities........ 173
Reda Maroufi, Jaber Mohammed Alketbi, and Marco Valeri

**Juma Al Majid Holding Group: Story of Success
and Achievement**... 201
Esra Qasemi, Hafsah Alderei, and Grisna Anggadwita

**M Glory Holding: The Aspiration to Establish an Automobile
Manufacturing Industry in the United Arab Emirates**.............. 213
Khaula Alkaabi and Majida Alazazi

About the Editors

Khaula A. Alkaabi is a Professor in the Geography and Urban Sustainability Department at UAEU. She holds a BA degree from UAEU; an MA and a Ph.D. in Geography from UNCG in the USA; and a Public Sector Innovation Diploma from the University of Cambridge in the UK. Her research interests include transportation, land use planning, spatial analysis and geostatistics, GIS, drone applications, economic geography, smart cities, entrepreneurship, and innovation. She was the Chair of the Geography Department from 2013 to 2017, and the Chief Innovation Officer for UAEU from 2015 to 2022. She has published several academic articles in scientific international journals like the Journal of Transport Geography, Frontiers, Journal of Enterprising Communities, Geomatics Natural Hazards and Risk, Journal of Cleaner Production, and Transportation Research Part F. She has published several book chapters with Ashgate, Routledge, and Springer. She has received several research grants and rewards including UAEU's "University Excellence Award for Service Excellence" in 2022, "Outstanding Leadership Awards in Education" in 2022, "Feminine Monitoring for Sustainable Environment Award" in 2019, and the "Best Academic Research at Sustainable Transport Competition" by RTA in 2018.

Veland Ramadani is a Professor of Entrepreneurship and Family Business at the Faculty of Business and Economics, South East European University, North Macedonia. His research interests include entrepreneurship, small business management, and family businesses. He authored or co-authored around 200 research articles and book chapters, 12 textbooks, and 28 edited books. He has published in *Journal of Business Research, International Entrepreneurship and Management Journal, International Journal of Entrepreneurial Behavior and Research,* and *Technological Forecasting and Social Change,* among others. Dr. Ramadani is co-Editor-in-Chief of *Journal of Enterprising Communities* (JEC). He has received the Award for Excellence 2016—Outstanding Paper by Emerald Group Publishing. In addition, Dr. Ramadani was invited as a keynote speaker in several international conferences and as a guest lecturer by President University, Indonesia, and Telkom University, Indonesia. During the 2017-2021, he served as a member of Supervisory Board of Development Bank of North Macedonia, where for 10 months acted as Chief Operating Officer (COO), as well. In 2023, four times in a row, based on the Stanford University's study, he was ranked among the Top 2% of the most influential scientists in the world.

Al Masaood Group: Through Diversification and Geographical Expansion to Success

Khaula Alkaabi and Abdul Samad Farooq

Abstract

By examining the perspectives and insights of family-owned businesses in the United Arab Emirates (UAE), one can gain a better comprehension of the continuity of such enterprises, which account for a significant portion of the GDP in Gulf Corporation Council countries. This chapter aims to provide a concise overview of Al Masaood Group, an Emirati company that is family owned and headquartered in Abu Dhabi, UAE, with operations and partnerships spanning 18 different market segments. The business profile and market segments of Al Masaood Group, as well as its geographic reach and diversification, are summarized in this chapter. Moreover, this chapter touches on several noteworthy insights into Al Masaood Group's response to the operational challenges posed by the pandemic, their effective human resource policies, financial planning strategies, initiatives aimed at promoting gender equality, and their sound governance and leadership practices. Additionally, this chapter briefly discusses several of the company's corporate social responsibility (CSR) initiatives.

K. Alkaabi (✉)
Geography and Urban Sustainability Department, United Arab Emirates University, Al Ain City, United Arab Emirates
e-mail: khaula.alkaabi@uaeu.ac.ae

A. S. Farooq
School of Mechanical Engineering, Shanghai Jiao Tong University, Shanghai, China
e-mail: abdulsamad@sjtu.edu.cn

© The Author(s), under exclusive license to Springer Nature Switzerland AG 2023
K. Alkaabi, V. Ramadani (eds.), *Family Business Cases*, Springer Business Cases,
https://doi.org/10.1007/978-3-031-39252-8_1

1 Introduction

Family businesses are the foundation of economic growth in both developed and developing nations, and they are crucial to the sustainability and development of the global economy, promoting economic stability and wealth creation. In the realm of free economies, family businesses account for more than 80% of all businesses (Ramadani et al., 2023). Therefore, at least two-thirds of all businesses globally are family businesses, which generate between 70 and 90% of the global GDP and more than half of all employment in industrialized nations (Oudah et al., 2018).

In terms of the Gulf Cooperation Council (GCC) region, family-owned businesses are responsible for generating over 90% of the private sector's employment and contribute to 80% of the non-oil and gas GDP of the region (Darwish et al., 2020). Similarly, family-owned businesses make up 90% of the private sector in the UAE (Darwish et al., 2020), highlighting their essential role in driving the GCC economy forward. According to the Federal Competitiveness and Statistics Center's latest data, the UAE's non-oil sector's contribution to the country's GDP has risen from 71.3% in 2020 to 72.3% in 2021 (Gulf Business, 2022), as depicted in Fig. 1.

Family businesses can come in various forms, such as small and medium-sized enterprises, start-ups, and large family-run conglomerates (Alkaabi, 2020). In most cases, these businesses are controlled by a small group of insiders or a single family member. While this structure provides several advantages, it can also result in some drawbacks. Family influence can potentially interfere with corporate governance if decisions are made exclusively within the family circle. This can lead to talented outsiders from other families becoming frustrated and disengaged. However, as noted by Sorenson and Bierman (2009), a firm directive from a family member or a small number of family stakeholders usually results in the best performance for family businesses. Figure 2 provides an overview of the crucial factors that influence the success of family businesses.

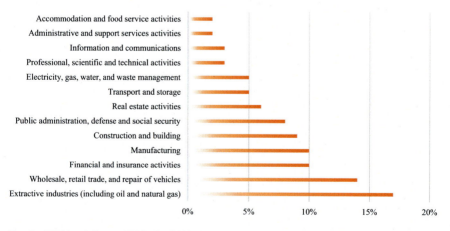

Fig. 1 GDP breakdown of UAE by 2020. Source: Statista (2022)

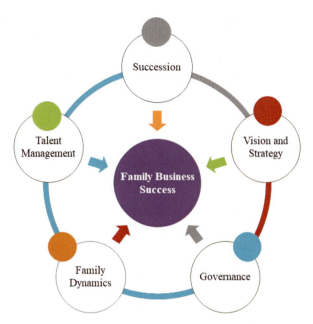

Fig. 2 Factors behind family business success. Source: Factors retrieved from the following references (Clauß et al., 2022; Abu Dhabi Chamber, 2019)

Succession planning can be challenging for family businesses due to the culture of secrecy surrounding them (Tharawat Magazine, 2013). It is essential for each firm to pass on its business obligations from one generation to the next, but the head of a family may face difficulties in making informed decisions that do not negatively impact the company's asset value. In surveys conducted among family business members, the long-term sustainability of a family business or conglomerate's business model was identified as one of the top concerns and risks. Finding a solution to these issues can be one of the most challenging aspects for family business owners, in addition to establishing and expanding the business successfully (Sharma et al., 2012).

The UAE government has recognized the importance of family businesses to the economy and has taken steps to improve the business environment for such enterprises. In 2015, the Abu Dhabi authorities established the Abu Dhabi Global Market on Al Maryah Island to support and facilitate private-sector asset management (ADGM, n.d.). This move has attracted investors from both inside and outside Abu Dhabi, who appreciate the ease of registration, numerous double tax treaties, lack of domestic taxes, status of a UAE company, common law jurisdiction, and other benefits offered under one roof. The government encourages investors with a background in family businesses to participate, creating opportunities for successful entrepreneurs. Additionally, the Tharawat Family Business Forum, founded in 2006 to provide thought leadership and networking opportunities, offers learning and educational programs to promote family businesses in the Arab world (Abu Dhabi Chamber, 2019).

Family businesses prioritize tangible areas such as family dynamics, business services, geographic distribution of firms, customers and business partners, leadership, gender equality, and values to ensure business stability and success. These factors are crucial for any well-established company, and in this regard, this chapter presents an overview of Al Masaood Group, a prominent family business-based enterprise in the UAE. The chapter highlights several attributes that have played a pivotal role in the company's remarkable growth over the years.

2 Business Overview

The Al Masaood Group is a family-owned enterprise headquartered in Abu Dhabi, UAE with businesses and partnerships spanning 18 different market segments. Al Masaood started as a family business in 1970 as a collaboration between three founding brothers: Ahmed Al Masaood, Rahma Al Masaood, and Abdulla Al Masaood. Al Masaood is one of the great trading families of Abu Dhabi, known as successful merchants in the UAE and the Arabian Gulf for more than five decades. The first chairman of the Al Masaood Group, the late Ahmed Al Masaood, also worked as the first president of the Abu Dhabi Chamber of Commerce, and the Al Masaood enterprises were among the first to be registered by the chamber in 1970. As a result, they have been a part of Abu Dhabi's commercial development since their inception (Al Masaood, n.d.).

Al Masaood has now adopted compliance and governance models to conduct all of its business transactions in a fair, ethical, and impartial manner, ensuring there is no appearance of impropriety. They are incorporated as an LLC (Limited Liability Company) under the control of family-appointed directors that oversee an independent management team of professionals and have adopted the latest international standards of company management. Reporting to the directors through an established authority matrix are the executive committee, the three CEOs of the primary business divisions, GMS, and the heads of corporate support functions. The directors represent the family ownership and are responsible for establishing the company's strategic vision, while the day-to-day operations of the company are handled by the C-level executives, who are accountable for the performance of the business unit. Establishing a proper legal and governance structure has been a key strategy of the second generation of leadership.

Al Masaood Group has a rich history of successful collaborations in various industries. One of its first partnerships was with British company John Brown Engineering to bring the first gas turbine to the Middle East in 1970. The Group later teamed up with Weir Westgarth to establish the UAE's inaugural desalination plant. The Al Masaood name has since become strongly associated with the automotive industry due to its more than 30-year affiliation with Nissan. Additionally, renowned companies such as Bridgestone, Fluor Corporation, and Volvo Penta have leveraged the Al Masaood platform to establish themselves in Abu Dhabi. Currently, the Al Masaood Group plays a crucial role in promoting the social, economic, and commercial development of the United Arab Emirates by operating, developing, and

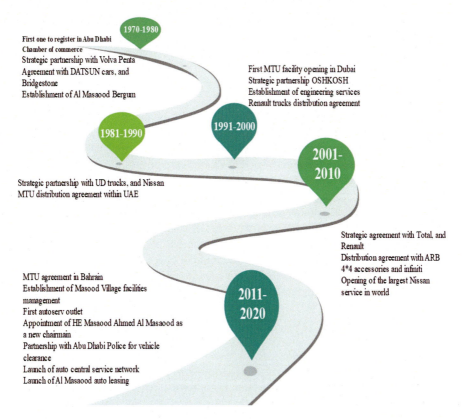

Fig. 3 A brief overview and history timeline of the Al Masaood Group. Source: Al Masaood (n.d.). Published with the company's permission

expanding a diverse network of businesses that demonstrate the robust and dynamic nature of Abu Dhabi's economy. Figure 3 illustrates a brief historical timeline of the Al Masaood Group, while the important market segments it covers are summarized in detail.

2.1 Automotive

With over 40 years of experience in the UAE's automobile industry, Al Masaood has established itself as a prominent dealer for Nissan, Infiniti, Renault, and Bridgestone in Abu Dhabi, Dubai, Al Ain, and the Western Region. In addition, they have expanded their network to include the Kingdom of Bahrain. The Group's automobile division boasts an extensive network of spare parts dealers and well-equipped service centers. Recently, they opened the Al Masaood Automobiles Nissan Service Centre, which is the most central service facility for Nissan globally. The division places great emphasis on maintaining the high service standards set by the Group, investing in its showroom and service facilities, and employing highly skilled personnel to ensure customer satisfaction and long-term relationships.

2.2 Industrial

Al Masaood LLC plays a vital role in the UAE's sustainable growth and economic diversity by offering a wide range of industrial solutions to strategic sectors, such as oil and gas, utilities, marine, heavy equipment and machinery, logistics, and modular construction. In addition, their Industrial Divisions cater to specific Retail industries, including the Automotive and Accessories sectors. They provide a diverse range of goods and services through collaborations with well-known international companies and locally developed manufacturing techniques. The company has developed some of the largest repair and maintenance, remanufacturing, and operational facilities in the UAE to support the nation and the region through its power, engineering, and industrial divisions. Al Masaood LLC is committed to advancing the UAE's industrial sectors by working with a portfolio of international brands, such as Volvo Penta, MTU, UD Trucks, Renault Trucks, KSB, BBV, MAN Energy, Bridgestone, Total, ARB, Leroy Somer, and TCM, among others.

2.3 Business Services

Al Masaood's Business Services Division is composed of several specialized areas, including insurance, law, IT, hotel, and hygiene services. Each of these entities is dedicated to delivering exceptional corporate services in line with Al Masaood's core values and commitment to excellence, providing essential support to the company's overall business operations.

2.4 Retail

Al Masaood has diversified interests in the retail industry, serving as a distributor of renowned brands and offering consumer and personal services. Its retail offerings span a range of products, including jewelry, flowers, hospitality, artwork, sporting goods, and leather items, available at its various stores.

2.5 Marine

The marine industry has been an integral part of Al Masaood's history since its inception, starting with the ownership of pearling dhows. Today, the Group has diversified into various areas within the marine sector, including commercial vessels, boat manufacturing, marine leisure equipment, marine engines, charter yachts, and yacht brokerage. With multiple waterside facilities, the Group provides comprehensive service and repair to commercial, military, and recreational ships. Al Masaood is the exclusive distributor in the UAE for a range of reputable brands, including MTU, Volvo Penta, 3 M, Hempel Paints, SP Systems, and Mares.

2.6 Real Estate

The construction division has successfully accomplished numerous projects adhering to global standards. They have provided essential services and product support for the development of real estate and infrastructure in the Middle East and North Africa regions. Moreover, the division has been actively involved in state-of-the-art production facilities projects in the UAE.

2.7 Power Division

Al Masaood Power Division, which was founded in 1972, has a rich history in the global diesel and gas-driven power generating industry. The division has formed a strong strategic alliance with key industry leaders in the UAE, such as DEWA, ADWEA, SEWA, and others. However, in recent years, the economies of the GCC countries have been preparing for a future without petroleum. Their policies have shifted away from relying solely on oil receipts to fuel their progress in modern society. Despite oil remaining a major player in the energy industry in the UAE, particularly with the discovery of new oil fields, the future direction is leaning toward embracing more renewable energy resources.

Based on the foregoing motivation, Al Masaood Group is planning to expand its portfolio into renewable energy. This change in direction is clearly reflected in the policy statement made by the current general manager of Al Masaood Power Division:

> We know how crucial our role is in the adoption and spread of various new technologies for energy generation, and we are committed to become the active partner of UAE government in help preparing the country for post-oil-era; Therefore, Al Masaood power division is looking forward to invest in developing smart grids and hydrogen, considering it as a fuel of future.

Furthermore, the Group plans to implement relevant initiatives according to top industry trends, including continued investments in renewable energy that have started over the last decade. All the strategies are essential to Al Masaood Power Division's path toward the future, and they will reshape its market leadership during the twenty-first century.

Figure 4 displays a brief organizational flow chart that highlights the essential business segments of the Al Masaood Group.

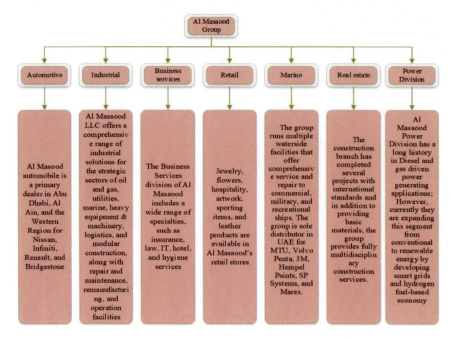

Fig. 4 Organizational flow chart of multiple business segments within the Al Masaood Group. Source: Al Masaood (n.d.). Published with the company's permission

3 Geographical Distribution and Diversification

The concept of geographical distribution diversification involves a company expanding its operations into various business segments and locations. It is considered a vital corporate and business strategy for many firms, including those in the service, IT, and retail industries. This strategy presents new market prospects for business expansion while also stabilizing overall returns across diverse economic situations and corporate laws in different market regions (Fang & van Lelyveld, 2014). Therefore, to achieve growth, family firms can adopt four key strategies: market penetration, development of new products or services, market development, and diversification of business (Hansen & Juslin, 2018).

Diversifying and geographical expansion offer several benefits; for instance, they increase brand exposure, attract new customers to the business, open up new revenue streams, and minimize seasonal risks due to economies of scope, as per below.

3.1 Benefits of Geographical Distribution and Diversification

3.1.1 More Customers

Customers are essential to the survival of any business, and sustained success largely depends on the ability to attract and retain a large customer base. One of the most effective ways for businesses to expand their reach is through vertical and conglomerate diversification. Vertical expansion allows organizations to benefit from both B2B and B2C sales, while conglomerate expansion introduces them to an entirely new group of consumers.

Diversification strategies can be particularly advantageous for small and medium-sized enterprises (SMEs) as they offer a means of attracting new clients without the need for significant investments in personnel or resources. Therefore, diversification is a sensible approach for business owners who want to expand their customer base without starting a new company or making radical changes to their existing business strategy.

3.1.2 Income Security

Operating a corporation always involves a certain amount of risk, and no business owner can predict what the future will bring, whether it is market disruptions or public health emergencies. Additionally, small organizations are often more vulnerable to difficulties due to their limited revenue sources, particularly if they are just starting out. However, business owners can take steps to mitigate these risks.

Expanding geographic reach and diversifying business lines can grant businesses immediate access to a wider range of markets. Successful implementation of this strategy has the potential to bolster a small business's revenue stream while simultaneously expanding its market presence.

3.1.3 Consistent Demand

Businesses that offer a limited range of goods or services may encounter recurring demand patterns, such as peak activity during the summer for a hospitality business or an increased demand for heating and snow removal services during the winter. Furthermore, cyclical businesses are susceptible to the overall economy, meaning that economic expansion or contraction can significantly impact their revenue.

Expanding geographically and diversifying their operations is an attractive option for businesses to cope with slow times and stabilize their seasonal sales. By doing so, businesses can increase their resilience to changing market demands, thus improving their long-term agility.

3.1.4 Broader Brand Recognition

Establishing ties with customers and entering new markets is vital to a business's success. This requires increased brand recognition, and small and medium-sized enterprises (SMEs) must take steps to improve their brand awareness. Diversification and expansion not only increase profits but they can also be utilized to promote a business effectively. Such efforts help to advertise the brand to new audiences and demographics, resulting in a more organic marketing approach that is highly effective in raising brand awareness compared to other marketing tactics.

3.2 Geographical Distribution and Diversification of Al Masaood Group

The Al Masaood Group, established in 1970, has diversified its business into 18 market segments, as discussed in the previous section. The Group's geographical distribution is well-formed as they operate their businesses across the UAE and have expanded to the Kingdom of Bahrain, making them one of the most reliable brands with significant outreach to customers.

Selecting the proper location is crucial for maximizing sales and revenue. The key characteristics for geographical distribution include being located in a central business district or at a convenient distance from it, accessibility to public transport and a developed road network, access to key markets, land price or average rental price, residential and industry density, availability of free parking, and pollution levels in the area. However, accessibility is considered the most important factor in deciding the location of a business, as it directly affects customer outreach.

Taking Al Masaood Automobiles in Abu Dhabi as an example, Fig. 5 shows that the Group has opened most of its automobile stores in prime locations in the central

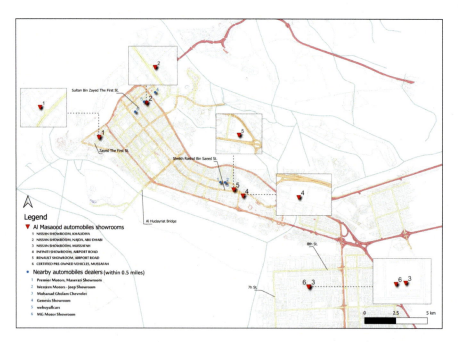

Fig. 5 Geographical distribution of Al Masaood automobiles in Abu Dhabi. Source: Information retrieved using Google Earth (October 20, 2022). Published with the company's permission

and industrial district, significantly enhancing their visibility and outreach to customers. Their stores are surrounded by developed road networks, near key landmarks, and have access to public transport. Furthermore, their stores are well-equipped with amenities such as attractive infrastructure, adequate parking space, highly qualified staff, and customer support, which differentiate them from their competitors.

The Al Masaood Group's diversified portfolio provides them with a wider reach to customers, as their stores offer various buying options such as Nissan, Infiniti, and Renault. Additionally, being located near competitors results in healthy competition, which ultimately leads to more customers in the area, resulting in increased business and higher revenues. The majority of their revenues are generated in Abu Dhabi, with 50% of the business being split between B2C, B2G, and B2B. As a result, Al Masaood Group has experienced significant growth in recent years. Despite the pandemic, they anticipate continued business growth and operational synergies across their diverse portfolio in the coming years.

4 Effective HR Policies

In a matter of months from December 2019, a severe acute respiratory syndrome coronavirus 2 transformed the entire world of work (Almeida & Santos, 2020). Due to the risks of catching the virus, businesses and consumers changed their behavior, resulting in millions of workers losing their jobs or being put on government assistance programs. Millions radically change their work mode, shifting to their homes from offices for the same reason, which increases the overall risk of job security (International Labour Organization, 2020). Similarly, the unemployment rate in the UAE increased from 2.23% in 2019 to 3.19% in 2020 (The Global Economy, 2021). The UAE government implemented various measures to support businesses and workers during the pandemic, including wage subsidies, loan programs, and allowing for remote work arrangements. These measures helped to mitigate some of the negative impacts of the pandemic on employment in the UAE. The subsequent challenge for HR is to make significant efforts in human resource management to eliminate the negative economic and social consequences of COVID-19. Nonetheless, Al Masaood Group's HR department worked tirelessly during the pandemic to secure the job and basic rights of their employees. According to the Head of Corporate Support and Group HR,

> We have not had to take extreme measures; however, we need to ensure we can protect the business through this crisis. When everything gets back to normal, and it's debatable what that might look like, companies that have let people go will need to get back up to speed. How that will work in practice is anyone's guess. We haven't been here before; however, undoubtedly, there will be an acceleration of hiring to meet customer demand for products and services that have been dormant during the crisis.

Furthermore, it is crucial to attract top talent since they possess specialized skills that allow them to carry out their tasks efficiently and effectively, meeting deadlines and making the most of available resources. However, one of the crucial questions is, where will the top talent decide to work, and what is the top talent today? According to the Head of Corporate Support and Group HR at Al Masaood Group,

> Top talents are the people who aim to exceed expectations consistently, are self-starters and are more accountable to themselves than others. They want enjoyable work experiences, including being with like-minded colleagues and having challenging and interesting work assignments. They want the freedom to deliver and won't stay long if their bosses are mediocre and apply outdated management practices. They are A-team platers that all employers in the industry want as part of their work community.

Furthermore, he also stated,

> We don't pick top talent anymore. It means that we have to work hard to build our employer's brand. Our approach during the crisis will reflect our values, which will be an important determining factor for top talent. Additionally, top talent will also be seeking competitive packages, career growth, training opportunities, and a healthy working environment.

In 2017, LinkedIn conducted a talent survey that involved over 14,000 professionals from more than 20 countries. The research revealed that, under normal circumstances, 90% of professionals worldwide express an interest in hearing about new job opportunities (LinkedIn, 2017). According to Thakkar (2022), 78% of the job market prioritizes a company's reputation and values, which are reflected in their actions and how they treat their employees. Conversely, 80% of employers emphasized that their company's employer brand significantly affects their ability to attract top talent. It is worth noting that nearly 75% of candidates are discouraged from working for a company with a poor reputation for leadership and negative online employer reviews, even if they are currently unemployed (Thakkar, 2022). Considering these factors, the Head of Corporate Support and Group HR at Al Masaood Group commented,

> We need to ensure our actions reveal our values of empowerment, optimism, engagement, excellence, and one team underpinned by our mission statement. It makes us attractive as an employer of choice and ensures our employees are happy and fulfilled at what they do, which drives our HR strategy, and I don't see a need to change that anytime soon.

5   Leadership and Governance

Good governance plays a significant role in developing influential leaders with the right vision when making decisions. Once incorporated, it empowers top management to better prepare for the company's future and achieves high transparency through an effective check and balance system.

Those at the helm are also provided with an opportunity to foster and encourage improved collaboration and communication, guaranteeing that everyone is on the same page when implementing a business strategy. Throughout the process, leadership skills are tested and enhanced as they work to address team differences and reach smart solutions while considering and appreciating different perspectives.

Therefore, effective corporate governance can be a good tool for leadership development and overcoming operational challenges. Consequently, allowing the leadership to collectively work towards meeting the company's overall objectives. Without a robust corporate governance structure in place, the long-term survival of a business enterprise will be impacted.

Building a resilient corporate governance structure necessitate putting together a strong board of directors. It is wise to have a group of people with proven expertise, diverse professional background, and impeccable integrity. The board is integral to establishing good corporate governance, especially if the executive members are current about the company's issues and concerns.

Additionally, it pays to engage with trusted team members who deeply value corporate governance as a living concept, ensuring they synchronize with the company's goals. When putting in place the right governance structure, we need to remember that the organization's best interests take precedence. Relevant policies and principles should be geared toward what is best for the business while fulfilling the commitment to stakeholders.

Furthermore, the effective business structure should manage the following objectives: succession at the top, quality and consistency of decision-making, and necessary checks in the decision-making process. All these and more are fundamental to business longevity, which ultimately is the primary objective. Having a right and clear outlook, goal, and approach are a few vital steps towards implementing reliable and effective governance.

6 Business in the Digital Era

Studies suggest that returning to the pre-pandemic era is a far-fetched fact. Digital spaces have replaced many of our human encounters, which has swiftly changed the game for brands. Brands that were not ahead of the digital curve lost their battle too soon, necessitating that brands encourage digital expansion. A digital growth plan involves more than merely launching social media campaigns and watching for material to receive likes, shares, and comments. A digital growth strategy examines all facets of your company's online presence and considers how to improve it with the specific goal of fostering commercial expansion. When properly implemented, a digital growth strategy boosts website traffic, increases online inquiries, and nurtures your prospects through the online sales funnel.

Realizing the importance of digital expansion, Al Masaood Group has focused on offering its products and services through the Internet and mobile apps. They are the very first automobile dealer to launch a Nissan e-commerce website for the Nissan brand. Moreover, they have launched virtual sales channels that offer a "Connected Live Interactive Experience." They have also launched a live and virtual customer feedback digital platform for developing an interactive customer experience and empowering positive changes in the business.

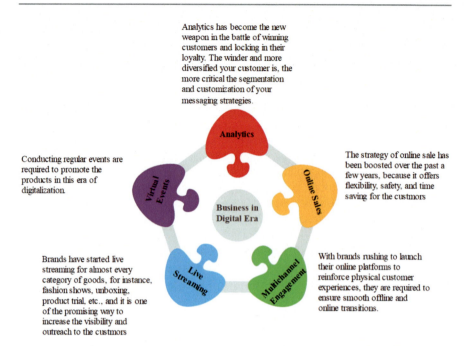

Fig. 6 Graphical illustration of essential characteristics of a business in digital era shortlisted by the head of Al Masaood Group marketing and corporate communication. Source: Al Masaood (n.d.). Published with the company's permission

Considering the importance of business in the digital era, the head of Al Masaood Group marketing and corporate communication shortlisted a few digital marketing strategies that have so far dominated the business front post-pandemic, as illustrated in Fig. 6.

6.1 Analytics

Using analytics has become a crucial tool in the competition for attracting and retaining customers. The broader and more diverse your customer base, the more crucial it is to segment and customize your messaging strategies.

6.2 Online Sales

While customers were predicted to one day give up on owning a car and the overall car market would plummet, according to Reuters, a few manufacturers have been gaining market share. Following such companies, Al Masaood Automobiles also experienced a surge in sales and their overall market share during the pandemic due to their efficient digital marketing strategies.

6.3 Multichannel Engagement

With brands rushing to launch their online platforms to reinforce physical customer experiences, they are required to ensure smooth offline and online transitions.

6.4 Livestreaming

Brands have started live streaming for almost every category of goods, for instance, fashion shows, unboxings, product trials, etc. Therefore, the Al Masaood Group's sales team believes that the "in-the-now" aspect of a live stream has connected customers and brands during the lockdown.

6.5 Virtual Events

Conducting regular events is required to promote the products in this era of digitalization. Realizing its importance, the marketing and corporate communication head of the Al Masaood Group stated,

> I have been part of the industry for many years now, yet I have never imagined that a time would come when I would launch a car or flagship product online.

Today, brands can easily connect with their customers and offer them an "I-will-come-to-you" service. Family businesses are now presented with an amazing opportunity to grow their enterprises simultaneously through cross-pollination of their customer base and omnichannel implementation. As the adaptation of new technologies accelerates even faster, businesses have also made a royal upgrade and amplified their digital marketing.

7 Women Empowerment

Empowerment is a motivational process that revolves around an individual's perception of having personal control or influence over their actions in the workplace, ultimately leading to enhanced performance, employee satisfaction, loyalty, and service delivery. The UAE has continuously supported women's empowerment across all disciplines. The successes and achievements of Emirati women in diverse domains reflect the vision of the UAE's founding father, Sheikh Zayed Bin Sultan Al Nahyan, who once said,

> The woman is half of the society, any country which pursues development should not leave her in poverty or illiteracy. (Tolba, 2022)

Since then, the UAE has come a long way toward improving Emirati women's status in all spheres of society. Today, this is evident in the fact that the nation has nine female ministers, making up 30% of all cabinet positions—one of the highest percentages in the region (The UAE Gender Balance Council, n.d.). Likewise, Al Masaood Group views Emirati women as partners in the company's success and is always working to provide them with the skills they need to support and advance in their professions as part of its mission to carry forward the vision of the company's wise leadership.

Recently, to celebrate Emirati Women's Day on August 22, the Al Masaood Group organized a female majlis with the theme "You Are a Gem." Emirati women from across the Group were invited to this event in honor of and appreciation for their motivational traits and significant contributions to the company's growth. They encourage female employees to pursue opportunities at every level of the corporate ladder to diversify their managerial and executive positions. Since Al Masaood is highly industrial and transportation-driven, the majority of the company's employee count is blue-collar: mechanics, service advisors, warehouse managers, construction workers, and drivers; hence, the majority of the workers are male. However, on the administration side of the business, Al Masaood provides ample managerial positions for women, with the majority of the corporate support businesses led by senior female leaders. They have developed effective HR policies for women employees, including equal pay, equal opportunity for growth, flexible hours, and work-from-home arrangements.

8 Financial Planning

Financial planning is the process of figuring out how a company will be able to fulfill its objectives and strategic goals. The development and implementation of effective financial planning necessitate several steps, such as determining the financial data and establishing future goals, analyzing and evaluating the data, strengths, and weaknesses, developing a financial plan, establishing the required action plan, reviewing and revising the program based on existing challenges, and so on, as shown in Fig. 7.

A chief financial officer (CFO) should approach planning and executing their role by focusing on four major areas: metrics, operational excellence, risk, and strategy. The finance function has traditionally been an early adopter of business technology, with the expectation that it will lead to improved metrics, operational excellence, and reduced risk. According to the CFO of Al Masaood Group,

> Finance interaction with compliance and risk management will be a pre-requisite. Through working with one of our key principles, the group has taken very significant steps forward in developing a risk management framework. Other principals are following closely behind as they also exist in a rapidly evolving world, where compliance is given and must now be part of the working relationship between principals, distributors, and suppliers. Having the appropriate compliance structures confers a competitive advantage, and the group is already

Fig. 7 Illustration of a financial planning process within an organization. Source: Information retrieved from Deloitte Ireland LLP (n. d.)

receiving opportunities from one of the principals as a result of being positively accredited for its processes.

Over the past 50 years, the company has been profitable and has witnessed year-on-year growth with no exception due to its adoption of proper strategy and hiring of high-profile CEOs. It was able to witness growth even in the past 3 years, during the COVID pandemic, and continues to be profitable even in times of oil price fluctuation, economic inflation, and disruption of the supply chain. This goes back to a couple of reasons, such as great management of liquidity, access to capital and cash in Abu Dhabi, Abu Dhabi witnessing one of the world's highest growth rates in urbanization, the growing population of the UAE and the GCC region, and several ambitious industrial and infrastructure projects launched by the Abu Dhabi government.

Therefore, Al Masaood Group is looking for vertical expansion into manufacturing and fabrication as well as geographic expansion. The CFO of Al Masaood Group believes the future for the Group is very bright and exciting. Al Masaood Group is emerging strongly from the pandemic and is now starting to identify and exploit business and operational synergies across its diverse portfolio. The shared experience of the pandemic's impact has provided more strength, thereby anticipating further growth in the next 50 years.

9   Angel Investor

Representing almost 90% of businesses and accounting for over 50% of employment worldwide, small and medium enterprises (SMEs) are a major contributor to job creation and global economic development (Ramdani et al., 2022). Considered the backbone of many economies worldwide, the sector best represents the entrepreneurial spirit, flexibility, adaptability, and resilience in facing challenges and evolving market trends.

In the UAE, SMEs play a significant role in driving economic growth, as they accounted for more than 94% of the total number of companies operating in the UAE in 2020 (Information and eGovernment Sector of the Telecommunication Regulatory Authority, 2023). Out of these, 73% of them operated in the wholesale and retail sector, while 16% were involved in the services sector, and the remaining 11% were engaged in the industry sector. These enterprises also contributed significantly to the economy, employing more than 86% of the private sector's labor force and constituting over 60% of the GDP (Information and eGovernment Sector of the Telecommunication Regulatory Authority, 2023). Considering the sector's strategic role in driving socio-economic development in various countries worldwide, the UAE was among the first countries to empower SMEs and encourage entrepreneurs to pursue their innovative ideas and materialize them.

Capital is often considered one of the main obstacles for entrepreneurs. It is where "angel investments" play a significant role in supporting SMEs as they provide capital extending for long periods, thereby helping business growth. This type of investment generates opportunities to establish new companies, boost entrepreneurship, create new job opportunities, and diversify the economy.

According to Mr. Masaood Rahma Al Masaood, a director of Al Masaood Group,

> At Al Masaood Group, we strive to support the community and economy sectors in which we operate in various ways. For instance, enhancing the awareness and spreading the culture of angel investments, creating more partnerships, and strengthening the cooperation with stakeholders and concerned entities that support the country's SMEs sector.

Although Al Masaood's current strategy is focused on large, established brands and operations, they do not invest directly in SMEs or start-ups. However, Al Masaood family members and owners have their own entrepreneurial quests, with Mr. Masaood Rahma launching his own platform for angel investing, "Emirates Association for Angel Investors."

Realizing the importance of SMEs, certain steps are required to enhance awareness regarding angel investments, and the big business enterprises should understand their responsibility of encouraging new start-up by offering them angel investments, which is essentially required to refuel the economy and fulfill market demand. Unlike conventional loans, the favorable terms offered by angel investors are attractive for entrepreneurs, whereas, in return, investors can also benefit by receiving the equity in shares.

10 Summary

Family businesses are the most widespread form of corporate ownership worldwide, and they have a considerable positive impact on economic growth and national wealth creation. The growth and sustainability of a family business depend on various factors, such as effective leadership and governance, portfolio diversity, HR policies, adaptability to changing circumstances, women's empowerment, financial planning, and more. In this regard, this chapter examines the case of the Al Masaood Group and highlights several determinants that influence the growth of a family business.

To begin with, geographic distribution and diversification can provide greater control, brand recognition, access to new markets, and tax benefits. However, location should be carefully selected, as it significantly affects customer and employee attraction and retention, marketing expenses, and B2B and B2C relationships.

Secondly, effective corporate governance is a crucial tool for leadership development and overcoming operational challenges. Companies are exposed to varying environmental conditions and diversify their portfolios to enhance their sustainability. For example, the COVID-19 pandemic has disrupted many businesses, and digital platforms have replaced numerous human interactions, necessitating innovative strategies such as online analytics sales, multichannel engagement, live streaming, virtual events, and more.

Thirdly, establishing effective HR policies is essential in maintaining cultures of trust, fairness, and inclusiveness. Such policies can impact a company's reputation, ability to attract and retain talent, employee motivation, and overall performance and growth. Competitive packages, career growth opportunities, training, and a healthy work environment are significant drivers of employee retention and motivation.

Fourthly, women represent a vast economic power and comprise 49.58% of the world's population. They have a better understanding of the requirements and needs of female consumers, making them best placed to tap into that opportunity and bring valuable consumer insight to the table. Furthermore, gender diversity in the workforce has fostered creativity and innovation, and organizations across industries prioritize and benefit from a diverse and inclusive work environment.

Fifthly, developing an excellent financial plan helps keep a company focused and on track as it grows, encounters new challenges, and experiences unexpected crises. It facilitates clear communication with staff and investors and enables the building of a modern, transparent business.

Lastly, large business enterprises have a responsibility to encourage new start-ups by offering angel investments, which are essential for refueling the economy and fulfilling market demand. Unlike traditional loans, the favorable terms offered by angel investors are attractive to entrepreneurs, while investors can benefit by receiving equity in shares in return.

Questions for Discussion

1. What advantages and disadvantages come with diversifying a business portfolio?
2. What measures could be taken to ensure that the top-performing employees remain with the company?
3. In what ways does future planning play a crucial role in sustaining a family-owned business?
4. How can promoting women's empowerment contribute to the growth of a business?
5. To what extent are digital technologies significant for modern family businesses?
6. What is the significance of angel investors in revitalizing the economy?

References

Abu Dhabi Chamber. (2019). *Family Business in Abu Dhabi*. Retrieved May 4, 2023, from https://abudhabichamber.ae/-/media/Project/ADCCI/ADCCI/Media-Center%2D%2D-Publications/Research-and-Reports/2019/Family-business-sector-report_December-English.pdf

ADGM. (n.d.). *About Abu Dhabi Global Market*. Retrieved from https://www.adgm.com/about-adgm/overview

Alkaabi, K. (2020). Effects of geographic distribution of small and medium-size enterprises on growth, innovation, and economic contributions: A case study of UAE. *International Journal of Applied Geospatial Research (IJAGR).*, *11*(4), 23–41. https://doi.org/10.4018/IJAGR.2020100102

Al Masaood. (n.d.). *Our story*. https://www.masaood.com/en/

Almeida, F., & Santos, J. D. (2020). The effects of COVID-19 on job security and unemployment in Portugal. *International Journal of Sociology and Social Policy, 40*(9–10), 995–1003.

Clauß, T., Kraus, S., & Jones, P. (2022). Sustainability in family business: Mechanisms, technologies and business models for achieving economic prosperity, environmental quality and social equity. *Technological Forecasting and Social Change, 176*, 121450. https://doi.org/10.1016/j.techfore.2021.121450

Darwish, S., Gomes, A., & Bunagan, V. (2020). Family businesses (FBs) in gulf cooperation council (GCC): Review and strategic insights. *Academy of Strategic Management Journal, 19*(3), 1–13.

Deloitte Ireland LLP. (n.d.). *5 steps to financial planning success*. Retrieved May 4, 2023, from https://www2.deloitte.com/ie/en/pages/deloitte-private/articles/5-steps-financial-planning-success.html

Fang, Y., & van Lelyveld, I. (2014). Geographic diversification in banking. *Journal of Financial Stability, 15*, 172–181. https://doi.org/10.1016/j.jfs.2014.08.009

Gulf Business. (2022, April 19). *Non-oil contribution to UAE's GDP reaches 72.3% in 2021*. Retrieved May 4, 2023, from https://gulfbusiness.com/non-oil-contribution-to-uaes-gdp-reaches-72-3-in-2021/

Hansen, E., & Juslin, H. (2018). *Strategic marketing in the global forest industries*. Oregon State University. Retrieved from https://open.oregonstate.education/strategicmarketing/chapter/chapter-4-strategy-and-strategic-planning/

Information and eGovernment Sector of the Telecommunication Regulatory Authority. (2023). *Small and Medium Enterprises (SMEs)*. Retrieved from https://u.ae/en/information-and-services/business/small-and-medium-enterprises/small-and-medium-enterprises

International Labour Organization. (2020). *The impact of the COVID-19 pandemic on jobs and incomes in G20 economies*. Retrieved from https://www.ilo.org/wcmsp5/groups/public/%2D%2D-dgreports/%2D%2D-cabinet/documents/publication/wcms_756331.pdf

LinkedIn. (2017). *Inside the mind of today's candidate*. LinkedIn Talent Solutions. https://business.linkedin.com/content/dam/me/business/en-us/talent-solutions/resources/pdfs/inside-the-mind-of-todays-candidate1.pdf

Oudah, M., Jabeen, F., & Dixon, C. (2018). Determinants linked to family business sustainability in the UAE: An AHP approach. *Sustainability (Switzerland), 10*(1), 1–12.

Ramdani, B., Raja, S., & Kayumova, M. (2022). Digital innovation in SMEs: A systematic review, synthesis and research agenda. *Information Technology for Development, 28*(1), 56–80. https://doi.org/10.1080/02681102.2021.1893148

Ramadani, V., Aloulou, W., & Zainal, M. (2023). *Family business in gulf cooperation council countries*. Springer.

Sharma, P., Chrisman, J. J., & Gersick, K. E. (2012). 25 years of family business review: Reflections on the past and perspectives for the future. *Family Business Review, 25*(1), 5–15. https://doi.org/10.1177/0894486512437626

Sorenson, R., & Bierman, L. (2009). Family capital, family business, and free enterprise. *Family Business Review, 22*(3), 193–195. https://doi.org/10.1177/0894486509341178

Statista. (2022). *UAE: Distribution of Real GDP by Sector 2020*. Retrieved May 4, 2023, from https://www.statista.com/statistics/1143052/uae-distribution-of-real-gdp-by-sector/

Thakkar, R. (2022). *Top 100 hiring statistics for 2022*. LinkedIn. https://www.linkedin.com/pulse/top-100-hiring-statistics-2022-rinku-thakkar/

Tharawat Magazine. (2013). *Communication in family businesses - getting your brain in gear*. Retrieved May 4, 2023, from https://www.tharawat-magazine.com/communication/communication-family-businesses/

The Global Economy. (2021). *United Arab Emirates: Unemployment rate*. Retrieved from https://www.theglobaleconomy.com/United-Arab-Emirates/unemployment_rate/

The UAE Gender Balance Council. (n.d.). *UAE Women FAQs*. Retrieved from https://www.gbc.gov.ae/facts.html

Tolba, K. (2022). *Emirati Women's Day 2022: Meet the ambitious female leader aspiring to reshape the UAE's aviation landscape*. Retrieved from https://www.aviationbusinessme.com/interviews/emirati-womens-day-al-saffar

Khaula Alkaabi is a Professor in the Geography and Urban Sustainability Department at UAEU. She holds a BA degree from UAEU; an MA and a PhD in Geography from UNCG in the USA; and a Public Sector Innovation Diploma from the University of Cambridge in the UK. Her research interests include transportation, land use planning, spatial analysis and geostatistics, GIS, drone applications, economic geography, smart cities, entrepreneurship, and innovation. She was the Chair of the Geography Department from 2013 to 2017, and the Chief Innovation Officer for UAEU from 2015 to 2022. She has published several academic articles in scientific international journals like the *Journal of Transport Geography*, *Frontiers*, *Journal of Enterprising Communities*, *Geomatics Natural Hazards and Risk*, *Journal of Cleaner Production*, and *Transportation Research Part F*. She has published several book chapters with Ashgate, Routledge, and Springer. She has received several research grants and rewards, including UAEU's "University Excellence Award for Service Excellence" in 2022, "Outstanding Leadership Awards in Education" in 2022, "Feminine Monitoring for Sustainable Environment Award" in 2019, and the "Best Academic Research at Sustainable Transport Competition" by RTA in 2018.

Abdul Samad Farooq is currently a Doctoral Candidate in power engineering and engineering Thermo-physics at the School of Mechanical Engineering, Shanghai Jiao Tong University, Shanghai, China. He completed a Master's in Thermal Energy Engineering from the National University of Science and Technology, Pakistan, and a Bachelor's in Electrical Engineering from The University of Lahore, Pakistan. He worked as a research assistant at the College of Humanities and Social Sciences at the United Arab Emirates University, UAE, in 2022 and at the School of

Energy and Environment, Southeast University, China, in 2018–2019. His area of research is solar energy utilization, heat transfer, and material characterization, and he has published 10 peer-reviewed journal articles, one book chapter, and three conference papers. He has published in renewable and sustainable energy reviews, renewable energy, solar energy, composite's part A applied science and manufacturing, among others.

Barjeel Aerial Photography Services: A Successful Geospatial Data Acquisition Company

Marwa Mohammed Al Suwaidi and Cristina I. Fernandes

Abstract

Family businesses are the major contributors to the strength and dynamism of the Emirati economy, sustainability, and long-term stability. This chapter recognizes the importance of family businesses in the UAE by covering deep insights into Barjeel Ariel Photography Services (BAPS) and providing an example of a successful family-owned Emirati business enterprise. The family dynamics, business overview, products, services, and projects completed by the BAPS are briefly summarized in this chapter. Furthermore, the effect of sustainability-related challenges, particularly during the pandemic, is analyzed. In the end, the alignment of the BAPS project with Sustainable Development Goals (SDGs) 13 and 14 set by the United Nations is briefly discussed, providing them with an effective way of mitigating climate change and ensuring the sustainability of marine resources.

M. M. Al Suwaidi (✉)
College of Humanities and Social Sciences, United Arab Emirates University, Al Ain, UAE
e-mail: 201304634@uaeu.ac.ae

C. I. Fernandes
University of Beira Interior, Department of Management and Economics & NECE Research Unit in Business Sciences, Covilhã, Portugal

Centre for Corporate Entrepreneurship and Innovation at Loughborough University, Loughborough, UK
e-mail: cristina.isabel.fernandes@ubi.pt

© The Author(s), under exclusive license to Springer Nature Switzerland AG 2023
K. Alkaabi, V. Ramadani (eds.), *Family Business Cases*, Springer Business Cases,
https://doi.org/10.1007/978-3-031-39252-8_2

1 Introduction

Barjeel Aerial Photography Services (BAPS) is a geospatial data acquisition company established in 2015 with expertise in aerial photography, thermal imagery mapping, topographic/land survey, hydrographic/bathymetric survey (sensors and satellite), environmental research, and satellite imagery analysis. It is a member of the Dubai Small and Medium Enterprises (SMEs) program.

Aerial photogrammetry is one of the earliest forms of remote sensing employed for photographing the Earth's surface (Ceraudo, 2013). It is one of the emerging fields in the geospatial world to collect data for different types of applications with the help of various multispectral sensors and computers (Herrero & Castañeda, 2022; McDonald et al., 2022). It typically refers to bird eye view images that focus on diverse landscapes and surface objects (de Joussineau, 2022; Gundlach et al., 2022). Aerial photogrammetry plays a vital role in UAE development and even in the scientific sector for completing various aerial photogrammetry projects using advanced multispectral sensors (Zahari et al., 2022; Howari et al., 2022).

BAPS is always dedicated to delivering services to clients in any condition, and the company is committed to meeting clients' requirements with high accuracy and precision. During the COVID-19 pandemic, BAPS worked remotely to successfully complete all their clients' projects and meet their deadlines. The BAPS team has earned a good reputation through partnerships with other companies worldwide and their footprints all over the UAE, including different sectors like municipalities, environmental agencies, GIS centers, and so forth.

This chapter will provide the business overview, products, services, and projects completed by the BAPS. Furthermore, it will focus on the BAPS's Alignment with the sustainable development goals (SDGs) set by the United Nations in 2030. BAPS has been working on various projects for the Ministry of Energy and Natural Resources and the Dubai Municipality's Environment Department that aim to preserve terrestrial and marine ecosystems and implement the necessary countermeasures for climate change.

2 Business Overview

The company was founded by Khalid Khamis Bin Dasmal, who is a retired UAE Armed Forces Coronel with 30 years of solid experience in terrestrial mapping from air, land, and water using different modes of techniques like satellite imagery, manned aircraft, drones, boats, and traditional field surveys. BAPS is equipped with a team of diverse professionals with national and international experiences to provide its clients with state-of-the-art services.

BAPS is a geospatial data acquisition company established and registered in Dubai on August 3, 2015, at the Department of Economics and Development (DED). It is one of Mohammed bin Rashid's SME development establishments, supervised by Hamdan Innovation and Incubator (HI2). It aims to "create a quality culture within the geospatial industry in which we develop employees' abilities and exceed the client's expectations", intending to deliver high-quality standard geospatial data products in innovative and affordable services from various platforms. It envisages being one of the leading geospatial acquisition companies amongst the SMEs in Dubai and the UAE, catering to the requirements of the private and public sectors.

3 Products and Services

BAPS provides its services in aerial photography, thermal imagery mapping, topographic/land survey, hydrographic/bathymetric survey (sensors and satellite), environmental research, and satellite imagery analysis. A brief description of each of its services is provided underneath:

3.1 Aerial Photography

BAPS offers a complete variety of expert aerial survey services with the potential to gather highly detailed data from various unmanned aircraft systems (UAVs). The company uses cutting-edge technology with high-quality sensor cameras for data collection for clients. The UAVs are operated by computerized navigators and employed as remote sensing instruments to capture ground surfaces. UAV data is utilized for GIS-based orthophoto, DTM and DEM generation, contour creation, volumetric reporting, or aerial still or oblique photographs.

3.2 Aerial Thermal Survey

BAPS specializes in advanced aerial thermal imagery and thermographic mapping. The team consists of airplane drivers experienced in thermography, environmental engineering, GIS, aerial thermal imagery, and mapping. Besides, the group specialized in thermal mapping by employing different techniques, including mobile mapping by collecting point cloud data, 360° photography, high-definition video, and thermal imagery for route corridors.

3.3 Hydrography/Bathymetry Survey

BAPS provides advanced analysis with the latest techniques used in the geospatial world to delineate watersheds or trace water flows, pre-processing elevation data so it will be suitable for hydrological modeling and analysis.

3.4 2D/3D Geospatial Data Acquisition

The team has knowledge of data conversion and experience with different types of 2D and 3D data creation and modeling of features based on the 3D data.

3.5 Orthophoto, DTM, DSM, and Map Production

Aerial photography for survey and mapping is the leading service BAPS provides, which can cover large areas or small blocks or lines of exposure. The company has successfully captured spectacular high-definition images for the property portfolio, structural inspections, and even archeological or industrial requirements.

3.6 Data Modeling and GIS Enterprise Solutions

BAPS is equipped with the latest technologies for data modeling and ArcGIS Enterprise solutions, which are the complete software package solution for all geospatial needs, which will be determined based on the client's requirements.

3.7 Smart Geospatial Solutions

BAPS provides comprehensive and accurate surveillance solutions for various industries and applications. For instance, flexible and easy access to premium satellite imagery and innovative geospatial analytics.

4 Base Map and Imagery Projects

A brief description of several mega projects accomplished by BAPS is briefly discussed below.

4.1 Dubai Base Map Update and Assets Verification

The project aims to verify all the assets belonging to Dubai Municipality (location and attributes) and update the base map vector data in all Dubai Municipality (plots, parks, conservation areas, etc.). Assets included benches and dustbins, amenity lights, umbrellas, etc., which were reviewed, integrated into the unified data model, then verified and captured in the field using GPS mobile devices. BAPS developed a unified database schema based on the updated assets catalog to store all Dubai Municipality asset data from different sources in one database schema. Then the metadata for each asset was entered according to the Dubai Municipality metadata standard. A data dictionary web-based application was developed based

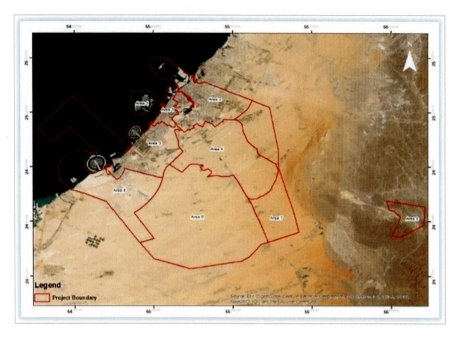

Fig. 1 Dubai Base Map Update, Phase 1. Source: BAPS. Published with the company's permission

on the newly created Dubai Municipality assets catalog, according to the GEO-DUBAI application in terms of look and feel (Fig. 1).

4.2 Fujairah and Khawr Fakkan Drone Imagery

BAPS was a subcontractor for drone surveys in the Fujairah and Khawr Fakkan areas. The project involves the data acquisition of aerial imagery using UAVs. The imagery was captured and processed using BAPS equipment and software. Large amounts of data must be processed for the project to manage all the data consistently and effectively. BAPS has created project standards and automated workflows when needed. Table 1 summarizes the BAPS's significant projects associated with mapping and imagery services (Fig. 2).

4.3 BAPS Projects Aligned with SDGs

The UN's member nations endorsed the 2030 Agenda, which includes 17 sustainable development goals, in September 2015. The UN's Rio+20 conference's promises of

Table 1 A brief description of BAPS's projects regarding the base map and imagery services

Sr. No.	Projects	Associated body	Status
1.	Provision of Aerial Imagery of the Al Ain Region	Al Ain Municipality	Ongoing
2.	Study of fundamental biological diversity spaces in the Al Marmoum Area, including preparation of natural resources and habitat mapping	Dubai Municipality	Completed (2017)
3.	Fresh Water Spring Study on Coastal Areas in the UAE	Ministry of Energy	Completed (2017)
4.	Workshop for Conservations Area in Dubai	Dubai Municipality	Completed (2017)
5.	Urban Heat Island Study for Dubai	Dubai Municipality	Completed (2018)
6.	Biodiversity Baseline Survey for Dubai	Dubai Municipality	Ongoing
7.	Dubai Base Map Update Project Phase One	Dubai Municipality	Completed (2019)
8.	Dubai Base Map Updating "Ortho Imagery and Assets" Phase 2	Dubai Municipality	Completed (2021)
9.	Drone Survey for Fujairah and Khor Fakan	Ministry of Infrastructure Development	Ongoing
10.	Dubai Protected Area Network Sustainable Development Policy	Dubai Municipality	Ongoing

Source: BAPS. Published with the company's permission

Fig. 2 Fujairah and Khawr Fakkan Drone Imagery. Source: BAPS. Published with the company's permission

sustainable development were paired with the renewal of the Millennium Development Goals, carried out between 2000 and 2015.

The 17 sustainable development goals will all be implemented differently in various nations due to the 2030 agenda's global scope. For instance, other countries should be more focused on encouraging a healthy diet and fighting obesity, while some continue to battle hunger. Another example is that some nations waste a third of their food supply, while others lose a significant amount of their harvest due to insufficient storage. Additionally, although some cultures worry about having access to energy, several other communities consume tremendous amount of energy. They need to find a way to decrease their consumption and its adverse environmental effects.

Companies worldwide are changing how they conduct business in response to public awareness of sustainable development and stringent environmental protection laws and regulations. BAPS provides ecological engineering solutions that can benefit public and private customers for the design, development, analysis, and improvement of public works infrastructure.

The environmental sciences are increasingly relying on GIS as a tool. GIS is more than a simple digital evolution from cartography to IT-based geographic data, and digital mapping offers enormous advantages for research, engineering, project management, and resource distribution. It is beneficial to give decision makers in both the public and private sectors the ability to restructure and maneuver by utilizing more data more efficiently and quickly. Numerous more applications in the field of environmental engineering services solutions include urban planning, waste management, oil spill clean-up operations, creating new road networks and planning infrastructure for those roads, and natural disaster relief. BAPS's primary expertise highlights several environmental fields, including climate resilience studies, archaeology and heritage, hydrometry and bathymetry, natural environment and ecology, and so on, as summarized in Fig. 3.

In addition, BAPS is working on data analysis in the GIS labs using updated systems and helping environmental data analysts in the field. For instance, BAPS assists clients by providing professional services in the field using GIS. Waste storage sites can be mapped by an environmental inspector, who can also identify the condition of waste containers, their volume, and their content. Besides environmental studies, hydrological studies are one of the primary services BAPS provides. BAPS focuses specifically on performing the latest techniques of bathymetric surveys using multi-beam echo sounders for a wide range of purposes.

The BAPS team can carry out advanced analysis with the latest techniques used in the geospatial world to delineate watersheds or trace water flows, pre-processing elevation data to make it suitable for hydrological modeling and analysis. They believe in creating hydrological models based on quality checks. These are the complex types of analysis enforced by elevation data with watersheds that require professional expertise to overcome the problems. Flood studies and DAM modeling are core services included in hydrography and bathymetry. Table 2 highlights three SDGs—climate change, life on land, and life below water—that Barjeel Company implements in their projects for their customers.

Fig. 3 Service provided by BAPS in environmental aspects. Source: BAPS. Published with the company's permission

A detailed description of a few significant projects that align with the SDGs is given below.

4.3.1 Urban Heat Islands Study

BAPS worked with the Dubai Municipality on a study to identify urban heat islands and recommend suitable mitigation measures. Dubai is acknowledged as the first modern city in the Arabian Gulf. It will remain one of the most amazing cities in the world due to the size and quality of its infrastructure and facilities for housing, commerce, leisure, and trade. In line with the Dubai Plan 2021 and UAE Vision 2021, the Environmental Department-Environmental Planning and Studies Section (ED-EPSS) of Dubai Municipality (DM), supported by the Executive Council of Dubai, has decided to research the consequences of urban heat islands. This study has been initiated to ensure Dubai can meet the challenges of climate change.

There are several internationally referenced methodologies used to conduct the UHI studies. This study has utilized three survey tools to cover Dubai's city, district, and building surface thermal characteristics, which include manned aerial vehicles (MAV), unmanned aerial vehicles (UAV), and building-level ground surveys.

The data received will then be processed to produce an updated thermal map for the study area. It will identify locations affected by the urban heat island effect, as illustrated in Fig. 4. Mitigation measures will then be developed for these areas. The study requires the processing of large volumes of remotely sensed data.

Table 2 Barjeel company alignments with SDGs

SDG #	Target	Company projects, initiatives, etc.	Numbers
SDG 13: Take urgent action to combat climate change and its impacts	13.2: Integrate climate change measures into national policies, strategies, and planning	Project 1: Urban Heat Islands Study Dubai	1
SDG 15: Protect, restore, and promote sustainable use of terrestrial ecosystems; sustainably manage forests; combat desertification; halt and reverse land degradation; and halt biodiversity loss	15.5: Take urgent and significant action to reduce the degradation of natural habitats, halt the loss of biodiversity, and, by 2020, protect and prevent the extinction of threatened species 15.9: By 2020, integrate ecosystem and biodiversity values into national and local planning, development processes, poverty reduction strategies, and accounts	Project 1: Biodiversity Map for Dubai Emirates: Project 2: Biodiversity Baseline Survey Project 3: Al Marmoum Habitat Mapping	3
SDG 14: Conserve and sustainably use the oceans, seas, and marine resources for sustainable development	14.1: Increase scientific knowledge, develop research capacity, and transfer marine technology, taking into account the Intergovernmental Oceanographic Commission Criteria and Guidelines on the Transfer of Marine Technology, to improve ocean health and enhance the contribution of marine biodiversity to the development of developing countries, in particular small island developing states and least developed countries	Project 1: Fresh Water Spring Study	1

Source: BAPS. Published with the company's permission

4.3.2 Biodiversity Map for Dubai Emirates

BAPS has been working on preparing the Biodiversity Map for Dubai Emirates to conduct a baseline survey on non-protected surrounding areas around ± 2500 km^2 in terrestrial regions with a particular focus on local communities, cultural heritage, and land use, as illustrated in Fig. 5a. It will be conducted with sampling events and comprises terrestrial, marine, and coastal habitat assessment and species monitoring (avifauna, turtles), besides providing a geo-referenced database for the preparation of a meta-database with data collection and management protocol and developing GIS maps as well as technical and non-technical reports for submission to authorities.

Fig. 4 Urban Heat Islands Study: Dubai. Source: BAPS. Published with the company's permission

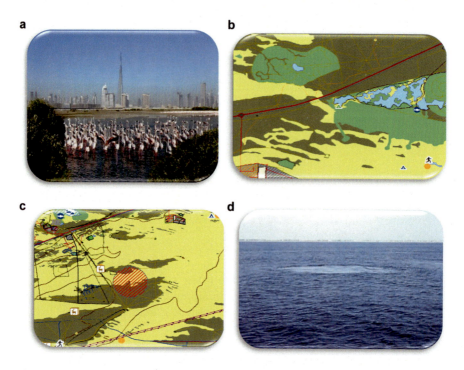

Fig. 5 (**a**) Biodiversity Map for Dubai Emirates, (**b**) Biodiversity Baseline Survey for Dubai Emirates, (**c**) Al Marmoum Habitat Mapping, (**d**) Fresh Water Springs Study. Source: BAPS. Published with the company's permission

4.3.3 Biodiversity Baseline Survey

BAPS and Proteus (TCARTA) completed the pilot project for the Dubai Municipality, Environment Department, and Environment and Natural Conservation Resources Section by submitting an ecological field survey report detailing a description of methods used, observations, and quality control methods, as shown in Fig. 5b.

4.3.4 Al Marmoum Habitat Mapping

BAPS and Proteus (TCARTA) completed the pilot project for the Dubai Municipality, Environment Department, and Environment and Natural Conservation Resources Section by providing a biodiversity baseline study for an extended area of Al Marmoum protected area in the Emirate of Dubai, as shown in Fig. 5c.

4.3.5 Freshwater Springs Study

BAPS and Proteus (TCARTA) completed the pilot project for the Ministry of Energy and Natural Resources (MOENR), as illustrated in Fig. 5d. In the United Arab Emirates and the Gulf region, groundwater is a limited resource needed to maintain a growing population. Relying on desalinated water affects marine ecology due to the rising hypersalinity in the Arabian Gulf. The Ministry of Energy, UAE, has awarded this pilot project to identify submarine freshwater springs via remote sensing. Submarine freshwater springs may still exist within the UAE shores. A report has been compiled to provide the Ministry of Energy with several alternative approaches to consider regarding technologies and searching for optimal areas.

5 Summary

GIS is crucial for the analysis and creation of efficient plans for environmental studies. Also, it is considered one of the essential instruments for digital data transmission standards, data validation, retrieval, visualization, dissemination, and analysis in the environmental data framework. Since it provides the technical foundation for applying various multimedia approaches to environmental decision-making, it can be used to communicate environmental information to the public and policymakers.

The Dubai SMEs program provides unlimited support for Emirati nationals to start them in everything from planning finances, simplifying official procedures, and helping the establishment of businesses from start to finish (Ramadani et al., 2023; Alkaabi, 2020). They guide BAPS as a business development partner through starting their enterprise. As an outcome of this trust that has been given, BAPS makes sure to pay it back by providing high-quality products for their customers that aim to serve environmental cases such as the urban heat island effect, detect freshwater springs, and maintain biodiversity by conducting ecological field surveys, which all fall under SDGs 13, 14, and 15.

Questions for Discussion

1. What is the BAPS Vision?
2. What registration certifications has the BAPS company earned?
3. What types of products and services does BAPS offer?
4. In which fields do BAPS projects operate?
5. Which BAPS projects are aligned with the SDGs?

Acknowledgments The authors express their heartfelt gratitude to Mr. Khalid Khamis Bin Dasmal, the Director of Barjeel Company, for granting permission to use all the necessary materials to complete this chapter. They would also like to extend a special thanks to Sajid Ali, a GIS Engineer at BAPS, for his assistance in assembling the components and providing valuable input on the project.

References

Alkaabi, K. (2020). Effects of geographic distribution of small and medium-size enterprises on growth, innovation, and economic contributions: A case study of UAE. *International Journal of Applied Geospatial Research (IJAGR).*, *11*(4), 23–41. https://doi.org/10.4018/IJAGR.2020100102

Barjeel Aerial Photography Services. (n.d.). Retrieved September 23, 2022, from https://baps.ae/

Ceraudo, G. (2013). Aerial photography in archaeology. *Good Practice in Archaeological Diagnostics, 11*–30. https://doi.org/10.1007/978-3-319-01784-6_2

BAPS. (n.d.). Data dictionary application, SRS document, prepared for Dubai municipality, prepared by BAPS. Retrieved September 23, 2022, from documentation provided by the Barjeel Aerial Photography Services Company.

de Joussineau, G. (2022). The geometrical properties of fracture corridors. *Tectonophysics, 846*, 229637. https://doi.org/10.1016/j.tecto.2022.229637

Zahari, F., Harun, A., & Nasrijal, N. M. H. (2022). A systematic literature review on the usage of digital photography at crime scene investigation process. *Journal of Pharmaceutical Negative Results, 13*(6), 2061–2069. https://doi.org/10.47750/pnr.2022.13.s06.269

Gundlach, E. R., Bonte, M., Story, N. I., & Iroakasi, O. (2022). Using high-resolution imagery from 2013 and 2020 to establish baseline vegetation in oil-damaged mangrove habitat prior to large-scale post-remediation planting in Bodo, Eastern Niger Delta, Nigeria. *Remote Sensing Applications: Society and Environment, 28*, 100831. https://doi.org/10.1016/j.rsase.2022.100831

Herrero, J., & Castañeda, C. (2022). A dataset of aerial photographs of 1972 from an irrigated area in Monegros, Spain. *Data in Brief, 42*, 108325. https://doi.org/10.1016/j.dib.2022.108325

Howari, F. M., Sharma, M., Nazzal, Y., El-Keblawy, A., Mir, S., Xavier, C. M., Salem, I. B., Al-Taani, A. A., & Alaydaroos, F. (2022). Changes in the invasion rate of Prosopis juliflora and its impact on depletion of groundwater in the northern part of The United Arab Emirates. *Plants, 11*(5). https://doi.org/10.3390/plants11050682

McDonald, M. R., Tayviah, C. S., & Gossen, B. D. (2022). Human vs. machine, the eyes have it. Assessment of Stemphylium leaf blight on onion using aerial photographs from an NIR camera. *Remote Sensing, 14*(2). https://doi.org/10.3390/rs14020293

Profile of BARJEEL Aerial Photography Services. (n.d.). Retrieved September 23, 2022, from documentation provided by the Barjeel Aerial Photography Services Company.

Ramadani, V., Aloulou, W., & Zainal, M. (2023). *Family business in gulf cooperation council countries*. Springer.

United Nations. (n.d.). *Do you know all 17 SDGs?* Retrieved September 23, 2022, from https://sdgs.un.org/goals

Marwa Al Suwaidi is a PhD Student of Geography and Geographic Inf. Sys, United Arab Emirates University, United Arab Emirates. Her research interests include geographic information system, remote sensing, environmental studies, statistics, and population. Marwa has authored or co-authored approximately four research articles, which have been published in distinguished academic journals, including *XXIV ISPRS Congress, Open Journal of Social Sciences, The Arab World Geographer*, and *ISI World Statistics Congress*. In May 2017, Marwa received her bachelor's degree in GIS with honors from United Arab Emirates University. In December 2020, she attained a master's degree in science in Remote Sensing and Geographic Information System with honors from the same university. Besides her academic success, Marwa has a very successful career path discovering different domains in the geographic information system and remote sensing. She started her professional journey as a GIS analyst and advanced to become a LiDAR analyst at Al Ain Municipality. Later, Marwa was appointed as a specialist GIS, and subsequently, as an acting section manager GIS at Statistics Centre, Abu Dhabi.

Cristina Fernandes is an Assistant Professor with Habilitation at the University of Beira Interior (UBI), Portugal. She holds a PhD in Management from the University of Beira Interior. She is a researcher at the NECE Center for Studies in Business Sciences at the University of Beira Interior and at the Centre for Corporate Entrepreneurship and Innovation at Loughborough University, UK. She is part of the editorial board of Management Decision; has several dozen scientific articles published in international journals including: *Journal of Technology Transfer, Journal of Knowledge Management, R&D Management,* and *Journal of Business Research*. Actively participates in scientific meetings and international conferences on these topics, having been distinguished several times with awards for best article. Has participated in several international projects.

Innovation Floor: 4.0 Technologies and Information Solutions

Khaled Khamis Al Arafati and Léo-Paul Dana

Abstract

This chapter explores the strategies family businesses can utilize to improve their success by providing an example of the Innovation Floor, one of the leading Emirati business enterprises. It is a technology-based company offering services in artificial intelligence, gamification, GIS-based solution development, and so forth. This chapter explores Innovation Floor, its business profile, and services related to artificial intelligence, robotics applications, gaming, and simulations for the education sector, GIS and enterprise solutions, smart devices, and a sample of its wearable technology incorporating augmented reality and virtual reality solutions. Besides, the geographical distribution of numerous projects and initiatives completed by the innovation floor is briefly discussed. In the end, several insights regarding the alignment of their projects with sustainable development goals are summarized and discussed.

1 Introduction

Due to growing interconnectedness and intelligent automation, the Fourth Industrial Revolution (also known as Industry 4.0) predicts rapid change in technology, industries, and societal patterns and processes in the twenty-first century

---

K. K. Al Arafati (✉)
Al Ain Town Planning and Survey, Al Ain City Municipality, Al Ain City, Abu Dhabi, UAE
e-mail: 200850014@uaeu.ac.ae; khaled.alarfati@aam.gov.ae

L.-P. Dana
Ecole de commerce Paris – ICD Business School, Groupe IGS, Paris, France

LUT School of Business and Management, Lappeenranta University of Technology, Lappeenranta, Finland
e-mail: lpdana@groupe-igs.fr

© The Author(s), under exclusive license to Springer Nature Switzerland AG 2023
K. Alkaabi, V. Ramadani (eds.), *Family Business Cases*, Springer Business Cases,
https://doi.org/10.1007/978-3-031-39252-8_3

(Castelo-Branco et al., 2022; David et al., 2022; Malomane et al., 2022). It is employed to boost operational efficiency, enhance demand forecasting, remove data silos, carry out predictive maintenance, give staff members virtual training, and more (Barrett & Rose, 2022; Kocdar et al., 2021). The industrial revolution introduced technology like artificial intelligence, gene editing, and smart robots, eliminating the barriers between the physical, digital, and biological worlds (Farooq & Zhang, 2022). Due to the continuous automation of conventional manufacturing and industrial methods, smart technologies, extensive M2M connectivity, and the Internet of Things, profound changes in the world's production and supply networks are taking place (Jamwal et al., 2021). Its adoption has a wide range of effects on the entire supply chain and forces businesses to reconsider how they plan and handle their supply chains. Industry 4.0 technologies assist manufacturers in bridging the gap between the aforementioned distinct processes and a more transparent, viewable perspective across the entire business with valuable insights. Due to the imperative significance of 4.0 technologies, the UAE continues to invest in them to boost its global competitiveness and accelerate the digital transformation of its industrial sector to be a global hub for 4IR. As a result, several national tech businesses, such as Innovation Floor, have emerged in alignment with the UAE's 4IR strategy.

Innovation Floor (Ardhiyat Alibdaa) is a technology-based company offering services in artificial intelligence, gamification, GIS-based solution development, and so forth. The company was founded in 2017 to explore and develop upcoming disruptive innovations and technologies to create solutions that bring value to the community and improve the customer experience. Therefore, this study explores Innovation Floor, its business profile, key artificial intelligence and robotics applications, gaming and simulations for the education sector, GIS and enterprise solutions, smart devices, and a sample of its wearable technology incorporating augmented reality and virtual reality solutions (Innovation Floor, 2021).

2 Business Overview

Ardhiyat Alibdaa Information Solutions means Innovation Floor. It is a technology-focused corporation that develops and supports advanced solutions specialized in newly emerging and disruptive technologies. The innovation floor is a customer-focused organization. It offers innovative subsystems to enhance the user experience and optimize the final output to support the customer's digital transformation strategies, thereby contributing to industrial revolution trends and technologies focusing on the major four segments: (1) AI, (2) robotics, (3) games and simulations, and (4) GIS and Enterprise.

The company was established by an emirate entrepreneur, Ibrahim Al Obaidly, who has been in the field of technology since the early 1990s. The company was launched in 2017 as a commitment by him and his team to have a place to host their creativity and research. They decided to materialize their efforts under the initiative of the Prime Minister of the UAE, Mohammed Bin Rashed Al Maktoum, to support small and medium enterprises. The primary goal was to make a meaningful move

Innovation Floor: 4.0 Technologies and Information Solutions

Fig. 1 Ibrahim Al Obaidly, The Founder. Source: Innovation Floor. Published with the company's permission

toward capitalizing on the team's domain experience and producing products and solutions resulting from the R&D efforts (Fig. 1).

Since its establishment, Innovation Floor has aimed to invest in disruptive innovations that are demanded and contribute to community awareness to ensure efficient technology utilization. They aim to host solutions that can be accessed by the community and thereby achieve the leading position in domestic manufacturing by 2030 through efficient participation in community development and awareness, with a vision to saddle the technology with excellence and passion for benefiting the community. The Innovation Floor has adopted several core values involving client value creation, customer focus, innovation and creativity, integrity, and transparency, as illustrated in Fig. 2, to distinguish it from competitors.

3 Products and Services

The innovation floor believes in the importance of technology integration by interrelating the four verticals (artificial intelligence, robotics, gaming, and GIS) to form a disruptive experience. This interdisciplinary knowledge and expertise granted the company a competitive advantage in delivering newly trending applications such as the metaverse, extended reality, and autonomous driving.

Innovation Floor works with domain experts in artificial intelligence, gaming, and geographic information systems to deliver an integrated solution using the above-mentioned interconnected disciplines to fulfill customers' business requirements and expectations. The journey starts with understanding the customer's mission

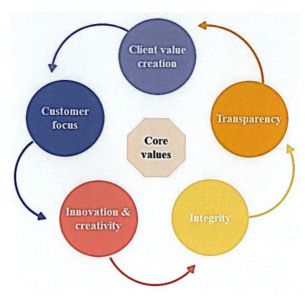

Fig. 2 The list of core values shortlisted by the management of the Innovation Floor to achieve their goals and objectives. Source: Innovation Floor. Published with the company's permission

requirements, analyzing the current situation, and proposing solutions that efficiently serve the business needs and increase the ROI. Their extraordinary characteristics, including the combined value of the industry, the proven technologies, and the expertise, ensure maximum utilization and efficiency at reduced risk, cost, and complexity. Figure 3 summarizes the several products and services offered by the Innovation Floor.

Following is a list of the products and services mapped to the main scope of business.

3.1 Artificial Intelligence Solutions Development

A wider range of sectors is transforming due to the emergence of artificial intelligence (AI). For instance, AI is anticipated to impact various domains, including global productivity, equality and inclusion, and environmental results (Ramadani et al., 2023). Considering the undoubted significance of AI in nearly every industry, the Innovation Floor is providing AI-based solutions in the following areas: (1) computer vision and machine learning, (2) facial expression analysis, and (3) human and animals gait analysis.

3.2 Robotics and Autonomous Driving Solutions Development

Robotics deals with machines constructed to carry out preprogrammed activities without additional human involvement. This broad concept encompasses everything

Innovation Floor: 4.0 Technologies and Information Solutions 41

Fig. 3 Types of products and services offered by the innovation floor. Source: Innovation Floor. Published with the company's permission

from a bare mechanical arm used to assemble autos to science fiction creations like Wall-E or Amazon's planned Astro "Alexa on wheels" household robot. Typically, robots are designed and programmed to perform specific tasks; however, the incorporation of AI in robotics has enabled more sophisticated designs and dynamic operations while performing various activities simultaneously with higher accuracy. It is a vast field covering several applications in business, health care, aerospace, the military, and so forth. Therefore, being one of the leading companies in AI, the Innovation Floor is keen on research and development in automation as well as developing a multi-mission autonomous vehicle (HIND-G30).

3.3 Gaming and Simulations

The gaming industry requires artificial intelligence to model its animated objects in games and simulations to act autonomously and smartly. The goal of AI in gaming is to improve the user experience. These AI-powered interactive experiences are typically created by NPCs, or non-player characters, that behave intelligently or imaginatively as though a human participant was directing them, as illustrated in Fig. 4. The Innovation Floor provides services in the following areas of gaming as

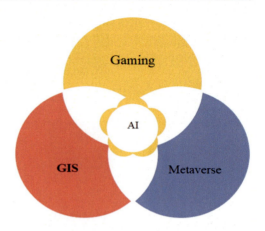

Fig. 4 Graphical illustration of the integration of AI into gaming. Source: Innovation Floor. Published with the company's permission

simulations: (1) 3D Graphic Design and Animation Production, (2) Game Development, (3) Simulation Development and Modelling, (4) Motion Platform-based Gaming, and (5) Integration with Geo-enabled Technology.

3.4 Geographic Information Systems

Artificial intelligence (AI) has made significant strides in recent years. It is now as accurate as or even more so than humans in tasks like text translation, image recognition, and reading comprehension. Possibilities that were before inconceivable are now becoming possible due to the convergence of AI and GIS. The term "AI GIS" refers to a range of technologies that combine artificial intelligence (AI) with GIS functions, such as geographical data processing and analysis techniques (GeoAI). In recent years, geoscience research and application have increasingly centered on AI GIS. Considering the importance of AI in GIS, the Innovation Floor is providing services in the following areas: (1) web mapping solutions; (2) web mapping integration; (3) smart data acquisition; (4) geoprocessing automation; (5) virtual reality, mixed reality, and extended reality geoenable applications; (6) 3D city modeling; and (7) Ground Station Development for Data downlink and processing.

4 Projects and Geographical Distribution

As illustrated in Table 1, numerous projects and initiatives were started throughout the previous years and will continue until September 2022. All of these initiatives and projects are being carried out in India and the United Arab Emirates, with the project in India serving as a first step in expanding operations outside. Figure 5 depicts the geographical locations of the projects carried out by the Innovation Floor

Table 1 Overview of projects carried out by the Innovation Floor over the years

Project/Initiative	Stage	Size	Location	Customer	Technology	Delivery
Smart Police Patrol	Awarded	1.7 M	Dubai	Dubai Police	The extended reality motion platform	Simulation system
Classic Car Driving	Awarded	600 K	Sharjah	Government	3D city modeling, motion platform	Simulation system
Smart University	Finished	300 K	India	University	Robotics, artificial intelligence	Robots and artificial intelligence research platform
HorseOSS	Ongoing	10 M	UAE	Joint Venture	Cloud computing, IOST, GIS	One-stop shop services for enquire industry
UEA Mission to Mars	R&D	1 M	UAE	Self-Product	Unreal Engine	Space game with UAE national theme/mission
Hazza Mission to ISS	R&D	500 K	UAE	Self-Product	Unreal Engine/Augmented Reality	Ar Game, smart-T-Shirts
EzTaxi Indoor Taxi	Ongoing	200 K	UAE	ExxTaxi	Cloud	Digital transformation
Civil Defense Training	Opportunity	2 M	UAE	Civil Defense	Unreal engine. Virtual reality. 3D	Firefight simulation
HINO-G30	R&D	8 M	Dubai	Self-Product	Car modeling, cloud, AI	Autonomous car (multi-mission)
Money Laundry Training	R&D	1 M	Abu Dhabi	MOI	3D, Unreal Engine, VR	Interactive training system
MARS ATLAS/Echo System	R&D	1 M	UAE	Self-Product	3D, Unity, Unreal Engine, AR/VR	Interactive room

Source: Innovation Floor. Published with the company's permission

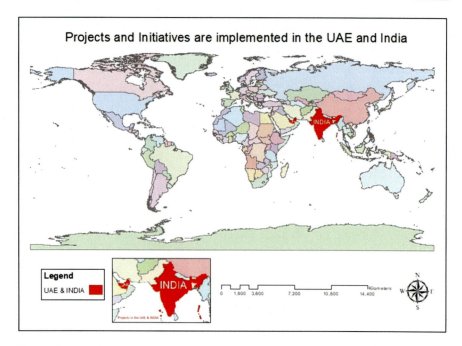

Fig. 5 Geographical distribution of projects carried out by the Innovation Floor. Source: Innovation Floor. Published with the company's permission

over the years. Depending on goals and market demands, the company plans to grow its commercial activity in the GCC nations and other countries.

5   Projects Alignment with SDGs

The 2030 Agenda for Sustainable Development offers a comprehensive plan for world peace and prosperity for both people and the environment. It constitutes 17 Sustainable Development Goals (SDGs), an urgent call to action for both rich and developing countries to work together in a global partnership. The idea was to eradicate poverty and other forms of deprivation through collaborative efforts to improve health and education, reduce inequality, spur economic growth, confront climate change, and defend the environment. The UN, notably the UN Department of Economic and Social Affairs, has been working on the SDGs for decades.

The UN System collaborates with the Secretary-General of the UN to produce the annual SDG Progress Report based on the global indicator framework, data from national statistics systems, and local knowledge (Are you familiar with all 17 SDGs? 2022). The list of initiatives and projects carried out by the Innovation Floor following SDGs 9, 11, and 17 are summarized in Table 2.

Table 2 List of projects carried out by the Innovation Floor in line with SDGs

SDG goals and targets for 2030	Indicators	UNSD indicator codes	Company projects	Total projects
Goal 9. Build resilient infrastructure, promote inclusive and sustainable industrialization, and foster innovation				
9.4 By 2030, all nations should take action in their own capacities to modernize infrastructure, remodel industries to make them sustainable, and adopt cleaner, more environmentally friendly technology and industrial processes	9.4.1 CO_2 emissions per unit of added value	C090401	1. Patrol Training System 2. Sharjah Classic Cars	2
9.5 Enhance scientific research, modernize industrial sectors' technical prowess in all nations, particularly emerging nations, and, by 2030, promote innovation and greatly raise the ratio of R&D personnel to every 1 million people, as well as public and private R&D expenditure	9.5.1 Research and development expenditure as a proportion of GDP	C090501	1. Hazza Mission to Mars 2. AI Autonomous Vehicle 3. Mars Atlas	3
9.c By 2020, significantly expand access to information and communications technologies and work toward granting all people in the world affordable Internet access	9.c.1 Population proportion with mobile network access.	C090c01	Service Robots	1
Goal 11. Make cities and human settlements inclusive, safe, resilient, and sustainable				
11.2 Improve road safety by expanding public transportation and ensuring that everyone has access to safe, affordable, accessible, and sustainable transportation systems by the year 2030. Pay particular attention to the needs of the elderly, women, children, people with disabilities, and those in vulnerable situations	11.2.1 Population proportion with public transport access	C110201	1. Patrol Training System 2. Sharjah Classic Cars	2

(continued)

Table 2 (continued)

SDG goals and targets for 2030	Indicators	UNSD indicator codes	Company projects	Total projects
Goal 16. Promote peaceful and inclusive societies for sustainable development, provide access to justice for all, and build effective, accountable, and inclusive institutions at all levels				
16.5 Substantially reduce corruption and bribery in all their forms	16.5.1 Proportion of persons who had at least one contact with a public official throughout the previous 12 months and who either paid a bribe to a public official or were requested to do so by them	C160501	Money Laundry System	1
Goal 17. Partnership for the goals				
17.6 Enhance knowledge-sharing on mutually agreed upon terms, including through improved coordination among existing mechanisms, particularly at the UN level, a global technology facilitation mechanism, and innovation	17.6.1 Fixed Internet broadband subscriptions per 100 inhabitants, by speed	C170602	1. Hazza Mission to Mars 2. AI Autonomous Vehicle 3. Mars Atlas	3

Source: Innovation Floor. Published with the company's permission

6 Innovation Floor as a Success Story

Innovation Floor is classified as a "success story" of Dubai Emirate in their SME Support strategies due to considerable innovation and valuable contribution to the emirate and the country. Being under the Umbrella of Dubai SME granted the Innovation Floor considerable exposure to the government projects that fall under the Digital Transformation initiatives.

Innovation Floor predicts successful graduation from the Dubai SME program; aiming to compete in the domestic and international markets with their products and services. The company has invested in developing its organization model, commercial and operational strategies that can execute its mission toward success and competence.

7 Joint Venture

A company, INOI, has proposed a joint business collaboration model for establishing a METAVERSE startup, including a venture studio setup. The new JV is called INOI Meta Dubai. Both companies' involvement will be in providing the business plan for potential investment and collaboration. The INOI invented:

- The first ever Web 3.0 mobile phone.
- *Mobile phone is DID, mobile phone is a wallet.*
- *The mobile phone is Node, and the mobile phone is Miner.*

Additionally, Innovation Floor has agreed with an international partner to establish an earth observation startup for delivering ground receiving stations and remote sensing solutions. Young-generation education is another primary scope for supporting professionals and students from age 9 years and older.

8 Conclusion

Innovation Floor (Ardhiyat Alibdaa) invests in disruptive innovation aligned with the UAE Industry Revolution strategy. The company is expanding by introducing new products to the market, merging with international businesses, and acquiring innovations from researchers worldwide.

The company is appreciated by the Dubai government and considered a success story or role model among other SMEs. Their experts are motivated by the work environment, enjoy innovation, and believe in their ambitious strategy and achievements. The company is contributing to social responsibility. In 2020, the company decided to deploy all its robots to support COVID-19 pandemic prevention; they also educate students at schools and campuses and work with different government entities to prove the concepts and facilitate their decision-making. Innovation Floor created several projects aligned with the Sustainable Development Goals, particularly SDGs 9, 11, and 17.

Questions for Discussion

1. What is the most important factor in an organization's success?
2. How can you overcome the influence of giant companies?
3. Do you have to invest your time in setting the strategy and the business model? Or will this come in time?
4. Do you have to work full time on your business?
5. Do you need to plan for an exit strategy? When should you plan for this?
6. What challenges would you face during the establishment of a new, innovative business?
7. Will robotics and artificial intelligence take over people's jobs?

Acknowledgments We would like to express our heartfelt gratitude to Dr. Khaula Abdulla Al Kaabi and Mr. Ibrahim Yousif Al Obaidly for giving us the opportunity to write about Innovation Company, one of the most innovative firms in the UAE. We are confident that the brand will expand rapidly and establish tens of branches worldwide in a short period.

References

Barrett, H., & Rose, D. C. (2022). Perceptions of the fourth agricultural revolution: What's in, what's out, and what consequences are anticipated? *Sociologia Ruralis, 62*(2), 162–189. https://doi.org/10.1111/soru.12324

Castelo-Branco, I., Oliveira, T., Simões-Coelho, P., Portugal, J., & Filipe, I. (2022). Measuring the fourth industrial revolution through the Industry 4.0 lens: The relevance of resources, capabilities and the value chain. *Computers in Industry, 138*(1), 103639. https://doi.org/10.1016/j.compind.2022.103639

David, L. O., Nwulu, N. I., Aigbavboa, C. O., & Adepoju, O. O. (2022). Integrating fourth industrial revolution (4IR) technologies into the water, energy & food nexus for sustainable security: A bibliometric analysis. *Journal of Cleaner Production, 363*, 132522. https://doi.org/10.1016/j.jclepro.2022.132522

Do you know all 17 SDGs? (2022). *United nation.* Department of Economic and Social Affairs, Sustainable Development. Retrieved from https://sdgs.un.org/goals

Farooq, A. S., & Zhang, P. (2022). Sensors and actuators: A. Physical A comprehensive review on the prospects of next-generation wearable electronics for individualized health monitoring, assistive robotics, and communication. *Sensors and Actuators: A. Physical, 344*, 113715. https://doi.org/10.1016/j.sna.2022.113715

Innovation Floor. (2021). Retrieved from https://innovationfloor.com/

Jamwal, A., Agrawal, R., Sharma, M., & Giallanza, A. (2021). Industry 4.0 technologies for manufacturing sustainability: A systematic review and future research directions. *Applied Sciences, 11*(12). https://doi.org/10.3390/app11125725

Kocdar, S., Bozkurt, A., & Goru Dogan, T. (2021). Engineering through distance education in the time of the fourth industrial revolution: Reflections from three decades of peer reviewed studies. *Computer Applications in Engineering Education, 29*(4), 931–949. https://doi.org/10.1002/cae.22367

Malomane, R., Musonda, I., & Okoro, C. S. (2022). The opportunities and challenges associated with the implementation of fourth industrial revolution technologies to manage health and safety. *International Journal of Environmental Research and Public Health, 19*(2). https://doi.org/10.3390/ijerph19020846

Ramadani, V., Istrefi-Jahja, A., Zeqiri, J., & Ribeiro-Soriano, D. (2023). COVID-19 and SMEs digital transformation. *IEEE Transactions on Engineering Management., 70*, 2864. https://doi.org/10.1109/TEM.2022.3174628

Khaled Khamis Al Arafati with over three decades of experience working for Governmental Entities, has gained extensive knowledge and expertise in Leadership, Land Survey, Cartography, Aerial Survey, Remote Sensing, Photogrammetry, and GIS. This experience has equipped him with the skills needed to thoroughly understand successful managerial and technical techniques. Khaled had the privilege of leading exceptional teams, units, sections, and departments during his tenure at the Military Survey Department for 22 years, BAYANAT for approximately 6 years, and YAHSAT for nearly 2 years. The focus of Khaled and his teams was on delivering projects on time while maintaining high-quality standards. Currently, Khaled is part of the Town Planning and Survey Sector at Al Ain Municipality, where he joined in May 2019. He works closely with the Spatial Data Division Head and other sections to update all geospatial records of the Al Ain sector. Khaled is responsible for managing several Geospatial projects related to Remote Sensing, Photogrammetry, Geographical Information Systems, Terrestrial Survey, Aerial Surveys, and Mapping. Additionally, Khaled and his teams handle Innovative Management connected to Team Management, Project Management, Information Systems Management, Quality Assurance Management, Risk Management, and Change Management.

Léo-Paul Dana is a Professor at ICD Business School Paris and affiliated with Lappeenranta University of Technology School of Business and Management. A graduate of the Faculty of Management at McGill University and of HEC-Montreal, he has served as Marie Curie Fellow at Princeton University and Visiting Professor at INSEAD. He has published extensively in a variety of journals and is the author of several books.

Secuira Technologies: Re-innovating Smart Technology

Abdulla Al Naqbi and Cristina Blanco González Tejero

Abstract

Family enterprises are an essential component of the Middle East's economy. They play a significant role in vital industries such as banking, construction, manufacturing, information technology (IT), and so forth, thereby accounting for a substantial share of the region's private sector GDP. As a part of one of the leading family businesses within the United Arab Emirates (UAE), here we provide a brief overview of Securia Technologies. The study will address the company's business plans through deep market analysis, the challenges of building the team, and financial and legal challenges. Furthermore, Secuira's projects and applications are highlighted in line with the UAE's vision for smart and safe city development by implementing artificial intelligence (AI) and innovative technologies. In the end, Secuira's initiatives aligned with the Sustainable Development Goals (SDGs), particularly those related to building resilient infrastructure and sustainable communities, as well as the protection of residents, are briefly summarized.

A. Al Naqbi (✉)
National Space Science and Technology Center (NSSTC), College of Humanities and Social Sciences, United Arab Emirates University (UAEU), Al Ain, Abu Dhabi, UAE
e-mail: 202190029@uaeu.ac.ae

C. B. G. Tejero
University of Alcalá, Madrid, Spain
e-mail: cristina.blancog@uah.es

© The Author(s), under exclusive license to Springer Nature Switzerland AG 2023
K. Alkaabi, V. Ramadani (eds.), *Family Business Cases*, Springer Business Cases,
https://doi.org/10.1007/978-3-031-39252-8_4

1   Introduction

In recent years, considerable attention has been paid to the rapid technological progress and the ever-expanding integration of information and communication technology (ICT) in the operations of business organizations (Gërguri-Rashiti et al., 2017). Moreover, massive development and progress in technology and artificial intelligence (AI) are rapidly advancing. The process of digitization has profound impacts on both the economy and the broader community (Buck et al., 2023). The government of the United Arab Emirates (UAE), through its leaders, took the initiative to adopt the new technologies in the early stages to place the country on the map of the leading nations in technological innovation. One of the main initiatives in the country is the development of smart cities to facilitate decision-making and ensure sustainable development. As a result, local entrepreneurs and technology enthusiasts have taken the lead to align with this vision and contribute to the country's progress in AI and innovative technologies, such as Secuira Technologies (Nummi, 2019).

Cities need to face new challenges, and in this regard, there are various innovative methods aimed at improving urban services based on the use of different technologies, which allows the concept of smart cities to be established (Albino et al., 2015). Thus, smart cities refer to technologically advanced urban areas. In smart cities, a diverse range of electronically managed methods, like automated sensors on the road, are used to collect specific data.

In today's digital age, there is a vast quantity of data being produced from almost every industry (Reddy et al., 2020). The information is utilized to operate assets and different services efficiently. Along with the growth of technologies in the contemporary era, the development of smart cities has become an integral part of government strategies, especially in developed countries (Asmyatullin, 2020). The UAE has been a pioneer in developing exemplary smart cities like Abu Dhabi and Dubai. In 2018, Abu Dhabi launched a pilot project to convert one of the cities into a city named Zayed Smart City using blockchain technologies and AI in different public and private sector activities (Hafifi, 2021). In addition, using technologies to convert Dubai into an innovative and sustainable city, the Emirati government has implemented a project called "Smart City Vision". The project contains six target areas to improve: easy and open accessibility of data; smarter transport; optimization of energy resources; more innovative city parks and beaches; more ingenious apps for the police department; and a new master control unit (UAE, 2022). Additionally, the project has been designed to improve almost 1000 government services.

Secuira is a national company established in 2016 with national expertise and competencies that provide multiple services and focused smart and safe cities innovative solutions. Secuira is heavily involved in software development in several fields, such as AI, the Internet of Things, big data, unmanned aerial vehicles, and anti-aircraft systems. Secuira also provides advisory services, management, and implementation of projects in the field of the security industry and the associated smart technologies that contribute to building safe and smart city systems (Nummi, 2019), which is done through a work team, and national cadres backed by extensive security and technical expertise. This study will explore the UAE's vision for smart and safe city development by implementing AI and innovative technologies. Furthermore, Secuira's projects and applications are highlighted, which enrich their role and management in aligning with the UAE vision (Lin & Bergmann, 2016). Additionally, the concept of the business model has been the subject of study in the academic literature throughout the history of management, with three main interpretations: business models as attributes of firms, as cognitive/linguistic schemas, and as formal conceptual representations of how a firm works (Massa et al., 2017). The study will address the company's business plans through deep market analysis, the challenges in building the team, and financial and legal challenges. Finally, Secuira's alignment with the United Nations Sustainable Development Goals (UNSDGs) will be explored and mapped to various projects developed by the company.

2 Business Overview

Digital transformation entails the reconfiguration of business models by leveraging cutting-edge digital technologies (Li et al., 2023). In that sense, the significance of enterprises that provide cutting-edge technology-driven amenities is enormous for implementing smart city projects. In the UAE, several companies that provide such services have been part of the government's plans to convert cities like Abu Dhabi and Dubai into innovative and sustainable cities. Secuira is one of these companies that have been designed and built to deliver such advanced and cutting-edge technologies that might further improve the quality of life of Emirati society using AI, IoT, and blockchain tools.

The firm was founded in 2016, and in such a short period, it has achieved a range of successful inventions powered by these advanced technologies, such as face recognition, smart home solutions, and so on. The business's inception was by professionals with experience of more than 20 years in the technological sector in different departments such as data security and solutions, IT-related project management, and hardware and software development (Wani, 2022). Hence, from the very beginning, the firm has been powered by the true expertise of the top management in the technological aspects, which has supported it in delivering such exemplary tech solutions. From the very beginning of the business operations, it started to focus on large-scale projects, especially government projects, which has been the key reason that Secuira has been a significant contributor to the government's strategy to develop Abu Dhabi as a sustainable and smarter city. Only 1 year after its inception, the firm has successfully integrated projects like the data security enhancement project at Homeland Security Consulting and the solutions project. The outstanding success in increasing data security by integrating IoT-powered tools into the project resulted in the firm's early success. Thus, it supported Secuira in establishing a positive brand reputation in Emirati society from the very beginning of its business operations. Moreover, these projects in 2017 supported Secuira in attaining adequate

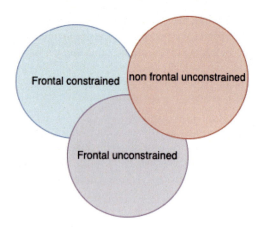

Fig. 1 Secuira face recognition solution. Source: Secuira Technologies. Published with the company's permission

brand recall within a short period by achieving responsibility for managing different government projects in the later part of the business life cycle.

In the following year, 2018, Secuira further developed its position in the technology-based service delivery industry by delivering advanced facilities. For instance, it invented software that is capable of face recognition. The exemplary software can detect faces from a long distance of the camera and deliver flexible credit from multiple angles of the camera. Figure 1 shows the effective solutions offered by Secuira in face recognition, which has supported law enforcement agencies in avoiding any possible threat of identity hiding. Secuira's face recognition technology can detect faces from frontal and non-frontal constrained angles. Moreover, it can overcome any partial camera obstruction while detecting any face. This face recognition technology is differentiated as it recognizes faces covered with make-up or sunglasses. Moreover, the facility is adequate due to its real-time intelligence, which can recognize 3.4 million faces within a second (Secuira, 2022a, b).

The face recognition technologies offered by Secuira have supported law enforcement agencies in different ways, as shown in Fig. 2. The visual representation on the firm's website is presented here, which shows how the system supports identifying age, gender, and facial gesture in terms of mental state and if there is any issue in the security checking. Hence, this technology-driven service delivery enabled the firm to increase its brand reputation, as this is considered a supportive tool for law enforcement agencies such as national security forces and border security forces.

Figure 3 illustrates the firm's offering in managing business activities in terms of using technologies to predict and prevent any possible threat related to crime, which supports improving the quality of life. The success of the facial recognition system created further opportunities for businesses to serve the government's smart city projects. For example, in 2018, it invented a technique to detect crime scenes from the heat map. It developed AI-powered tools that have supported law enforcement authority in different aspects, such as integrating with Google Maps, developing city-wise heat maps, and filtering locations regarding crime type, location,

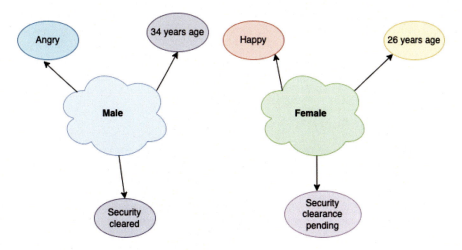

Fig. 2 Secuira's face recognition example. Source: Secuira Technologies. Published with the company's permission

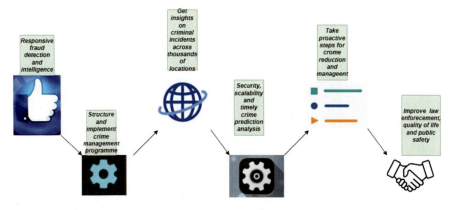

Fig. 3 Crime heat map of Secuira. Source: Secuira Technologies. Published with the company's permission

registration, gender, or marital status. Hence, it helped the police authorities significantly to continue crime-free societal activities in Abu Dhabi and the UAE (Khaleej Times, 2022).

Furthermore, the firm continued to focus on innovation and delivered different innovative outcomes, such as sentiment analysis. It has supported businesses in tracking the trends in the market and the ups and downs in business activities. In addition, it has supported setting benchmarks for business leaders. Moreover, this facility has supported analyzing customer preferences by analyzing customer activities on the social media platform. In addition, it contributed to smart city projects by developing an innovative facility titled License Plate Recognition

(LPR). It supported the traffic police department in activities like preventing car theft, collecting e-tolls, and analyzing accident cases in a hyper-localized manner. As the smart city projects in the UAE are focused on further improving transportation and traffic control procedures, this inclusion from Securia has been a pivotal contribution to the success of these projects.

3 Market Analysis

3.1 Overview

The integration of business analytics has transformed decision-making support, generating a surge in executives' interest in quantitative decision aids and analytical models, fueled by massive data sets, pattern extraction algorithms, and user-friendly software systems (Lessmann et al., 2021). Therefore, market analysis has gained relevance as the tactical method taken up for analyzing and understanding a particular market relevant to the quantitative and qualitative standards (Abuzeinab et al., 2017). In this section, the market analysis for Securia is conducted by researching the resources available on the Internet and the frameworks for the market analysis.

3.2 Demographics and Segmentation

Securia is laid in the digital market and is re-innovating smart city technology through current tactics of modernization and also considering the overall implied benefits (Oberlo, 2021; Pan et al., 2019). From a demographic point of view, the contribution of the different cities in the Middle East region is represented and hence implies benefits. In this consideration, the case of the UAE has shown an overall representation of about 13.6% of the total Gulf Cooperation Council, which is the most considerable contribution of any single nation. AI has been identified as the best combination alongside the development of smart city infrastructure (PWC, 2022).

The contributions in terms of the development of infrastructure for smart cities will eventually consider the overall technological uprising and improved communication technologies under focus (Qureshi et al., 2020). In this aspect, the development of the share for high-tech information outcomes is thus implied by the increased spending on Internet technology. Figure 4 denotes the construction industry's claim in 2024 for information and communication technologies (ICT), which shall substantially increase the share of Internet usage and information technological outcomes in place (Rosati et al., 2019).

The share for the construction and manufacturing industries is a part of the combination of usage, at around 9% and 7%, which has been implied with the developmental outcomes for technology aspects for Securia (Statista, 2022). On the other hand, the use of AI and its sector-wise share are represented in Table 1, which shows that Securia has tremendous scope for growth and expansion under the reigns

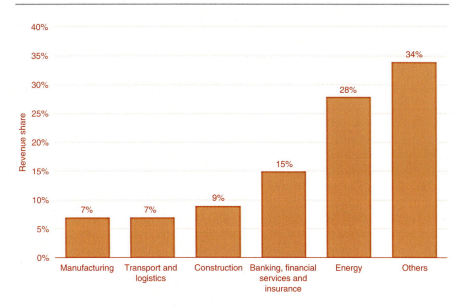

Fig. 4 Forecasted ICT spending share in the UAE in 2024. Source: Statista (2022)

Table 1 Contribution of AI to the industry in 2030

Industry	Contribution (Billion $)	Contribution (%)
Construction, manufacturing	$99	12
Energy, utility	$78	6
Public health, education	$59	19
Financial, professional	$38	14
Consumer, retail	$23	19
Transport, logistics	$12	15
Tech, media, telecom	$10	14

Source: Deloitte (2022)

of the UAE, wherein the denoted outcomes are associated directly with the target market (Deloitte, 2022).

3.3 Target Market Identification

The target market is identified as those wherein the products manufactured by the company are extensively sold (Sainidis & Robson, 2019). Segmentation, targeting, and positioning are crucial to marketing strategy, but while Big Data has enabled micro-segmentation, the global limitations of the Internet and concerns about data privacy and accessibility can pose challenges for global companies (Schlegelmilch, 2022). For the company under consideration, Secuira, the target market is the UAE market, where the smart cities are re-innovated, and the company is a determinant in the provision of technical support in infrastructural development. The target market, as identified, determines the quality of spending of the people within the cities and hence is associated with the developed outcomes in standardized results (Supena et al., 2021). The market potential for this sector is identified under the growth outputs for the differentiated results and hence considers the outcomes in place, which settles the consequences in nature (Taghinezhad et al., 2021). The industrial developments for using smart technologies have been considered beneficial outcomes for adequate support, hence the situational factors under review.

The market need within the UAE is to develop at least five (5) more smart cities and considerably develop their overall approaches in terms of effective outcomes (U. ae, 2022a, b, c). The first smart city in the UAE is Dubai, and the second one is Abu Dhabi. Further, Masdar City is also being initiated for development, which shall be considered the third smart city in the UAE. Currently, analysis of the rankings determines the position of Abu Dhabi and Dubai as the 28th and 29th smart cities across the globe, respectively. Secuira has these cities as its major clients.

The target market has grown at a percentage of 9% year on year, and this has created a positive effect on the structural and institutional results (U.ae, 2022a, b, c). For these results, the growth is determined by the potential for the spread of practical outcomes, hence the particular focus on conditional factors. The UAE's location and demographics have helped it flourish, and consequently, business growth has focused on standards of development within the country.

3.4 Analysis of Competitive Forces

The analysis of competitive pressures in the market is generally evaluated by Porter's five forces model, wherein the main motive is to identify and analyze the current outcomes for the company (Sainidis & Robson, 2019). Michael Porter's concepts of the new economy provide a valuable basis for investigating the environment (Karagiannopoulos et al., 2005). Despite being a highly recognized model, the practical application of the Five Forces framework has proven to be challenging (Dobbs, 2012). In this consideration, the defined results are evaluated using the four main factors, which creates inference for the fifth one, as shown in Fig. 5.

3.4.1 The Threat of a New Entrant

Secuira's business is in the information and technology sector, which supplies AI-oriented solutions for the smart cities under focus. Thereby, it is well focused that the organization has implemented several moats under consideration (Vyakina, 2019). The threat of new entrants is, therefore, shallow, as there is a requirement for substantially larger investment options and hence the usage of developed infrastructure.

3.4.2 Threat of Substitution

The company currently has established amicable relations with the governance councils and other members of its operations in the market. There is a significant

Secuira Technologies: Re-innovating Smart Technology

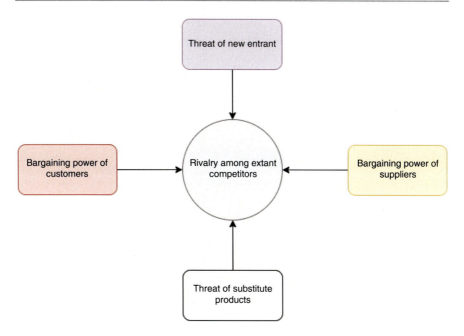

Fig. 5 Porter's five forces. Source: Secuira Technologies. Published with the company's permission

requirement for the defined outcomes in this consideration. Hence, the contracts are sizable, allowing a lesser threat of substitution and considering the consequences under focus (Zhou & Wen, 2020). The threat of substitution relates to the cheaper version of the same services and products launched by the company, in this case, Secuira, wherein the market reputation is damaged.

3.4.3 Bargaining Power of Suppliers
The supplier numbers in the same industry are considerably higher, allowing the substantiation of the numbers, thus implicating the beneficial outcomes in place (Sainidis & Robson, 2019). The defined credibility for the market holder is greater and considers the developments in the area for reduced benefits; hence, it is evaluated that the bargaining power for the supplier is considerably lesser.

3.4.4 Bargaining Power of Buyers
The buyers differ from the suppliers; hence, the bargaining power is considerably higher as they spend money on luxurious properties and infrastructure. The consideration under the defined outcomes has been seen as a positive focus for the maintenance of the competitiveness of the overall business (Demirkesen & Ozorhon, 2017).

3.4.5 Industry Rivalry

The industry rivalry is mainly present with the other companies in congruence with Secuira. It hence evaluates the current standards of operations under the company, highlighting the subsequent competition between the companies (Sainidis & Robson, 2019). The company under focus, Secuira, has perpetuated the delivery of effective services alongside increased prospects for growth.

3.5 Differentiation Among Competitors

Secuira is a leading AI service provider in the UAE, and it has been successful in having a trustable brand image in terms of providing smart city-related services, including LPR (License Plate Recognition) and face recognition technology (Secuira, 2022b, c, d). On the evaluation of the technology consulting industry in the UAE, the potential competitors of Secuira are Emtech Solution and Euclidz.ai. These have successfully captured around 56% of the total market share of the respective industries in the nation (Gulf News, 2022a). Table 2 explains the services the companies deliver under consideration and their details regarding the establishment.

The first and foremost differentiation of Secuira is its efficiency in developing customized kinds of AI technology or software solutions as per the customers' needs, along with following the standard of the state of the art (Secuira, 2022e, f). It means that if the administration of the UAE uses machine learning and AI-related services to develop smart cities, it will successfully accomplish the project without deviating from the standard internal quality related to technology and sustainability. On the other hand, evaluating the USP (unique selling proposition) of Emtech Solution, it is found that its management and team are not very efficient in providing any dedicated AI solution related to smart city development and management (Emtech, 2022a). The business head of Emtech Solution's expertise is related to cloud solutions, data protection, and cyber security, due to which it has been found efficient in providing digital data management-related solutions to the entities of the UAE. Since the business head of Secuira lacks expertise in delivering cloud solutions and cybersecurity-related services, Emtech Solution might get an edge over it in boosting the digital platform of the UAE.

The administration of Emtech Solution can boost the digital infrastructure of the cities of the UAE by transforming them into smart cities through the development of real-time digital fraud and crime management portals, and this will eventually help the nation be more technologically advanced than others. To develop a compelling smart city, its management or authority must have an information system capable of digitally recognizing and tracking each citizen's details without any manual effort. In developing live recognition of demographic and professional information about citizens, the business perspective of Secuira is found to be more competitive than that of its rivals, including Emtech Solution (Secuira, 2022f). The rationale behind the competitiveness of Secuira over its competitors is its efficiency in developing machine learning algorithms for face recognition, capable of recognizing more than

Table 2 The particular services that are delivered by Secuira and its competitors

Particular	Services	About
Secuira	• Face Recognition • License Plate Recognition • Crime Heat Maps • Sentiment Analysis • Internet of Things (IoT)	• Founded in 2016 • Operational only in the UAE • Working with both private companies and the government agencies of the UAE (Secuira, 2022b)
Emtech Solution (Competitor of Secuira)	• ICT Solutions • Cloud Solutions • Data Protection • Cyber Security • Professional services like managed IT Services	• Incorporated in 1993 (Emtech, 2022a) • Only available in the UAE • Provide services to both corporate and government agencies (Emtech, 2022b)
Euclidz.ai (Euclidz Technologies Pvt Ltd) (Competitor of Secuira)	• Business Analytics • AI (artificial intelligence) • Data Management • Cloud Solutions • Digital Transformation • Robotic Process • Automation • Data Governance • Managed Business Service	• Founded on December 12, 2019 (Euclid, 2022) • Available in the UAE and other international markets like India (Euclidz, 2022a)

Source: Secuira Technologies. Published with the company's permission

3.4 million faces simultaneously without any data accuracy-related error. On the other hand, in terms of providing AI services with a diverse cloud solution, the business perspective of Euclidz Technologies Pvt. Ltd. is found to be more competitive than that of Secuira, as the earlier one is efficient in providing automation-related solutions along with delivering digital services as well (Euclidz, 2022b). To have succeeded in developing a sustainable smart city, its authority needs to develop a real-time crime monitoring and tracking system so that the possibility of any unfortunate incidents might be curbed on time.

In terms of developing a real-time crime monitoring and management-related trait within the cities of the UAE, Secuira is found to be more competitive than its rivals like Emtech Solution and Euclidz Technologies Pvt. Ltd., as the earlier one is capable of running a crime heat map system in real time. Secuira efficiently displays real-time crime heat maps for each location in the UAE, along with transportation details. The nation's authorities can access all these facilities digitally without any manual intervention (Secuira, 2022f). Besides this, the business head of Secuira is more competitive than other companies in developing a driver-free transportation system and a digitally controlled traffic system with the strategic usage of its sentiment analysis and neural network features. It means that Secuira is more efficient than its rivals, like Emtech, in developing a crime-free and automatically controlled traffic system-based smart city. Above all, Secuira is more competitive than its rivals, like Emtech Solution, in developing an unmanned shopping system with the tactful usage of its sentiment analysis-related algorithm. It will eventually help the authority of the UAE to have fast and crowdless shopping facilities within its cities.

3.6 Regulation in the Market

The market for information technology and building infrastructure is considerably regulated within the UAE, substantially influencing developing businesses. In terms of effective corporate governance and infrastructural development, it has focused on overall growth in effective outcomes defined under regulated conditions (Vyakina, 2019). Therefore, the regulations in the market are placed under the government's capacity to be competent in effective service delivery.

3.7 Summary

The market analysis has thus identified the potential causes of the issues in place and has conditionally outlined the factors under consideration for which the company's value proposition is identified. From the analysis, it is clear that the situational factors and considerable outcomes in effective results are significant standards for outlining the features under consideration.

4 Challenges in the Incorporation

4.1 Evaluation of Challenges

The significant challenges within the incorporation are outlined through the ineffective solution generation and conditional to the clear values, which outcomes the characteristic features under consideration. The defined benefits are also seeded through successive significant initiatives for the outcomes under consideration. The challenges are also of two main kinds: operational and leadership. Therefore, the challenges within team development have been seeded under the prospective conditions under which the distinct standards are further aligned.

4.2 Operational Challenges

Secuira has faced several challenges since its inception and has shown great skill sets, caliber, and effectiveness to overcome them efficiently. The operational challenges are associated with the lack of a supply chain for the company and the lack of skilled employees, which have determined its weaknesses (Oberlo, 2021). The operational challenges are therefore outlined with the instances for supportive outcomes under consideration, and hence the operational challenges are outlined through the conclusive circumstances. The main challenge hereafter was found to be related to ineffective result delivery and hence associated with the principles for outcomes where there is substantial evidence for the outcomes in place. The challenges are mitigated through the outlined standards, thus considering the beneficial basis has the implied outcomes throughout the industry.

4.3 Leadership Challenges

Leadership challenges are therefore found to be implied by the fact that leadership is fragile and contemplates other issues like psychosocial characteristics. The leadership challenges are thus outlined by applying an overall perspective under focus related to the situational factors for the company's preferences (Asbari, 2020). The company has been capable of mitigating its challenges with improved recruitment measures for the staff and outlines the categorical decision-making standards under review (Andersen, 2018). The main challenge in leadership outcomes is thus contemplated with the defined outcomes for the undertaking organization. Therefore, it has been outlined that the company, Secuira, has been functional throughout the pandemic condition and hence considered the beneficial needs under which throughput and outlines the figurative requirements of review (Sainidis & Robson, 2019). The general conditions are therefore situated under the beneficial outcomes for focus, considering the technical capacity, and hence outline the factors under review. Hence, it has been outlined that the general issues in place are thus related to the factors under consideration, wherein the structural outcomes are in place.

4.4 Challenges in Building the Team

The process of team building is associated with the defined benefits under which the derived outcomes and hence considers the challenges under review, considering the benefits under overall conditions (Crowe, 2017). The defined outcomes for the team are constituted essentially with like-minded people, and hence the challenges for team building have been a result of the ineffective design. The hiring process and frequency were highly impacted due to the company's operational issues, wherein the standards were not reached through the criteria under consideration (Supena et al., 2021). The process has been impacted by the defined circumstances, which have been defined under the team building process. The defined outcomes for the challenges have been outlined through the defined perjury of information; hence, there is a tactical difference. The challenges are therefore governed by finding like-minded people and formulating a team of professionals. The main focus is on the perspective of information sharing, considering the beneficial outcomes in place. In the case of Secuira, therefore, it has been effectively outlined that the information transfer is seeded within the defined outcomes for review.

4.5 Financial and Legal Challenges

On the evaluation of the organizational strategy of Secuira, it is found that the primary financial challenge that the management of Secuira faces while executing its operational activities is cost and capital arrangements. Table 3 discusses the economic and legal challenges that a company providing similar services might encounter.

In developing AI solutions like facial recognition and crime heat maps, huge capital investment is required by Secuira, while the tendency of the customers of the UAE to pay a higher price for the service is moderate due to the availability of a higher number of service providers (Secuira, 2022e, f). The consequence of the requirement of huge capital for AI services and the higher bargaining power of customers is that the management of Secuira will face obstacles in having a higher return on employed capital. Suppose the business head of Secuira plans to contribute to developing a smart city within the UAE. The primary financial challenge that might be faced is related to fund shortages and huge investments. Since automating entire transportation, municipality, and crime management-related practices will require a considerable amount of money, the administration of Secuira might face a fund shortage-related situation (UAE Gov, 2022). Continuous maintenance activities will be necessary to keep the autonomous features of smart features active. It might add additional costs to Secuira as its management will have to deploy a dedicated team.

The primary legal challenge the administration of Secuira might face is related to quality standards in the event of the unavailability of a proper license for AI solution development. The authority of the UAE might put legal charges against companies violating business laws (Gulf News, 2022b, c). Apart from this, in case any AI

Table 3 Perspectives of financial and legal challenges

Financial challenges	Legal challenges
• Huge capital investment in developing AI solutions and lower return • Higher maintenance costs • Shortage of funds • Breach in the accounting system in case of digitalization of all sources of income	• Possibility of fines for not meeting legal and standardization-related obligations • Confidential breach due to encroachment in the AI system or solution • Political differences about the effectiveness of smart cities

Source: Secuira Technologies. Published with the company's permission

system is compromised by hackers and a third-party unethically accesses confidential data of the public, Secuira might face legal fines for a confidentiality breach.

5 Smart Infrastructures Through Secuira

Smart infrastructure is essentially defined as the virtual-physical system that helps to provide unified management of all elements through the use of technological tools that assist in analyzing and compiling information (Haenlein et al., 2019). It also helps meet efficiency, productivity, sustainability, and safety objectives. The factors that ensure the creation of a prosperous smart city depend on the development of innovative solutions within six domains: environment and energy, economy, living and health, government and education, and security and mobility (Hong et al., 2020). In a flourishing smart city, the economy and lifestyle conditions are entirely digital, and more people get all the services online in the comfort of their homes (Treleaven et al., 2018).

In regard to the creation of smart infrastructure for the amalgamation of all the aspects that are included within a smart infrastructure, Secuira is quite helpful. Secuira assists in creating a broader spectrum linked with innovative AI, blockchain solutions, and IoT for the unique needs of the collaboration of various systems (Schwalbe, 2020). The implementation of this term often integrates multiple solutions in a seamless and hassle-free way to provide optimum results to a greater extent. The creation of smart infrastructure within a city constitutes the creation of digital currency and the linking of individuals' bank accounts to their smartphones. It also helps people book bus rides or ensure proper commuting is possible directly from the doorstep (Kirpichnikov et al., 2020). To achieve all these aspects of smart infrastructure, four principles are followed for the unification of all the systems: data, analytics, feedback, and adaptability (Paudel & Sharma, 2020).

Data is the essential element, and smart cities are tightly linked to the governmental departments concerning education, health, environment, sociability, and mobility (Noothigattu et al., 2018). Thus, all the information is stored in the system so that citizens can access every piece of information with just one click. Secuira makes AI implementation possible, which helps get the information more quickly (Vaishya et al., 2020). The second principle is analytics, where the AI statistically automatically analyzes the data and provides the appropriate information to the customers (Haenlein et al., 2019). For example, in a smart city like the UAE, when customers search for a specific item of a certain quality within a particular budget, the AI app of Secuira analyzes the information and provides relevant results instantaneously.

The next part of the smart infrastructure is feedback and adaptability, where the input is associated with continuous communication with the customers through the AI apps. It also helps the customers procure information from AI (Dahi & Ezziane, 2019). Additionally, adaptability is enhanced when AI interacts with the human interface and updates itself along with the overall development of the research process.

6 Secuira Alignment to SDG

The United Nations 2030 Agenda for Sustainable Development laid down 17 Sustainable Development Goals (SDGs) to be met by all countries. The SDGs were established in 2016 as an evidence-based framework for sustainable development, and policymakers face the challenge of implementing them in a coherent and integrated way (Allen et al., 2018). Since then, the UAE has implemented extensive efforts toward meeting these goals through its public and private sectors. Hence, Secuira's vision aligns with the UN Sustainable Development Goals (SDGs), especially SDG9, SDG11, and SDG16. The contribution to the SDGs is part of the company's assessment when selecting projects. All employees have been made aware of the progress of the UN SDGs so that Secuira is aligned with the SDGs at all levels. Table 4 illustrates Secuira's alignment with the SDGs.

Secuira is aligned with SDG 11, which is developing sustainable cities and communities. It includes making cities and human settlements inclusive, safe, resilient, and sustainable. Secuira is preparing a multimillion-dollar project to establish AI-based smart cities equipped with modern facilities like risk management, disaster control systems, sustainable modern transports, well-structured human settlements, smart security, Wi-Fi-enabled cities, and proper waste management systems.

The biggest challenge for Secuira to develop a smart city in the UAE is due to the hot and dry climatic conditions. Most of the country's regions are covered in a desert, which is quite difficult for the construction teams to work on. Similarly, sandstorms and disturbances in the climate are frequent in this region. Secuira is trying to create technologies that enable proper sustainable development and help improve these adverse climatic conditions (Secuira, 2022f). Some critical sectors that will be highlighted and enhanced with smart cities are transport systems, water, sanitation, proper waste management, and education. Secuira is building sources of fresh and clean drinking water, which is essential for an urban city. Similarly, sanitation and the disposal of waste are managed effectively to maintain clean atmosphere and surroundings.

Other than SDG11, the Secuira app also helps fulfill SGD9 and SDG16 of the sustainable development goals, where SDG9 constitutes the development of industry, innovation, and infrastructure (UNDP, 2022). The UAE government plans to fulfill SDG 9 within the year 2030 by upgrading infrastructure and retrofitting industries to create sustainability (Dahi & Ezziane, 2019). It also helps to increase competence through the efficient use of resources and the creation of environmentally sound technologies throughout the city as a whole (Ghosh et al., 2019). Also, to make cities and human settlements inclusive, resilient, safe, and sustainable, the Secuira app helps collaborate and provides accessible roads by improving safety through public transport and providing exceptional care for vulnerable persons.

SDG16 creates a peaceful society, which can also be fulfilled by utilizing the Secuira app that reduces all kinds of violence and connected death rates within the UAE (UNDP, 2022). Moreover, the Secuira app helps develop accountable, effective, and transparent institutions at all levels, ensuring the right decision-making for

Table 4 Secuira's alignment with SDGs

SDG No.	Target	Company projects	Number of projects
SDG9: Build resilient Infra, promote inclusive and sustainable industrialization, and foster innovation	9.4 By 2030, upgrade infrastructure and retrofit industries to make them sustainable, with increased resource-use efficiency and greater adoption of clean and environmentally sound technologies and industrial processes, with all countries taking action following their respective capabilities	Project 1. LPR (License Plate Recognition)	1
SDG11: Make cities and human settlements inclusive, safe, resilient, and sustainable	11.2 By 2030, provide access to safe, affordable, accessible, and sustainable transport systems for all, improving road safety, notably by expanding public transport, with particular attention to the needs of those in vulnerable situations, women, children, persons with disabilities and older persons	Project 1. LPR (License Plate Recognition)	1
SDG16: Promote peaceful and inclusive societies for sustainable development, provide access to justice for all, and build effective, accountable, and inclusive institutions at all levels	16.1 Significantly reduce all forms of violence and related death rates everywhere 16.6 Develop effective, accountable, and transparent institutions at all levels 16.7 Ensure responsive, inclusive, participatory, and representative decision-making at all levels	Project 1. Crime Prediction Heat map Project 2. Safe Community App.	2

Source: Secuira Technologies. Published with the company's permission

individuals (Secuira, 2022a). With the increase in population, crime reduction helps increase the uphill task for the judiciaries, policymakers, police forces, and civic bodies to a greater extent (Kim et al., 2020). The main requirement at this point is taking the actionable and vast scale of available crime information and protecting the public from safety hazards.

To protect the public and fulfill SDG 16 of creating a peaceful society, the heat maps and prediction of crime spots are pretty substantial. It helps create an intelligent link with Google Maps and helps understand the crime trends in a specific area. Also, a list of offenders is made, which helps in understanding the crime rate within an exact spot, and the socio-economic and demographic variables of a particular case are considered to a considerable extent.

7 Conclusion

The development of smart cities in the UAE is associated with technological implementation in all walks of life. To be precise, the technical implementation of smart infrastructure is related to intelligent solutions in the economy, health, government work, education, security, and mobility. To achieve this particular aim, Secuira helps in providing innovative solutions with the help of AI, which creates the unification of all these projects. The factors of the economy are controlled by the initiative of making a digital currency and by creating mobile apps to ensure the proper transaction process with security.

It is also observed that Secuira ensures the development of AI by utilizing proper infrastructure. It is found that most of the unification is possible by connecting the interface. For example, security is observed to be maintained using encrypted forms within the infrastructure, ensuring the digital transaction's safety. Moreover, it is also found that the Secuira Company improves government activities like health and education by storing information and sharing the report whenever needed.

In the UAE's smart cities, Secuira uses AI to guide ordinary citizens to fill out any online form. Also, it helps in getting admission to universities within the UAE. Secuira also uses medical records and information stored in the health app. It is also linked to the overall analysis process used in the entire research context. Also, it is seen that mobility is immensely enhanced by the use of an AI interface within the Secuira app, which helps in using AI to detect a person's live location and send the vehicles for pick-up whenever it is required.

The report has also observed that the UN sustainability goals are also fulfilled with the help of Secuira, where SDG9, SDG11, and SDG16 are mainly satisfied. The SDG9 fulfillment constitutes building resilient infrastructure and sustainable industrialization for fostering innovation. The realization of SDG11 is done using sustainable building cities, which are achievable by employing smart infrastructure to a vast extent. Along with that, SDG 16 is also fulfilled. The AI apps are used for building peaceful societies by continuously monitoring several places in the city and providing the appropriate safety to its citizens.

In particular, with the analysis of the proposed case study and the consideration of the globalization and implementation of smart technologies in different areas of society, an overview of the benefits that can be derived from the implementation of such digital technologies in urban areas is observed. Due to that, the importance of smart projects and solutions in various fields is highlighted. In addition, the use of innovative solutions with the help of AI can improve efficiency and security in the process of digital transactions and the storage and sharing of information. However, there is also a need to address potential negative impacts in terms of inequality and privacy and to further research and develop policies that promote equity and the well-being of society at large. In conclusion, the analysis of the case study provides important insights and reflections on the benefits and challenges of implementing digital technologies in urban areas and generates a call for reflection and future research linked to the issue.

Questions for Discussion

1. What is Secuira technology?
2. How Secuira technology help in building smart cities in the UAE?
3. Do you think smart infrastructure is required for cities, and why?
4. How could Secuira technology be used to address specific city challenges?
5. What advantages may arise from implementing digital technologies in urban environments?

References

Abuzeinab, Arif, M., & Qadri. (2017). Barriers to MNEs green business models in the UK construction sector: An ISM analysis. *Journal of Cleaner Production, 68*(5), 27–37.

Albino, V., Berardi, U., & Dangelico, R. M. (2015). Smart cities: Definitions, dimensions, performance, and initiatives. *Journal of Urban Technology, 22*(1), 3–21. https://doi.org/10.1080/10630732.2014.942092

Allen, C., Metternicht, G., & Wiedmann, T. (2018). Initial progress in implementing the sustainable development goals (SDGs): A review of evidence from countries. *Sustainability Science, 13*, 1453–1467. https://doi.org/10.1007/s11625-018-0572-3

Andersen. (2018). Servant leadership and transformational leadership: From comparisons to farewells. *Leadership & Organization Development Journal, 39*(6), 762–774. https://doi.org/10.1108/LODJ-01-2018-0053

Asbari, M. (2020). Transformational leadership suitable for future organisational needs? *International Journal of Social, Policy and Law, 1*(1), 51–55. https://doi.org/10.1221/joop.19616

Asmyatullin, R. (2020) Smart cities in GCC: Comparative study of economic dimension. Presented in IOP conference series: Earth and environmental science. https://doi.org/10.1088/1755-1315/459/6/062045

Buck, C., Clarke, J., de Oliveira, R. T., Desouza, K. C., & Maroufkhani, P. (2023). Digital transformation in asset-intensive organisations: The light and the dark side. *Journal of Innovation & Knowledge, 8*(2), 100335. https://doi.org/10.1016/j.jik.2023.100335

Crowe. (2017). Defining components of team leadership and membership in prehospital emergency medical services. *Prehospital Emergency Care, 21*(5), 645–651.

Dahi, M., & Ezziane, Z. (2019). Measuring e-government adoption in Abu Dhabi with technology acceptance model (TAM). *International Journal of Electronic Governance, 17*(6), 206–231. https://doi.org/10.1504/IJEG.2015.071564

Deloitte. (2022). *Deloitte evaluates AI Readiness in the Middle East*. Retrieved October 13 2022, from https://www2.deloitte.com/xe/en/pages/about-deloitte/press-releases/deloitte-evaluates-ai-readiness-in-the-middle-east.html

Demirkesen, S., & Ozorhon, B. (2017). Impact of integration management on construction project management performance. *International Journal of Project Management, 35*(8), 1639–1654. https://doi.org/10.1016/j.ijproman.2017.09.008

Dobbs, M. E. (2012). Porter's five forces in practice: Templates for firm and case analysis. In *Competition forum* (Vol. 10, No. 1, p. 22). American Society for Competitiveness.

Emtech. (2022a). *About Us*. Retrieved October 13, 2022, from https://emtech.ae/about-us/

Emtech. (2022b). *News*. Retrieved October 13, 2022, from https://emtech.ae/news-listing/

Euclidz. (2022a). *About*. Retrieved October 13, 2022, from https://euclidz.ai/about/
Euclidz. (2022b). *Contact Us*. Retrieved October 13, 2022, from https://euclidz.ai/contact-us/
Gërguri-Rashiti, S., Ramadani, V., Abazi-Alili, H., Dana, L. P., & Ratten, V. (2017). ICT, innovation and firm performance: The transition economies context. *Thunderbird International Business Review, 59*(1), 93–102. https://doi.org/10.1002/tie.21772
Ghosh, A., Maeder, A., Baker, M., & Chandramouli, D. (2019). 5G evolution: A view on 5G cellular technology beyond 3GPP release 15. *IEEE access, 7*(1), 127639–127651. https://doi.org/10.1109/ACCESS.2019.2939938
Gulf News. (2022a). *Artificial Intelligence and Robotics are the major investment trends that will define the decade*. Retrieved October 13, 2022, from https://gulfnews.com/business/corporate-news/artificial-intelligence-and-robotics-are-the-major-investment-trends-that-will-define-the-decade-1.1628581195704
Gulf News. (2022b). *The-promise-and-possibilities-of-smart-cities*. Retrieved October 13, 2022, from https://gulfnews.com/opinion/op-eds/the-promise-and-possibilities-of-smart-cities-1.68944216
Gulf News. (2022c). *Dubai-silicon-oasis-kicks-off-sandbox-programme-with-12-startups*. Retrieved from Gulf News: https://gulfnews.com/business/dubai-silicon-oasis-kicks-off-sandbox-programme-with-12-startups-1.86107834
Haenlein, M., Kaplan, A., Tan, C., & Zhang, P. (2019). Artificial intelligence (AI) and management analytics. *Journal of Management Analytics, 6*(4), 341–343. https://doi.org/10.1080/23270012.2019.1671242
Hafifi, S. (2021). Blockchain technology as a method based on organising big data to build smart cities: The Dubai experience. *In Big Data Analytics Apple Academic Press, 8*(4), 145–157. https://doi.org/10.1201/9781003129660-16
Hong, J., Wang, Y., & Lanz, P. (2020). Why is artificial intelligence blamed more? Analysis of faulting artificial intelligence for self-driving car accidents in experimental settings. *International Journal of Human–Computer Interaction, 36*(18), 1768–1774.
Karagiannopoulos, G. D., Georgopoulos, N., & Nikolopoulos, K. (2005). Fathoming Porter's five forces model in the internet era. *Info, 7*(6), 66–76. https://doi.org/10.1108/14636690510628328
Khaleej times. (2022, October 22). *UAE: Obvious Technologies bet big on data visualisation, ML and digital twin cities*. Retrieved from Khaleej times: https://www.khaleejtimes.com/uae/uae-obvious-technologies-bet-big-on-data-visualisation-ml-and-digital-twin-cities
Kim, I., Ku, T., & Lee, B. (2020). Business model schema: Business model innovation tool based on direct causal mechanisms of profit. *Technology Analysis & Strategic Management, 32*(4), 379–396. https://doi.org/10.1080/09537325.2019
Kirpichnikov, D., Pavlyuk, A., Grebneva, Y., & Okagbue, H. (2020). Criminal liability of artificial intelligence. In E3S web of conferences. EDP Sciences. *EDP Sciences, 159*(1), 04025. https://doi.org/10.1051/e3sconf/202015904025
Lessmann, S., Haupt, J., Coussement, K., & De Bock, K. W. (2021). Targeting customers for profit: An ensemble learning framework to support marketing decision-making. *Information Sciences, 557*, 286–301. https://doi.org/10.1016/j.ins.2019.05.027
Li, S., Gao, L., Han, C., Gupta, B., Alhalabi, W., & Almakdi, S. (2023). Exploring the effect of digital transformation on firms' innovation performance. *Journal of Innovation & Knowledge, 8*(1), 100317. https://doi.org/10.1016/j.jik.2023.100317
Lin, H., & Bergmann, N. W. (2016). IoT privacy and security challenges for smart home environments. *Information, 7*(3), 40–44. https://doi.org/10.3390/info7030044
Massa, L., Tucci, C. L., & Afuah, A. (2017). A critical assessment of business model research. *Academy of Management Annals, 11*(1), 73–104. https://doi.org/10.5465/annals.2014.0072
Noothigattu, R., Gaikwad, S., Awad, E., Dsouza, S., Rahwan, I., Ravikumar, P., & Procaccia, A. (2018). A voting-based system for ethical decision making. In *Proceedings of the AAAI Conference on Artificial Intelligence* (p. 32). https://doi.org/10.1007/s10676-006-0004-4

Nummi, P. (2019). Hallitsematon tekijä? - Sosiaalisen median rooli kaupunkisuunnittelussa. Aalto University. https://aaltodoc.aalto.fi:443/handle/123456789/46637 Accepted: 2020-09-25T09:00:16Z ISSN: 1799-4942 (electronic).

Oberlo. (2021). *Why you desperately need a defined target market and target audience.* Retrieved November 27, 2021, from https://www.oberlo.com/blog/target-audience

Pan, W., Chen, L., & Zhan, W. (2019). PESTEL analysis of construction productivity enhancement strategies: A case study of three economies. *Journal of Management in Engineering, 35*(1), 05018013. https://doi.org/10.1061/(ASCE)ME.1943-5479.0000662

Paudel, S., & Sharma, H. (2020). Success models of information technology outsourcing. *Journal of Multidisciplinary Research, 3*(2), 37–52. https://doi.org/10.3126/njmr.v3i2.33022

PwC. (2022). *US$320 billion by 2030?* Retrieved October 13, 2022, from https://www.pwc.com/m1/en/publications/potential-impact-artificial-intelligence-middle-east.html#:~:text=The%20US%24320%20billion%20impact%20of%20AI%20for%20the%20Middle%20East&text=When%20we%20look%20at%20the,equivalent%20to%20US%24320%20billion

Qureshi, M., Kirkerud, S., Theresa, K., & Ahsan, T. (2020). The impact of sustainability (environmental, social, and governance) disclosure and board diversity on firm value: The moderating role of industry sensitivity. *Business Strategy and the Environment, 29*(3), 1199–1214. https://doi.org/10.1002/bse.2427

Reddy, G. T., Reddy, M. P. K., Lakshmanna, K., Kaluri, R., Rajput, D. S., Srivastava, G., & Baker, T. (2020). Analysis of dimensionality reduction techniques on big data. *IEEE Access, 8*, 54776–54788. https://doi.org/10.1109/ACCESS.2020.2980942

Rosati, F., Faria, & L.G.D. (2019). Business contribution to the sustainable development agenda: Organisational factors related to early adoption of SDG reporting. *Corporate Social Responsibility and Environmental Management, 26*(3), 588–597. https://doi.org/10.1002/csr.1705

Sainidis, & Robson. (2019). Environmental turbulence and the role of business functions in the manufacturing strategy debate: The case of UK-based SMEs and the great recession. *Journal of General Management, 45*(1), 190–208.

Schlegelmilch, B. B. (2022). Segmenting targeting and positioning in global markets. In: *Global marketing strategy. Management for Professionals.* Springer. https://doi.org/10.1007/978-3-030-90665-8_6

Schwalbe, K. (2020). *Information technology project management* (1st ed.). Cengage Learning. ISBN: 9780357235126.

Secuira. (2022a). *About Secuira.* Retrieved October 13, 2022, from Secuira: https://secuira.com/

Secuira. (2022b). *About Us.* Retrieved October 13, 2022, from https://www.secuira.com/about-us

Secuira. (2022c). *Home.* Retrieved October 13, 2022, from https://www.secuira.com/home

Secuira. (2022d). *Our values.* Retrieved October 13, 2022, from Secuira: https://secuira.com/#.

Secuira. (2022e). *Secuira.* Retrieved October 13, 2022, from https://www.secuira.com/

Secuira. (2022f). *Solutions.* Retrieved October 13, 2022, from https://www.secuira.com/Solutions

Statista. (2022). *Forecasted information and communication technology (ICT) spending share in the United Arab Emirates (UAE) in 2024, by segment.* Retrieved October 13, 2022, from https://www.statista.com/statistics/1135590/uae-forecasted-ict-spending-share-by-segment/

Supena, I., Darmuki, A., & Hariyadi, A. (2021). The influence of 4C (constructive, critical, creativity, collaborative) learning model on students' learning outcomes. *International Journal of Instruction*, 873–892. ISSN: 2684-7086.

Taghinezhad, A., Jafari, A., Kermanshachi, S., & Nipa, T. (2021). Construction project management dimensions in transportation agencies: Case study of the US Department of Transportation. *Practice Periodical on Structural Design and Construction, 26*(3), 06021002. https://doi.org/10.1061/(ASCE)SC.1943-5576.0000579

Treleaven, P., Brown, R., & Yang, D. (2018). Blockchain technology in finance. *Computer, 50*(9), 14–17. https://doi.org/10.1109/MC.2017.3571047

U.ae. (2022a). *The State of Play of Sustainable Cities and Buildings in the Arab Region Report.* Retrieved October 13, 2022, from https://u.ae/-/media/About-UAE/Smart-UAE/EN_SSCBAR_UN_2017.ashx

U.ae. (2022b). *What is a smart sustainable city?* Retrieved October 13, 2022, from https://u.ae/en/about-the-uae/digital-uae/smart-sustainable-cities

U.ae. (2022c, October 22). *Smart sustainable cities*. Retrieved October 22, 2022, from https://u.ae/en/about-the-uae/digital-uae/smart-sustainable-cities

UAE Gov. (2022). *Smart sustainable cities*. Retrieved October 13, 2022, from https://u.ae/en/about-the-uae/digital-uae/smart-sustainable-cities#:~:text=Dubai's%20Smart%20City%20project%20adopts,services%2C%20urban%20planning%20and%20electricity

UAE. (2022). *Smart sustainable cities*. Retrieved October 13, 2022, from UAE https://u.ae/en/about-the-uae/digital-uae/smart-sustainable-cities#:~:text=Dubai's%20Smart%20City%20project%20adopts,services%2C%20urban%20planning%20and%20electricity

UNDP. (2022). *THE SDGS IN ACTION*. Retrieved October 13, 2022, from https://www.undp.org/sustainable-development-goals

Vaishya, R., Javaid, M., Khan, I., & Haleem, A. (2020). Artificial intelligence (AI) applications for COVID-19 pandemic. *Diabetes & Metabolic Syndrome: Clinical Research & Reviews, 14*(4), 337–339. https://doi.org/10.1016/j.dsx.2020.04.012

Vyakina. (2019). Security of business operations and supervisory functions of the state as characteristics of the business environment. *Journal of Advanced Research in Law and Economics (JARLE), 56*(1), 1696–1705.

Wani, T. A. (2022). Innovation diffusion theory. *Journal of General Management Research, 3*(2), 101–118.

Zhou, P., & Wen, W. (2020). Carbon-constrained firm decisions: From business strategies to operations modeling. *European Journal of Operational Research, 281*(1), 1–15. https://doi.org/10.1016/j.ejor.2019.02.050

Abdulla Al Naqbi is a PhD candidate in the College of Humanities and Social Sciences, Geography, and Urban Sustainability Department. He is also a GNSS Engineer and researcher at the National Space Science and Technology Center (NSSTC), UAEU. His research interests include the characterization of different GNSS errors over the UAE, development of a spatial model to predict GNSS errors using machine learning, and multipath mitigation using wavelet transforms. Currently, he is working on a national project addressing the alternative PNT solution using LEO-PNT augmentation from Low Earth Orbit small satellites. He authored or co-authored different research articles in recognized scientific journals specialized in GNSS and Earth observations, such as the *Journal of the Royal Institute of Navigation*.

Cristina Blanco González Tejero is the associate editor of the *Review of Accounting and Finance* and a member of the editorial board of the *International Journal of Intellectual Property Management*. She holds a PhD in Economy and Business Management from the University of Alcala (Spain). She has published widely on topics such as entrepreneurship, intrapreneurship, soft skills, and social networks. Some publications are in *Technological Forecasting and Social Change* (2022), *Journal of Business Research* (2022 and 2023), *Review of Managerial Science* (2022), among others. Moreover, she has previous experience in the marketing division in the private sector.

Safe City Group: Enable Cities Safety

Aaesha Saif Ahmed Shehhi and Veland Ramadani

Abstract

The United Arab Emirates (UAE) is widely prevalent in small, medium, and even large-sized family businesses. Family businesses confront the same pressures and challenges as any major organization when they expand, since they are a vital part of every economy and play a significant role in fostering economic progress. To be successful, they must stay one step ahead of the competition, establish sound corporate governance procedures, and masterfully handle market fluctuations. Based on the motivation of covering leading Emirati family businesses, this chapter covers an in-depth analysis of Safe City Group (SCG), uncovering its approaches and processes to deliver high-quality service packages to consumers across the Middle East. It addresses several issues, including customer distribution, practice and intervention, performance, ethics and corporate values, globalization, and succession planning. It also covers business operations and practice. This study further emphasizes SCG's business overview, geographic distribution, firm performance, and the value of having such technology in enabling the plan and supporting the vision for smart cities. In the end, several brief insights regarding the projects and initiatives completed by SCG are briefly summarized, and their alignment with the Sustainable Development Goals (SDGs) has been outlined.

A. S. A. Shehhi (✉)
College of Humanities and Social Sciences, United Arab Emirates University, Al Ain, UAE

RAK GIS Center, Ras al Khaimah, UAE
e-mail: 200310043@uaeu.ac.ae

V. Ramadani
Faculty of Business and Economics, South East European University, Tetovo, North Macedonia
e-mail: v.ramadani@seeu.edu.mk

1 Introduction

Most governments focus on municipal safety due to escalating issues worldwide (Ho, 2002; Hong, 2022; Paté-Cornell, 2002). The UAE is moving towards planning based on sustainability and city safety (Al Manhali et al., 2022). As a result, this component has been agreed upon in numerous strategic plans and activities. Private sector companies have led many initiatives in the government sector, and one of the prominent companies in this field is SCG.

SCG is a UAE-based security and IT solutions company that is a regional leader in offering IT solutions to clients across the region, preventing illegal access to sensitive information and locations. SCG's business interest is cybersecurity, and the company strives to offer cutting-edge IT solutions to institutional/corporate clients across the Middle East. Through the latest IT solutions, advancements, and innovative ideas for security intelligence, SCG offers complete solutions for smart and safe cities. The SCG's vision focuses on achieving international standards in innovation, with the vision statement "A UAE inspiration and international innovation hub delivering futuristic smart, safe, and healthy city solutions."

The organization offers various products, ranging from CCTV cameras to advanced technological security solutions, to protect its clients from malicious attacks. It was founded in 2016, with its main headquarters in Masdar City, UAE. The company is led by Ali Omari, the CEO, who has over 20 years of experience in the field of cybersecurity and is responsible for the relentless growth that the firm has witnessed since its founding (Safe City Group, 2022a). A brief overview of the organizational structure of SCG is summarized in Fig. 1. Based on the motivation of covering leading Emirati family businesses, this chapter covers an in-depth analysis of SCG, uncovering its approaches and processes to deliver high-quality service packages to consumers across the Middle East. It includes the coverage of business operations, customer distribution, resource allocation for different types of projects, practice and interventions, performance, ethics and corporate values, globalization,

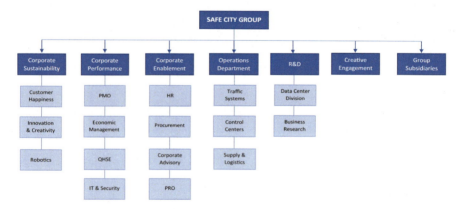

Fig. 1 Organization structure for safe city group. Source: Safe City Group. Published with the company's permission

and succession planning. Moreover, this study focuses on SCG's business overview, geographic distribution, company performance, and the benefit of having such technology in supporting the smart city vision and enabling the strategy.

2   Business Overview

The strength of Safe City lies in its all-rounded approach to security, offering a barrage of physical security solutions and cutting-edge technology to protect its clients from malice. With the growing need for safety for organizations and individual players, Safe City has stepped in to offer advanced technological solutions that guarantee protection for its customers across the region (Mishra & Kumar, 2013). The top-down approach makes Safe City a key player in the field, as it handles all security needs for its clients, making them a formidable player in the industry.

Through the latest IT solutions, advancements, and innovative ideas for security intelligence, SCG offers complete solutions for smart and safe cities. The company is headed by Ali Omari, who has led the company into dominance of the sector in the region. Mr. Omari is regarded as a security visionary, and he understands the critical role of IT in offering complete and all-rounded security solutions to institutions and individuals alike. The company has numerous partnerships with government organizations, including police departments, private institutions, and multinationals seeking a reliable security partner in the Middle East region. Cybersecurity is a significant concern for organizations and individuals alike owing to the advancement and criticality of technology in daily life across the globe (Ristvej et al., 2020). The need to secure data and systems from malicious intent and unauthorized access continues to rise, and organizations are constantly seeking the best technological solutions to reduce this menace (Unit, 2018). SCG offers an all-in-one package that allows organizations to focus on their core objectives, with the firm handling all security needs and protective mechanisms required for the smooth running of the institution. The approach has proven successful, with the company operating in over ten countries across the Middle East region with numerous customers and partners across the board.

The company values are embedded into a regular employee recognition program called Team Member Salute, where they recognize high performers who live the company values through their 6-monthly employee performance reviews. Employees are assessed against living the importance, and our individual-themed months focus on each company's value. The ISO9001 Quality Management System is the foundation of the organization. Quality is not just a word; it is something they build into all processes and controls within the organization. SCG continues to improve quality controls and reduce errors or undesired process variation. The SCGs' staff is trained in Lean Sigma principles and continual improvement processes and practices, such as taking ownership, solutions thinking, streamlining delivery, teamwork, innovation, and so on.

2.1 Corporate Values and Ethics

Company values are key pillars behind the operation and success of SCG: "values are the key building block of the Safe City performance and delivery culture" (Safe City Group, 2022a). The firm relies heavily on its workforce and has strengthened its corporate culture to ensure quality and consistency in service delivery. The values guide the organization's decision-making strategy and processes and represent the nature of SCG and its scope of operations to the clients. To ensure that the corporate culture seeps through the entire company structure, the organization runs its monthly employee recognition program, which seeks to recognize and reward high performers within set values and organizational parameters. The program is called Team Member Salute and aims to assess staff performance against set corporate values and goals. The program has successfully nurtured corporate values, strengthening partnerships, growth, and overall customer satisfaction.

To represent each of the values that SCG holds, the company dedicates a special corporate deal every month to ingrain them amongst its workforce. The most critical one is the company's value for partnerships with its stakeholders, namely customers, suppliers, subcontractors, and staff. Emphasis is placed on staff partnerships, as the workforce goes out to meet clients and spread the corporate culture. Additionally, the company respects quality in service delivery and the products it uses to meet customer needs. Timeliness, teamwork, critical thinking, and innovativeness are core values guiding the corporate culture at SCG. A broad workforce with specialized skills is crucial to organizational success, and through forging teamwork, the firm achieves the set goals and objectives (Safe City Group, 2022a). Flexibility is also essential to guaranteeing customer satisfaction, especially when dealing with problems on-site. Passion and keeping its word are also core values for SCG. Respect, integrity, and giving back represent the epitome of SCG's corporate values, striving to constantly better the environment and the communities in which it operates.

3 Geographic Distribution of Customers

SCG operates in 13 Middle Eastern countries, including the UAE, Saudi Arabia, Qatar, Egypt, Bahrain, Oman, Turkey, Morocco, Jordan, Kuwait, Tunisia, Libya, and Algeria, as illustrated in Fig. 2. Founded and located in the UAE's Masdar City, SCG has achieved numerous successes in the country, positioning itself as the IT security go-to company. It offers all-rounded IT security solutions and works with the government of Abu Dhabi and Dubai to ensure that these cities are developed to meet the required security protocols to prevent malicious attacks and hacks that can be detrimental to the functioning of these cities (Ristvej et al., 2020). The UAE is emerging as a tech leader in terms of creating smart cities and leveraging the growth of technology to create more functional and efficient cities. Dubai is the best example, as it is a top destination for global travel. IT-related security solutions have played a critical role in protecting citizens and tourists when in the city (Shires,

Safe City Group: Enable Cities Safety

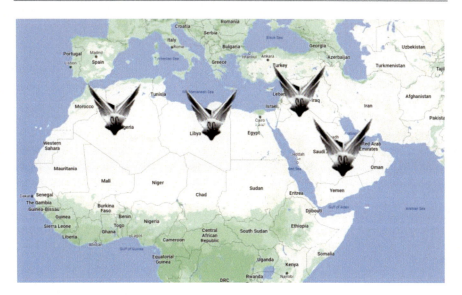

Fig. 2 Geographical distribution of SCG. Source: Safe City Group. Published with the company's permission

2022). The Economist's Global Safe Cities Index ranks Dubai and Abu Dhabi as the safest cities globally, a source of pride for SCG and other industry players (Unit, 2019). Such achievements could not have been possible without adopting cutting-edge technological solutions vital for protecting IT systems and products, which SCG specializes in regionally.

Masdar City is also a key partner for SCG, as the UAE strives to create one of the world's leading smart city projects. SCG has its headquarters in the city and partners with the government to offer leading-edge technological solutions to guarantee the city's safety. The company has worked on transport systems, government IT infrastructure, and schools, among other institutions, to alleviate loopholes and counterattacks on the developed infrastructure. The firm is also targeting the NEOM City project in Saudi Arabia, another smart city in the region, and intends to be the lead IT security partner. NEOM is a mega project, and working with the Saudi government would significantly boost SCG's portfolio and revenue owing to the size of the planned project and the expanse of the required system's security to guarantee safety within the city (Ahmed & Nanath, 2021). The company has a significant stake in Algeria and Libya, where it aims to be a leader in the industry by offering advanced IT solutions to institutions, governments, and cities in the countries. With over 20 years of experience in the field, the company's leadership is a formidable force in the industry, especially in the Middle Eastern region, where it specializes and focuses much of its attention.

4 Projects

As denoted, SCG focuses on an all-rounded approach to guaranteeing safety within cities. In this regard, the organization has ventured into offering technological and IT solutions for cities, schools, transportation, children's centers, and law enforcement, among others. It has resulted in the development of numerous company products and projects. SCG's specialties include safe city AI robotics, mobile control rooms, smart kiosks, command and control centers, facial recognition, ICCC, Super CAM-puter & Surveillance, smart video walls, gates, keyboards, specially crafted police, ANPR, crisis management rooms, and futuristic vehicles, among others (Safe City Group, 2022b). The company has significantly advanced technological capabilities, allowing it to offer and exceed global standards in these critical areas. The company guarantees its clients the installation, supervision, and operation of these systems. It makes it a key player with a strong position in the industry, owing to its all-rounded approach. Table 1 and Fig. 3 summarize the several significant projects completed by the SCG.

4.1 Projects Alignment with SDGs

The United Nations General Assembly endorsed the 2030 Agenda for Sustainable Development in 2015 as a "plan of action for people, planet, and prosperity" that "seeks to build universal peace in broader freedom." The United Nations released 17 Sustainable Development Goals (SDGs) and 169 targets as part of the 2030 Agenda for Sustainable Development. According to UN Secretary-General Ban Ki-moon, these goals and targets serve as a concrete action plan and road map for success for all people (UNDP, 2022). The SDGs include objectives including balancing economic, social, and environmental development by 2030 and taking immediate action to address climate change and its effects. Table 2. Summarize SCGs' projects in line with the SDGs.

5 Resource Allocation, Leveraging, and Performance

SCG has three tiers for project classification. The tiers represent the scope and nature of the work based on expected deliverables, confidentiality, cost, and priority to the organization (Safe City Group, 2022b). High-cost projects receive a higher capital allocation compared to low-cost projects since more resources are required. The size and scope of the project are also critical, as some projects may require minimal funds but a large team to complete within specified timelines and specifications. Such considerations determine the tier on which the project is placed. Tier 3 projects require minimal resource allocation since they are smaller or less demanding than tiers 1 and 2. Tier 2 projects take up a considerable number of resources, requiring higher budgets, which may be labor or funding. Tier 1 projects are in the highest category of resource allocation owing to the need for increased investment and the

Table 1 List of projects completed by SCG

Emirate	Client	Project name	Description
Dubai	SAAED	SAAED Call center system	Implementation and training of solutions for Customer Relationships and call center for SAAED.
AUH	Abu Dhabi Police	Smart Traffic Center (Abu Dhabi)	Traffic Monitoring System Project of Abu Dhabi
All UAE	Ministry of Interior	Emergency Response Operations Room	Supply and Installation of an Emergency Response Operations Room for: – MOI Abu Dhabi – MOI Sharjah – MOI Ajman – MOI Umm Al Quwain – MOI Ras Al Khaimah – MOI Fujairah
All UAE	Abu Dhabi Police	Traffic Violation Recorders	Supply and Installation of Traffic Volition Recorders. (TVRS) for Abu Dhabi Police at different locations in Abu Dhabi, Alain, Ajman, Umm al Quwain, and Fujairah.
AUH	Hemaya Security Services Co.	Operational Control Room	Supply and Installation an Operational Control Room for Hemaya Security Services in Abu Dhabi.
AUH	SAAED	Operational Control Room	Supply and installation of two operational control rooms for SAAED traffic systems in Dubai and Abu Dhabi.
AJM, AUH	National Ambulance	Emergency Response Operations Room	Supply and Installation of an Emergency Response Operations Room for National Ambulance in Abu Dhabi.
AUH	Monitoring and Control Center	Operational Control Room	Supply and Installation of two Operational Control Rooms for MCC in Abu Dhabi.
DUBAI	SAAED	SAAED Portal	Implementation and training of the SAAED portal for organizational task management, communication management, documentation, and other organizational workflows.
DUBAI	Dubai Police	Smart inspector	Implementation and training of the Smart Inspector Application for Dubai Police.
DUBAI	Dubai Police	Crisis magnet application	Implementation and training of the Crisis Magnet Application for Dubai Police.
DUBAI	Dubai Police	Command and control centers	Supply and Installation of an Operational Control Room for Dubai Police.
AUH	SAAED	Traffic Incident Application	Implementation and training of the Traffic Incident Application for SAAED for Traffic Systems.
ALL UAE	Ministry of Interior	ICCC	Implementation and training of ICCC in 8 Emergency Response Operations Rooms of MOI in different emirates of UAE.
Dubai	Dubai Police	Ghiath Patrol	Joint venture project with W-motors

(continued)

Table 1 (continued)

Emirate	Client	Project name	Description
AUH	Abu Dhabi Police	Emirates Vehicle Gate	Implementation of the Emirates Vehicle Gate (EVG) for Abu Dhabi Police. EVG is an integrated application that provides in-one traffic and vehicle management services for users.

Source: Safe City Group. Published with the company's permission

purchase of products, equipment, labor, time, and other resources. Figure 4 summarizes the total employee count of the SCG.

The company leverages its skill-based workforce to offer competitive rates within the industry. Most of SCG's staff has undergone rigorous training, enabling them to work on the hardest problems with minimal supervision and promptly. The approach helps the company allocate far fewer resources, especially labor, than rival companies. Efficiency and productivity are crucial for SCG's operations, and the workforce is the most critical resource for the organization. The efficient workforce allows for high performance, lowers project turn-around time, and guarantees quality with minimal resource allocation (Safe City Group, 2022a). Leveraging the skill-based workforce allows the company to allocate far fewer resources and maintain high productivity, guaranteeing excellent performance, and customer satisfaction.

6 Globalization Trends and Succession Planning

SCG has adopted a regional approach to expansion, focusing mainly on the Middle East region before entering foreign markets. The approach is carefully calculated, as the company aspires to dominate a region in which it is well-versed and deeply rooted. Much of the operation of most Middle Eastern countries is harmonious, allowing SCG to grow in all markets with minimal losses stemming from expansion (West & Bernstein, 2017). Unlike the market-focused approach taken by most players in the field, which targets the most lucrative markets, SCG's approach focuses on dominating its region of operation before venturing out into foreign markets (Aboul-Enein, 2017). Despite being in process for a few years, the company has successfully entered new markets other than its founding country, the UAE, expanding into Egypt, Saudi Arabia, Qatar, and Kuwait, among others. The company aspires to further its dominance in overseas markets, such as Europe, North America, and East Asia. Still, it can only achieve this by first dominating its region and being the leading IT solutions company in the Middle East.

Succession planning for projects and organizational stewardship is carefully thought out in SCG. The project managers collaborate with the executive and steering committees, clients, and other stakeholders to ensure smooth handovers of completed projects. The company also liaises with a client to ensure that the project runs smoothly, even after official delivery. For organizational stewardship, the company adopts an internal approach to promotion, rewarding high performers

Fig. 3 Some of SCGs projects and clients. Source: Safe City Group (2022b)

with top positions before considering outsiders (Safe City Group, 2022a). It has enabled the firm to grow and develop without losing its core values, which are the pillars upon which it stands.

SCG is ISO certified and follows ISO 9001, 14,001, 45,001, and 27,001. Safe City is an equal opportunity organization that promotes young talent along with training and development for people of determination.

Table 2 Summary of SCGs' projects in line with the SDGs

SDG#	Target	Company project	Number of cities implementing such technology
SDG 11: Make cities and human settlements inclusive, safe, resilient, and sustainable	**11.2**: By 2030, provide access to safe, affordable, accessible, and sustainable transport systems for all, improving road safety, notably by expanding public transport, with special attention to the needs of those in vulnerable situations, including women, children, persons with disabilities, and older persons	Smart Visualization	7
SDG 11: Make cities and human settlements inclusive, safe, resilient, and sustainable	**11.1**: By 2030, ensure access for all to adequate, safe, and affordable housing and basic services, and upgrade slums Indicators	Crisis management room	7
SDG 11: Make cities and human settlements inclusive, safe, resilient, and sustainable	**11.3**: By 2030, enhance inclusive and sustainable urbanization and capacity for participatory, integrated, and sustainable human settlement planning and management in all countries	Smart Kiosk	3

Source: Safe City Group. Published with the company's permission

Using environmentally friendly and sustainable technologies is the top priority for SCG during its project implementation. Industrial innovation is one of the core values of SCG. A dedicated R&D team is assigned to work on futuristic and environmentally friendly innovations. Ergonomic and energy-saving equipment is used for all the projects.

7 Summary

SCG's all-rounded approach to cybersecurity and IT solutions makes it a formidable player in the industry, resulting in its market dominance in the Middle Eastern region. Despite being a relatively new company, SCG has successfully offered IT solutions packages to customers across the region, with advanced technological

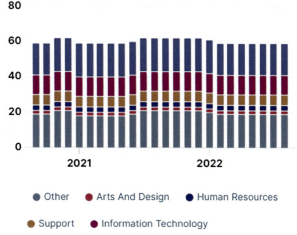

Fig. 4 Total employee count. Source: Safe City Group (2022a)

adoptions that enable it to remain ahead of the competition. A focus on workforce development has enabled the organization to strengthen its value proposition by offering competitive rates and quality solutions to various technological issues. The strict regard for the company values guides the corporate culture of SCG, streamlining operations, service delivery, and feedback processes. The importance of partnership and customer relations has enabled the company to soar to new heights with ever-increasing prospective growth. With its dominance in the Middle East market, SCG should look out to foreign markets in North America, Latin America, Europe, and East Asia for continued growth and complete dominance of the sector.

8   Questions for Discussion

1. What is the potential impact of Safe City initiatives on the achievement of Sustainable Development Goals?
2. To what extent will the Safe City group extend across the world?
3. How will Safe City technology help cities be more sustainable?
4. Can the Safe City solution be integrated with other AI solutions, such as Chat GPT?

References

Aboul-Enein, S. (2017). Cybersecurity challenges in the Middle East. *GCSP, 17*(1), 5–49.

Ahmed, N. N., & Nanath, K. (2021). Exploring cybersecurity ecosystem in the Middle East: Towards an SME recommender system. *Journal of Cyber Security and Mobility, 10*(3), 511–536.

Al Manhali, A. H., Al Kaabi, F., & Al Hanaee, M. (2022). We are all police-Abu Dhabi police community engagement initiative. *Policing, 16*(2), 236–248. https://doi.org/10.1093/police/paac013

Ho, A. T. K. (2002). Reinventing local governments and the E-government initiative. *Public Administration Review, 62*(4), 434–444. https://doi.org/10.1111/0033-3352.00197

Hong, C. (2022). "Safe cities" in Pakistan: Knowledge infrastructures, urban planning, and the security state. *Antipode, 54*(5), 1476–1496. https://doi.org/10.1111/anti.12799

Mishra, D., & Kumar, M. (2013, August 15). *Role of technology in smart governance: Smart city, Safe City*. Safe City.

Paté-Cornell, E. (2002). Risk and uncertainty analysis in government safety decisions. *Risk Analysis, 22*(3), 633–646. https://doi.org/10.1111/0272-4332.00043

Ristvej, J., Lacinák, M., & Ondrejka, R. (2020). On smart city and safe city concepts. *Mobile Networks and Applications, 25*(3), 836–845.

Safe City Group. (2022a). *About*. https://safecity.com/about.

Safe City Group. (2022b). *Products*. https://safecity.com/scproducts.

Shires, J. (2022). *The politics of cybersecurity in the Middle East*. Oxford University Press.

UNDP. (2022). *The SDGs in action*. Retrieved October 13, 2022, from https://www.undp.org/sustainable-development-goals

Unit, E. I. (2018). *Safe cities index 2017: Security in a rapidly urbanizing world*.

Unit, E. I. (2019). Safe cities index. *The Economist*. Intelligence.

West, D. M., & Bernstein, D. (2017). *Benefits and best practices of Safe City innovation*. Washington, DC, USA.

Aaesha Saif Ahmed Shehhi is currently leading the GIS center for their ambitious implementation of road map and enterprise GIS in the emirate of RAK. Her experience is in urban planning, Cadastral system, GIS Infrastructure, Building and engineering along with survey services. In addition, Aaesha represents the municipality in the Smart government committee in RAK government. Aaesha holds a master's degree in engineering project management from American university of RAK, UAE and a Bachelor of GIS from UAEU, Diploma in government performance management from Melbourne University. has received the Award for Excellence 6 times starting from 2016. In 2021, she graduated from the UAE leadership program in future leader category. In 2022, she graduated from RAK executive leadership program. She was awarded by the RAK Emirates leadership in 2022 as the outstanding ambassador for representing the UAE abroad.

Veland Ramadani is a Professor of Entrepreneurship and Family Business at the Faculty of Business and Economics, South-East European University, North Macedonia. His research interests include entrepreneurship, small business management, and family businesses. He authored or co-authored around 180 research articles and book chapters, 12 textbooks, and 25 edited books. He has published in the *Journal of Business Research, International Entrepreneurship and Management Journal, International Journal of Entrepreneurial Behavior and Research*, and *Technological Forecasting and Social Change*, among others. Dr. Ramadani has recently published the co-authored book *Entrepreneurial Family Business* (Springer). He has received the Award for Excellence 2016—Outstanding Paper by Emerald Group Publishing. In addition, Dr. Ramadani was invited as a keynote speaker at several international conferences and as a guest lecturer by several universities. During 2017–2021, he served as a member of the Supervisory Board of the Development Bank of North Macedonia, where for 10 months acted as Chief Operating Officer (COO), as well. In 2021, in a study conducted by Stanford University (USA), he was ranked among the Top 2% of the most influential scientists in the world.

MetaTouch: A Case of Successful Transformation of a Research Idea into a Start-Up During the COVID-19 Pandemic

Fady Alnajjar and Yehya Al Marzooqi

Abstract

Start-ups fuel innovation and economic growth by creating jobs and attracting investments in both developed and developing countries. The UAE exemplifies the significant impact of start-ups on the economy, with academia serving as a crucial catalyst for start-up development by providing research and development resources and human capital. The Emirati tech start-up MetaTouch, conceived at the United Arab Emirates University during the COVID-19 pandemic, showcases the fruitful collaboration between academia and industry in the UAE. This chapter explores MetaTouch's history, accomplishments, and challenges, emphasizing the essential roles of start-ups, academic institutions, and government support in fostering innovation and economic growth. Successful commercialization of lab-developed products and services necessitates the concerted efforts of academia, industry, and government. MetaTouch's launch in the UAE highlights the successful transition from lab concept to marketplace, with the commercialization process relying on a robust network for promotion and product trials.

F. Alnajjar (✉)
Department of Computer Science and Software Engineering, College of Information Technology, United Arab Emirates University, Al Ain City, UAE
e-mail: fady.alnajjar@uaeu.ac.ae

Y. A. Marzooqi
Meta Touch, Al Ain City, UAE
e-mail: dryehya@metatouchtech.com

© The Author(s), under exclusive license to Springer Nature Switzerland AG 2023
K. Alkaabi, V. Ramadani (eds.), *Family Business Cases*, Springer Business Cases,
https://doi.org/10.1007/978-3-031-39252-8_6

1 Introduction

Technology start-ups drive innovation in both developed and developing countries. As pioneers in finding solutions to untapped problems, these start-ups drive society forward by creating jobs, promoting the economy, making a social impact, and attracting investments. In terms of opportunities for creating new industries over time, they offer the most potential (Spender et al., 2017). They truly transform into money-making engines when they go public, contributing significantly to economic growth for everyone involved, including the owners, employees, and shareholders (Aishwarya, 2020).

In the UAE, start-ups and small and medium enterprises (SMEs) serve as modern pathways for establishing a robust economy and attracting foreign direct investments. SMEs account for 94% of all companies and institutions operating in the UAE and contribute to more than 50% of the country's gross domestic product (GDP) (Abu Dhabi Chamber, 2022). Since government policy plays a key role in the success of an entrepreneurial process, the UAE government has announced visa and business reforms to encourage start-ups and entrepreneurship and to entice more expats to work in the region. Additionally, the government plans to offer capital for start-ups in a variety of forms, including equity, direct lending, and loan guarantees, all of which are essential for a start-up's growth and success (Zarrouk et al., 2021).

It is well known that academia serves as both a hub of research and development and a catalyst for the development of human capital in any given country. The primary source of basic and applied research, which is the foundational element of any successful start-up, is academic research institutes. In traditional institutes, faculty members aim to publish their research findings in journals and conferences while paying little attention to applied research that can be commercialized (Mowery et al., 2015). However, those who risked taking their research ideas to market and launched their start-ups were able to make a significant impact on their communities. For instance, Google, the most popular search engine in the world, was conceived as a PhD research idea by two computer science doctoral students at Stanford University in 1996 (Davidson et al., 2017). The concept started with gathering web links and leveraging the students' expertise in mathematics and programming to build an algorithm that could evaluate and present the importance of those links. The resulting search engine was able to scale up to market with the assistance of the faculty, and within a few years, it turned into a multi-billion-dollar firm with a global impact. Likewise, Facebook, which was still a start-up back in 2004, was conceived at Harvard University. An online "hot or not" game where players merely compared students' photographs and chose the hottest faces was where the concept for Facebook first took root (Gwynne, 2018). The algorithm was enhanced gradually to identify the students' faces. Initially only available to Harvard University students, Facebook quickly expanded to cover all universities in the USA and Canada before becoming one of the most popular social media platforms globally. Multimillion-dollar companies like Snapchat, Reddit, WordPress, and FedEx were once successful student start-ups that originated at universities (Verma, 2021). These and other comparable start-ups around the world not only impact the economies of their respective countries but also change the world every single day.

MetaTouch is one such promising tech start-up project that Emirati researchers developed at the United Arab Emirates University (UAEU) during COVID-19 pandemic. The idea of MetaTouch was sparked by the laboratory for applied robotics research at UAEU. This chapter summarizes MetaTouch's history while highlighting its achievements and challenges.

2 MetaTouch Overview

2.1 Successful Innovation Out of a Pool of Inventions

In June 2020, an Emirati researcher at the UAEU and an Emirati investor came up with the concept for MetaTouch at the university's Science and Innovation Park (SIP) (UAEU, 2022). A research project at the Artificial Intelligence (AI) and Robotics Lab at UAEU gave rise to the idea of MetaTouch. The main aim of the laboratory was to build robotics applications to assist the health and education sectors (UAEU, n.d.). During the COVID-19 pandemic, researchers working on the project tried to exploit robotics and AI technologies to develop solutions that could help contain the spread of the coronavirus infection. Within a few weeks following the announcement of the pandemic in the UAE, the researchers were able to successfully develop various innovative technologies that can assess the protection and safety of students on campus, such as: (1) The laser-design doorknob hook, a hand-held hook that can be used to open/close doors without requiring the user to touch the doorknob, Fig. 1 (designed by mechanical engineer graduate students); (2) A humanoid robot "Pepper," a brand name of a semi-humanoid robot manufactured by SoftBank Robotics, with an animated interface to educate school children about COVID-19 (designed by computer science undergraduate students); (3) High-tech 3D printed face masks for heavy-duty task, Fig. 2 (designed by mechatronic and art graduate engineers); (4) 3D printed refillable hand sanitizer watch for children, Fig. 3 (designed by a mechanical engineering graduate student); (5) Smart arm motion sensor, a system to detect people's propensity for unintentionally touching their noses or mouths and alert them to refrain from such activities in order to stop the transmission of infectious diseases (Alnajjar et al., 2022); (6) a system for social distancing compliance (Gochoo et al., 2021) (Elkhodr et al., 2021); and (7) a mechanical robotics arm for touchless technology, the core trigger of MetaTouch, Fig. 4.

Regarding the mechanical touchless technology innovation, as shown in Fig. 4, the prototype was designed as a simple servomotor-based robotic arm that allowed the students to operate elevators without touching the elevator buttons. Simply pointing at the infrared proximity (IR) sensors from a distance activates the servomotor to push the elevator button. This unique mechanical idea was immediately patented by UAE University (Alnajjar et al., 2021).

Fig. 1 Laser design doorknob hook. Source: MetaTouch. Published with the company's permission

The touchless technology concept was discussed with a couple of local investors during a gathering at the SIP, which is a technology promoter and start-up incubator at the UAEU. A local investor not only provided MetaTouch with the financing it needed, but he also used his network to promote the product locally. During the early stages, MetaTouch was able to successfully develop two versions of its product, namely *TecK v1.0* and *TecK v2.0*. In the UAE, MetaTouch technology is considered as one of the top technological innovations in response to the COVID-19 outbreak (Bardsley, 2020). The government, through the Department of Government Support (DGS), awarded MetaTouch the contract to install the touchless technology at the Abu Dhabi International Airport. Once satisfied with the functionality and deployment of the technology, DGS awarded MetaTouch a further contract to install it in other governmental entities.

2.2 Locally Built Technology

To adjust to the restrictions imposed by the global lockdown during the COVID-19 period, MetaTouch adopted a local-oriented strategy that primarily relied on the local workforce and local technology for its production lines. Therefore, MetaTouch intensively trained and motivated graduate and undergraduate internship students with different academic backgrounds to operate its initial production line (see

MetaTouch: A Case of Successful Transformation of a Research Idea into... 89

Fig. 2 High-tech 3D printed face mask. Source: MetaTouch. Published with the company's permission

Fig. 3 3D printed refillable hand sanitizer watch for children. Source: MetaTouch. Published with the company's permission

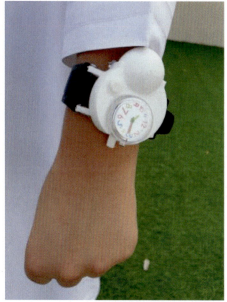

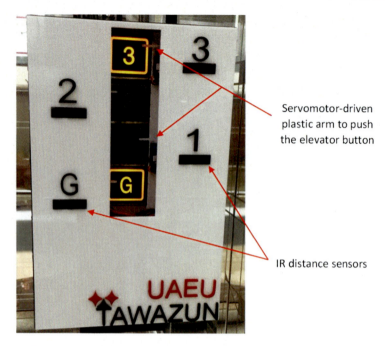

Fig. 4 The first version of MetaTouch, *TecK v1.0*, is a mechanical robot that can be mounted atop an elevator keyboard to help users operate elevator buttons by pointing to the desired floors from a distance of 1–2 cm without actually touching the buttons. This is made possible by IR-sensor technology. Source: MetaTouch. Published with the company's permission

Fig. 5 Undergraduate engineering students at UAEU working on a production line. Source: MetaTouch. Published with the company's permission

Fig. 5). For instance, engineering interns primarily concentrated on the electric design and assembly of components of touchless devices (see Fig. 6). Design engineering interns were mostly in charge of completing the 3D design of the product. Computer science interns were primarily responsible for programming the controller. Interdisciplinary faculty members oversaw all the aforementioned operations. During this extraordinary journey, MetaTouch has trained about 66 graduate and undergraduate students from engineering, IT, and business departments, contributing to the capacity building of UAEU students.

Fig. 6 Printed circuit board (PCB) of MetaTouch TecK v1.5, designed at UAEU. Source: MetaTouch. Published with the company's permission

Fig. 7 The latest version of MetaTouch, TecK-v3.1. TecK-v3.1 is designed to be a master button, i.e., it can replace any elevator button. TecK-v3.1 is designed to function as a hybrid button, supporting both touchless (using radio-based distance sensor) and touch technology (built-in button). Source: MetaTouch. Published with the company's permission

Because MetaTouch adheres to the philosophy of continuous research and development, it has been able to develop an innovative product that integrates touch and non-touch technologies into a single product, TecK v3.1 (see Fig. 7).

2.3 From Lab to Market

MetaTouch's initially successfully commercialized products, TecK v2.0 and TecK v2.1, were first installed at the Abu Dhabi International Airport, the first airport in the world to adopt such technology to secure its travelers during COVID-19 (Khaleej Times, 2020), and 53 elevators at the airport had the system in place by early June 2020. In less than 2 years, MetaTouch was able to accelerate the development of five different versions (see Fig. 8).

Given the value of Emirati start-ups to the UAE economy and the public's recognition of this, MetaTouch has received moral support from numerous

Fig. 8 MetaTouch progress overview. Source: MetaTouch. Published with the company's permission

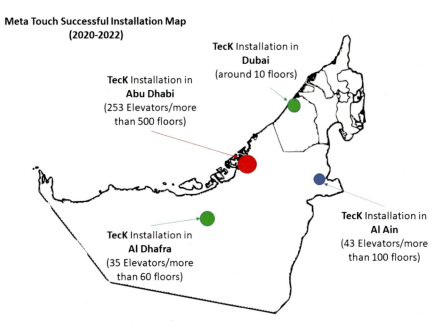

Fig. 9 Geographical distribution of MetaTouch TecK installations. Over 17,000 buttons have been installed in approximately 400 elevators in the UAE. Source: MetaTouch. Published with the company's permission

government and private institutions in the country that have facilitated their work. In only a few months, MetaTouch was able to secure the installation of over 17,000 buttons to cover approximately 400 elevators (see Fig. 9).

3 Conclusion

In this digital age, start-ups are at the core of an economy and drive innovation, creativity, and economic growth. Academic centers serve as incubators for start-ups and innovative companies, which often have the potential to create great economic value for society. Successful start-ups can stimulate economic growth and generate new jobs and are, therefore, the lifeblood of an economy. The UAE has a robust ecosystem that supports start-ups to grow and flourish. It is renowned for being among the first countries to adopt technologies that offer innovative solutions to the challenges faced by industries, society, and humanity. The UAE government always encourages its citizens to defy the odds, be innovative, and create commercially viable, competitive business industries both locally and globally. In this study, we showcase MetaTouch, an Emirati tech start-up that was conceived against the backdrop of the COVID-19 pandemic. The success of MetaTouch is largely attributable to the fruitful cooperation between UAEU and SIP, which provided the MetaTouch team with guidance, training, and information on the market situation, gave them the knowledge they needed, and connected them with parties who might help them bring their products to market. MetaTouch's vision now focuses on transforming existing and well-established technologies into contactless technologies in order to help limit contact with potentially contaminated areas and lower the risk of viral transmission.

It is important to highlight that bringing products and services developed in the lab to the marketplace calls for consolidated efforts from academia, industry, and government. The launch of MetaTouch in the UAE demonstrates how a concept can successfully transition from the lab to the marketplace. Any product's commercialization requires a strong network that can promote and open doors for product trials. In the case of MetaTouch, the customer's (in this case, Abu Dhabi International Airport) endorsement and praise for the product paved the way for securing subsequent contracts, which allowed research funding to be made available in order to address technical challenges related to touchless technology.

In order to build on its current success, MetaTouch is exploring international partnerships to take this successful product to other countries, as well as engaging with prospective investors for second-round fundraising to expand the boundaries of touchless technology to cover additional applications, including ATMs and vending machines, to name a few. With its "Know-How" and vast network, MetaTouch is in the process of exploring other technologies that will positively impact mankind, the community, and the environment. This, we envision, might be accomplished through in-house inventions or collaborations with other tech start-ups.

4 Questions for Discussion

1. How can universities encourage their students and facilitate idea generation in order to empower start-ups?
2. What effects do university-initiated start-ups have on students' technical and practical capacities? And how essential is that for re-programming students' mindsets from looking for jobs to creating jobs?
3. How does bridging the gap between academia, industry, and government help in the promotion of successful start-ups?

References

Abu Dhabi Chamber. (2022, June 1). *Seminar "UAE economy 2022 and beyond", in cooperation with ministry of Economy, Pakistan Business Professional Council and CSR UAE Fund.* Retrieved from https://abudhabichamber.ae/Media-Centre/News/uae-economy-2022

Aishwarya, C. (2020). Financing the startup economy-A critical study. *Journal of Entrepreneurship and Management, 9*(1), 35.

Alnajjar, F., Ahmed, W., & Gochoo, M. (2021). *Touchless elevator keyboard system,* US Patent Application No. 10,968,073.

Alnajjar, F., Aziz, M. A., Ahmed, W. K., & Gochoo, M. (2022). *Arm motion sensor system. U.S. Patent Application No. 11,231,437, 2022.*

Bardsley, D. (2020, June 21). Coronavirus: 5 technologies inspired by the pandemic. *The national news.* Retrieved from https://www.thenationalnews.com/uae/science/coronavirus-5-technologies-inspired-by-the-pandemic-1.1036287

Davidson, C. N., across America, A., Brin, S., & Page, L. (2017). *The surprising thing Google learned about its employees—and what it means for today's students.* The Washington Post, 20.

Elkhodr, M., Mubin, O., Iftikhar, Z., Masood, M., Alsinglawi, B., Shahid, S., & Alnajjar, F. (2021). Technology, privacy, and user opinions of COVID-19 mobile apps for contact tracing: Systematic search and content analysis. *Journal of Medical Internet Research, 23*(2), e23467.

Gochoo, M., Alnajjar, F., Ahmed, W. K., & Aziz, M. A. (2021). *System and method for social distancing compliance.* U.S. patent application no. 11,080,981, 2021.

Gwynne, J. (2018). Facebook bans reflect a lack of impartiality. *News Weekly, 3024,* 4.

Khaleej Times. (2020, June 10). *Combating coronavirus: New contactless elevators introduced at Abu Dhabi airport.* Retrieved from https://www.khaleejtimes.com/coronavirus/combating-coronavirus-new-contactless-elevators-introduced-at-abu-dhabi-airport

Mowery, D. C., Nelson, R. R., Sampat, B. N., & Ziedonis, A. A. (2015). *Ivory tower and industrial innovation: University-industry technology transfer before and after the Bayh-dole act.* Stanford University Press.

UAE University (UAEU). (n.d.). *AI and Robotics lab.* Retrieved from https://industry4.uaeu.ac.ae/en/robotics-lab.shtml

UAE University (UAEU). (2022, June 6). *Meta touch providing job opportunities for graduates.* Retrieved from https://www.uaeu.ac.ae/en/news/2020/june/meta-touch-providing-job-opportunities-for-graduates.shtml

Spender, J. C., Corvello, V., Grimaldi, M., & Rippa, P. (2017). Startups and open innovation: A review of the literature. *European Journal of Innovation Management., 20,* 4.

Verma, J. (2021, January 21). *Facebook, Google, Snapchat & 4 other companies that were founded on college campuses.* Retrieved March 19, 2023, from https://in.askmen.com/tech-news/1127519/article/facebook-google-snapchat-4-other-companies-that-were-founded-on-college-campuses

Zarrouk, H., El Ghak, T., & Bakhouche, A. (2021). Exploring economic and technological determinants of fintech startups' success and growth in The United Arab Emirates. *Journal of Open Innovation: Technology, Market, and Complexity, 7*(1), 50.

Fady Alnajjar is an Associate Professor in the Department of Computer Science and Software Engineering at the College of Information Technology, United Arab Emirates University. His primary research focus encompasses the exploration of human behavior, delving into the study of neuromuscular strategies for learning, adaptation, and recovery, as well as the examination of the brain's neural dynamics and cognitive functions. By merging his understanding of human behavior with his expertise in artificial intelligence and robotics design and control, Dr. Alnajjar's primary objective lies in developing innovative rehabilitation technologies to enhance the quality of life for individuals. To date, he has authored or co-authored approximately 200 research articles, conference proceedings, and book chapters, and has obtained eight registered US patents. In 2020, Dr. Alnajjar co-founded Meta-Touch.

Yehya Al Marzooqi joined Tawazun in 2009 after working at Abu Dhabi Company for Onshore Oil Operations (ADCO), currently called ADNOC Onshore for over 16 years. Prior to that, he had worked in the Resources Centre of a major bank in the USA. At Tawazun, he has led various people development initiatives such as Leadership Development Program, Establishment of MBA in Manufacturing, Excellence with UAE University, Integration of Female Emirati National in manufacturing, Facilitating the process of articulating vision, mission and values for the organization, Conducting various people development workshops for senior management, Attracting and enticing young Emirati National to pursue their education in STEM-C (Science, Technology, Engineering, Math, and Coding), Supporting SMEs and Facilitating projects from lab to market. Dr. Yehya had served on the Executive Committee of Tawteen Program and later as a Chairman of the Executive Committee. He also serves as: Member of the Executive Board of UAE University, College of Business and Economy, Board member of Executive Committee of Khalifa Innovation Center (KIC), Chairman of the board of Business and Economy at Hamdan Bin Mohammed Smart University, Chairman of the Engineering Innovation Solution Center; a consortium between Tawazun Council, Mubadala and Higher Colleges of Technologies. He has co-authored articles that were published in the *National HRD Journal* and *American Society for Training and Development* (ASTD) publication. Dr. Yehya has participated as a keynote speaker at local and international conferences. Dr. Yehya has completed his undergraduate and graduate studies in the USA and has obtained his Doctorate Degree from Bradford University in the UK. He currently serves as Executive Director, Collaboration, and Skills Development at Tawazun Council.

Nayel & Bin Harmal Group: Integrated Services in the Construction Sector

Hessa Alkalbani, Eiman Almazrouei, and Veland Ramadani

Abstract

This chapter offers a brief introduction to the Nayel & Bin Harmal (NBH) Group, a family-owned business in the United Arab Emirates (UAE). The NBH group has been one of the most versatile and thriving builders in the UAE since its inception, contributing significantly to the country's overall development. However, they are also active in several other sectors, including hotels and leisure, education, insurance, property and investment, among others. This study focuses on their market segments and growth as they strive to become the most renowned construction company in the Middle East, as well as their sustainability efforts and unwavering commitment to their values, principles, and ethics. Finally, this chapter briefly summarizes their various projects and initiatives aligned with the Sustainable Development Goals (SDGs).

1 Introduction

Over the past 20 years, urban development in the UAE has gradually improved. The Dubai Roads and Transport Authority has pushed for sustainable transport growth at all levels to address the implications of this development (Ahmed & Alali, 2022; Al Nahyan et al., 2012; Jha & Tandon, 2019). One of the significant financial drivers in the UAE is the construction and real estate sectors due to their increasing long-term

---

H. Alkalbani (✉) · E. Almazrouei
College of Humanities and Social Sciences, United Arab Emirates University, Al Ain, UAE
e-mail: 201903711@uaeu.ac.ae; 201902682@uaeu.ac.ae

V. Ramadani
Faculty of Business and Economics, South East European University, Tetovo, North Macedonia
e-mail: v.ramadani@seeu.edu.mk

© The Author(s), under exclusive license to Springer Nature Switzerland AG 2023
K. Alkaabi, V. Ramadani (eds.), *Family Business Cases*, Springer Business Cases,
https://doi.org/10.1007/978-3-031-39252-8_7

impact on economic growth. It allows commercial development, creates new jobs, and thereby increases income (Koelemaij, 2022).

The construction sector in the UAE accounts for up to 70% of all significant projects, with an estimated worth of 90 billion USD (ABIQ, 2022). The UAE government prioritizes investments in energy and infrastructure, such as utilities, transportation, decarbonization, nuclear and renewable energy production, and addressing the chronic water shortage. The government's substantial resources and commitment result in several projects and possibilities for UAE construction and engineering firms. As part of the Projects of the 50 initiative, the UAE government announced plans to put into action several projects aimed at accelerating the country's economic development and transforming it into a comprehensive hub for all sectors, with the goal of attracting $150 billion (AED550 bln) in foreign direct investment (FDI) over the following 9 years (Naar, 2021; U.S. Department of Commerce, 2022; The Information & eGovernment Sector, n.d.).

Being one of the largest construction groups, the Nayel & Bin Harmal Group (NBH) is one of the most versatile and thriving builders within the UAE and has contributed a great deal to the UAE's overall development. NBH aims to offer customers the highest standard of services, and its staff is well equipped with technical expertise and credentials. Since it was founded in 1991, NBH Hydro Export LLC has taken on and completed several large public and private sector projects in the UAE. With more than AED 1 billion in paid-up capital to support project needs, NBH continues to increase its market share with high-profile clients. NBH showed off its skills and abilities by working on some of the most prestigious government and private construction projects, such as the development of Yas Island and Al Raha Beach, oil and gas projects, police headquarters, former president guard command projects, private improvements, ADSSC projects, shopping malls, hotels, villas, and apartments, and so on (Nayel & Bin Harmal Hydroexport, n.d.-a).

The goal of NBH is to become the top infrastructure contractor in the UAE, continue looking for ways to expand into the GCC region, and offer the highest-quality construction services while completing projects on schedule. It aims to ensure continuing operations and to maintain the highest level of professionalism, honesty, integrity, and fairness in all our relationships with suppliers, subcontractors, professional associates, and clients by providing various services, including constructing structures, civil works, water reservoirs, water system systems, sewage treatment, and so forth.

This chapter briefly overviews NBH, its market segments, and completed projects. Furthermore, several useful attributes contributing to the NBH group's growth are identified. In the end, a few valuable insights regarding the corporate social responsibility-related activities of the NBH group are summarized.

2 Business Overview

NBH is an ISO and OHSAS certified investment firm. Since the beginning, NBH has been proud of and confident in its ability to be an innovative, competitive organization that is growing into new areas and quickly adapting to new market trends. NBH is one of the most successful and versatile contractors in the UAE. Each year, the company's construction projects consistently bring in more than 500 million AED in revenue. Abu Dhabi Municipality ranks the company as the best infrastructure contractor year after year. Therefore, NBH has become the partner of choice for several clients due to the quality of its work and its unwavering commitment to successfully finishing a wide range of projects (Nayel & Bin Harmal Hydroexport, n. d.-a).

With the aim of creating a lasting impact for their shareholders, the group comprises more than 50 companies spanning several sectors such as construction and architecture, manufacturing, engineering, medical facilities, tourism, real estate, information technology, and so forth. Furthermore, it is expanding into several asset classes, including platform investment, public equity, and venture capital. They leverage their shared platform to capture cross-asset-class opportunities in strategic focus areas. The NBH group is committed to social responsibility-related contributions through its annual initiatives and projects, serving the nation. A brief overview of various market segments of NBH is summarized in Fig. 1.

NBH started expanding its business to include real estate and major contracting companies, including Nile Contracting Co., NAYEL & BIN HARMAL HYDROEXPORT, and road and infrastructure companies such as AlFahjan and Cement Product Factories. Furthermore, it has been expanded to include

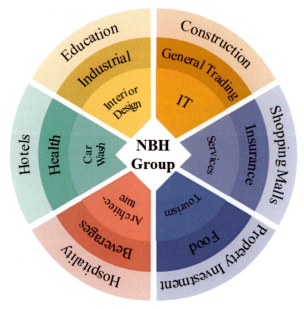

Fig. 1 Overview of NBH group's market segments. Source: Nayel and Bin Harmal Hydroexport (n.d.-a). Published with the company's permission

construction project contracting, oil and natural gas pipeline construction contracting, installation and contracting, and so on. A detailed overview of its essential market segments is summarized below.

2.1 Health Care

NBH Group serves the health sector of the UAE by providing state-of-the-art medical health-related services and turnkey projects in biomedical and electromechanical engineering services. Furthermore, they are also offering civil maintenance and medical equipment maintenance to several significant hospitals in the UAE, such as Tawam Hospital, Al Ain Hospital, Mafraq Hospital, and so on. The NBH group comprises several companies and hospitals, such as Dalma Medical Center, Nayel Medical Equipment, Al Reem HOSPICO, HOEPETIC International, Emirates International Hospital, International Hospital Technical EST, and EMIRATES International Policlinics.

2.2 Education Sector

Education is the process of hastening the process of learning and the acquisition of values and virtues. It promotes the growth of better people all throughout the world. It is a more long-lasting technique for teaching individuals knowledge, abilities, and morals. The NBH Group serves a pivotal role in the education sector of the UAE, and the list of schools and universities associated with the NBH Group includes Abu Dhabi University, Canadian International School, Al Khawarizmi International College, and Abu Dhabi University Knowledge Group.

2.3 Industrial Sector

By giving people jobs in secondary and tertiary sectors, the industrial sector not only assists in modernizing but also lessens the heavy reliance on an oil-based economy. The list of companies associated with the industrial segment of the NBH Group includes Nayel Cement Production, Hafeet Plastic Factory, United Agricultural Productions, Arabian Agriculture, and so forth.

2.4 General Trading Sector

The general trading sector of NBH Group aims to meet our customers' end-to-end requirements with the latest technology and highest quality at a minimum cost. The list of companies contributing to the general trading sector of the NBH Group is given as follows: Hafeet Traders Group of Companies, Al Reem General Trading, Al Ain General EST, and Al Jaheli Trading and Import.

2.5 Hospitality, Tourism, and Travel

The tourism and hospitality industry has established significance in the United Arab Emirates. It is estimated that by 2028, the travel and tourism sector will be responsible for up to 400,000 jobs. There are several companies of the NBH group that are contributing to this sector, as follows: Bin Harmal Travel & Tourism, Ayla Hotels & Resorts, Ayla Hotel (AL Ain), Ayla Grand Hotel (AL Ain), Ayla Bawadi Hotel (AL Ain), Ayla Hotel (Oman), Ayla Hotel (Djibouti).

2.6 Construction and Architecture

The construction and architecture segment of NBH Group provides solutions in building materials, construction and maintenance, agricultural solutions, electromechanical services, and so on. The list of companies associated with the construction and architecture segment of the NBH group is given as follows: Nayel Engineering, Nayel Construction, Nayel General Constructions, AG Drilling, Nayel Brick Factory, Nayel & Bin Harmal Construction, and so on.

2.7 Property Investments and Shopping Malls

The NBH Group has formed several property investment companies. Furthermore, the group has developed several shopping malls across the UAE and Oman. The list of the group's property investment companies and malls developed is as follows: "Magna Investments, Al Ain Tours Investments, Nayel & Bin Harmal Investments, Al Ain Central Market, and so forth."

2.8 Other Services

In addition to the aforementioned services, NBH Group provides state-of-the-art services in the IT sector, insurance, interior design, car wash stations, and so on.

3 Projects and Initiatives

3.1 Yas Island

NBH follows PCRS, PRRS, and PBRS guidelines from the Urban Planning Council for community development and sustainable development goals (SDGs) by ensuring the procurement of sustainable materials and taking initiatives to reduce waste through recycling and reuse. One of NBH's significant projects is the development of Yas Island, the region's leading destination for recreation and entertainment. The

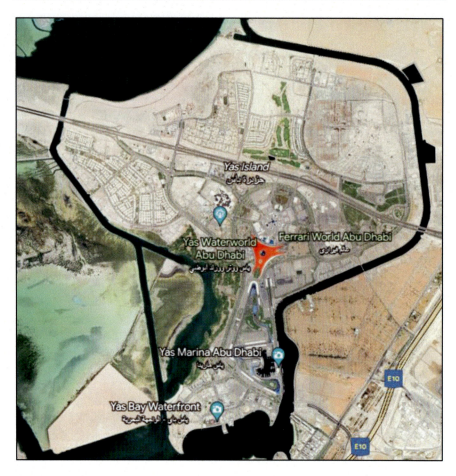

Fig. 2 Overview of Yas Island. Source: Google Earth (2023)

project aimed to build a multifunctional commerce, entertainment, and leisure complex.

Many amusement centers and theme parks provide visitors with unforgettable experiences. The Yas Island is surrounded or covered by clear water and contains some of Abu Dhabi's more recognizable attractions (Miral, 2021; UNESCWA, 2007), as illustrated in Fig. 2. The setting provides a fantastic encounter and creates unforgettable memories. It includes the Yas Links golf course, an exciting F1 racetrack, a world-class theme park, and enjoyment in the sun at Yas Beach. Yas Mall, one of the biggest malls, provides a range of culinary options, lodging alternatives, and hospitality services. Moreover, Yas Marina offers dining, exercise, and recreational opportunities.

The Yas Island theme park includes a range of attractions, including the award-winning Warner Bros., a branded hotel, serviced apartments, and an air-conditioned retail stroll. Along with these, the Yas village offers affordable and high-quality

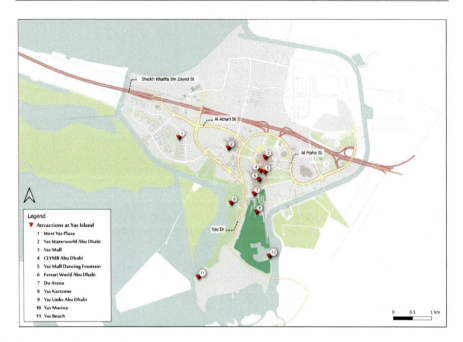

Fig. 3 Demographic illustration of Yas Island. Source: Authors constructed the map using QGIS software where map information was retrieved from Google Earth and Nayel and Bin Harmal Hydroexport (n.d.-a). Published with the company's permission

Table 1 Overview of a few projects established on Yas Island

Entertainment project	Cost (AED)	Client	Location	Number of visitors by years	Duration
Yas Island Theme Park	AED 14.5 billion	Miral	Yas Island, Abu Dhabi	27 million Visitors	12 years
Warner Bros. World Abu Dhabi	$ 1 billion	Miral	Yas Island, Abu Dhabi	27 million visitors	4 years

Source: Authors retrieved information from Nayel and Bin Harmal Hydroexport (n.d.-a) and Miral (2021). Published with the company's permission

housing to the residents of Yas Island. Moreover, visitors can enjoy a vibrant 80,000 square meter beachfront that spans half a kilometer along the corniche. For a better understanding of the land uses and attractions of Yas Island, refer to Fig. 3. Additionally, Table 1 displays the cost and revenue of a few projects established on the island.

3.2 Transportation Infrastructure

Transportation becomes even more crucial for the country when there are tourist spots or locations to visit. The modes of transportation offer people the necessary connectivity to enable easy transit from one location to another. The metro system in Dubai, United Arab Emirates, comprises a train network with dynamic connections. The Dubai Metro features 45 stations, 2 depots, and various operating controls. Almost 100,000 people, or 10% of the total population, used the Dubai Metro in the early days when services were first offered. The number of passengers it could hold up to 2011 was around 10 million. Dubai's metro system was considered the longest route on the planet until it began operating without a driver in 2016. During the development of the Dubai Metro, the NBH group contracted for utility relocation and protection works between 2005 and 2009.

In addition, NBH Group has completed several other projects with the road and transport authority of the UAE, such as the construction of an outer bypass from Umm Al Quwain, the development and upgrading of Al Ittihad Taween Road, the construction of the infrastructure in Khalifa City, Abu Dhabi, and so on. Table 2 summarizes the major projects completed by the NBH group for transportation infrastructure development.

4 Projects Alignments with Sustainable Development Goals

NBH is presently the go-to partner for many customers because of the quality of its work and its continued dedication to completing various unique projects. As they spread across the UAE and the region, the depth and breadth of the company's people, resources, and knowledge will be a source of strength. Due to their involvement in the construction project, they have been a part of several significant projects in line with the sustainable development goals, particularly SDGs 3, 4, 7, and 11 (United Nations, n.d.; Nayel & Bin Harmal Hydroexport, n.d.-a). They have completed several projects with key government agencies, including the Abu Dhabi Electricity and Water Agency, the Duba Board, the Abu Dhabi Water and Sewage Organization, the Al Ain Drainage Agency, the Al Ain Roads Agency, and so on (Nayel & Bin Harmal Hydroexport, n.d.-a). In order to ensure sustainability, NBH took significant measures while developing Yas Island. Yas Island was not produced by marine vessels that threw sand into the air. To achieve and accomplish their EHSMS Policy, NBH is committed to protecting the health and safety of all people (workers, visitors, and contractors) on their property, to environmental protection, and to protecting and developing their natural, constructed, and cultural environment.

In line with the sustainable development goal of providing good health and well-being, NBH Group is serving the health sector of the UAE by providing state-of-the-art medical health-related services and turnkey projects in biomedical and electromechanical engineering services. Furthermore, in order to ensure the implementation of quality education (SDG4), NBH has developed several

Table 2 Summary of the transportation infrastructure development projects by the NBH Group

No.	Contract description	Client	Location	Amount (AED)	Start date (mm/yy)	End date (mm/yy)
1	Dubai Metro—Utility relocation and protection works at Dubai Metro—Subcontract package to JTM JV.	Roads and Transport Authority	Dubai	412.000.000	Dec/05	Aug/09
2	Construction of outer bypass from Umm Al Quwain—Dhaid Road to Sajaa—Khawaneei Road—contract R/13/2006	Ministry of Public Works	Umm Al Quwain	155,358,456	Aug/06	Jan/08
3	Tender no. /49/2015, development and upgrading of Al Ittihad—Taween Road (second stage: From Al Ittihad R/A to Sheikh Mohammed Bin Zayed Interchange—E311)	Ministry of Public Works	Umm Al Quwain	139,990,000	Jan/16	May/18
4	Construction services—development of roads, infrastructure and streetscape at Khalifa City east sectors 22, 23, 24, and 34—contract 231-5	Department of Municipalities & Transport	Abu Dhabi	91,477.085	Jul/21	Dec/21
5	Heilo-Abu Al Abiyad Road in Dhafra region and Dualization of Tal Moreeb Road in Liwa	Aldar Projects	Dubai	576,000,000	May/21	Nov/23

Source: Authors retrieved information from Nayel and Bin Harmal Hydroexport (n.d.-a). Published with the company's permission

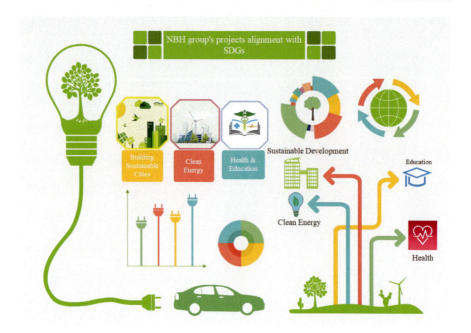

Fig. 4 Graphical illustration of NBH group's projects aligned with SDGs. Source: Authors retrieved information from Nayel and Bin Harmal Hydroexport (n.d.-a). Published with the company's permission

educational institutions, such as Abu Dhabi University. Moreover, they are contributing to achieving the country's goals for sustainable cities by employing their vast engineering knowledge and technical services. The skilled personnel at NBH are capable of working toward the fulfillment of the highest levels of quality (Nayel & Bin Harmal Hydroexport, n.d.-b). The wide fleet of technology we have available, which includes trenchers, shovels, and excavators, further strengthens the foundation of our business. Figure 4 illustrates the commitment of the NBH group toward the UAE government's agenda on sustainable development goals (United Nations, n.d.).

5 Summary

This chapter provides a brief overview of the Nael and Bin Harmal Hydroexport L.L.C. (NBH) group, one of the private sector enterprises operating in the Middle East. The building and real estate sector has been a critical driver of economic growth in the region, and it is essential to the UAE's overall GDP. The discussion highlights that the construction sector in the UAE plays a significant role in the nation's economy and is critical to achieving its socioeconomic development goals.

Economic growth depends heavily on the construction industry, which has a significant impact on almost every aspect of the economy.

The Nael & Bin Harmal Group (NBH) is among the largest construction groups and one of the most versatile and successful builders in the UAE, having made significant contributions to the overall development of the country. Since its inception in 1991, NBH Hydro Export LLC has successfully completed numerous large-scale public and private sector projects in the UAE. NBH has demonstrated its skills and capabilities by undertaking some of the most prestigious government and private construction projects, such as the development of Yas Island and Al Raha Beach, as well as oil and gas projects, police headquarters, former presidential guard command projects, private developments, ADSSC projects, shopping malls, hotels, villas, apartments, and more. NBH is an ISO and OHSAS-certified investment firm that has expanded its business to include real estate and significant contracting companies, such as Nael Construction & Contracting, Nael and Bin Hermel Hydroaxport, and Road and Infrastructure Companies like AlFahjan and Cement Product Factories. Additionally, NBH has expanded its scope to include construction projects, oil and natural gas pipeline construction, installation, and contracting.

The NBH group is committed to corporate social responsibility and is eager to contribute to the country's sustainable development goals. As such, the group has participated in several significant projects aligned with the sustainable development goals, with a particular focus on SDGs 3, 4, 7, and 11. These projects were carried out in collaboration with key government agencies, including the Abu Dhabi Electricity & Water Agency, the Dubai Board, the Abu Dhabi Water and Sewage Organization, the Al Ain Drainage Agency, the Al Ain Roads Agency, and others.

6 Questions for Discussion

1. What significant role do the real estate and construction sector play in the UAE economy?
2. List out the attraction at Yas Island that make it the most attractive destination for visitors.
3. How is the NBH Group participating in the development of the UAE?
4. What is the commitment of NBH to achieve the SDGs?

References

ABIQ. (2022, June 3). *The United Arab Emirates construction industry: 2022 overview*. Retrieved from https://www.abiq.io/the-united-arab-emirates-construction-industry-2022-overview

Ahmed, A., & Alali, H. (2022). Effect of technological orientation on Project Management process and infrastructure performance of RTA in UAE. *Journal of International Business and Management, 5*(3), 1–26. https://doi.org/10.37227/jibm-2022-03-5684

Al Nahyan, M. T., Sohal, A. S., Fildes, B. N., & Hawas, Y. E. (2012). Transportation infrastructure development in the UAE: Stakeholder perspectives on management practice. *Construction Innovation, 12*(4), 492–514. https://doi.org/10.1108/14714171211272234

Google Earth. (2023). *Yas Island Map*. Retrieved from https://earth.google.com/web/search/uas+island/@24.48585254,54.60297829,3.80421452a,16935.18649471d,35y,0h,0t,0r/data=CigiJgokCZ4IxdEwTz9AEaAIxdEwTz_AGQkEzZWQ7EtAIf2CN1IFkEzA

Jha, S. S., & Tandon, J. K. (2019). A study on the impact of transport and power infrastructure development on the economic growth of United Arab Emirates (UAE). *Journal of Management, 6*(2), 25–35. https://doi.org/10.34218/jom.6.2.2019.003

Koelemaij, J. (2022). The world's number 1 real estate development exporter? Assessing announced transnational projects from The United Arab Emirates between 2003–2014. *Environment and Planning A, 54*(2), 226–246. https://doi.org/10.1177/0308518X211054847

Miral. (2021). *Miral investment brochure*. Retrieved from https://miral.ae/wp-content/uploads/2021/02/Miral-Investment-Brochure-English-3.pdf

Naar, I. (2021, September 5). *Here are some of the UAE's projects of the 50 initiatives unveiled so far*. Al Arabiya news. Retrieved from https://english.alarabiya.net/features/2021/09/05/Here-are-some-of-the-UAE-s-Projects-of-the-50-initiatives-unveiled-so-far

Nayel & Bin Harmal Hydroexport. (n.d.-a). *Construction engineering & management solutions*. Retrieved from https://nbhh.ae/

Nayel & Bin Harmal Hydroexport. (n.d.-b). *Environmental health & safety policy*. Retrieved from https://nbhh.ae/about-us/environmental-health-safety-policy/

United Nations. (n.d.). *Sustainable development goals*. Retrieved from https://sdgs.un.org/goals

United Nations Economic and Social Commission for Western Asia (UNESCWA). (2007). *Plan Abu Dhabi 2030 Urban structure framework plan*. Retrieved from https://andp.unescwa.org/plans/1274

U.S. Department of Commerce. (2022, July 26). United *Arab Emirates–Country commercial guide: Design and construction*. Retrieved from https://www.trade.gov/country-commercial-guides/united-arab-emirates-design-and-construction

The Information & eGovernment Sector. (n.d.). *Initiatives of the Next 50*. Retrieved from https://u.ae/en/about-the-uae/uae-in-the-future/initiatives-of-the-next-50

Hessa Humaid Alkalbani studied Urban Planning at the Geography and Urban Sustainability Department at United Arab Emirates University. Her research interests include regional and urban planning, tourism policy and planning, demography, and land use.

Eiman Saeed Almazrouei studied Geographic Information Systems (GIS) at the Geography and Urban Sustainability Department at United Arab Emirates University. Her research interests include regional and urban planning, tourism policy and planning, demography, and land use.

Veland Ramadani is a Professor of Entrepreneurship and Family Business at the Faculty of Business and Economics, South-East European University, North Macedonia. His research interests include entrepreneurship, small business management, and family businesses. He authored or co-authored around 180 research articles and book chapters, 12 textbooks, and 25 edited books. He has published in the *Journal of Business Research, International Entrepreneurship and Management Journal, International Journal of Entrepreneurial Behavior and Research*, and *Technological Forecasting and Social Change*, among others. Dr. Ramadani has recently published the co-authored book *Entrepreneurial Family Business* (Springer). He has received the Award for Excellence 2016—Outstanding Paper by Emerald Group Publishing. In addition, Dr. Ramadani was invited as a keynote speaker at several international conferences and as a guest lecturer by several universities. During 2017–2021, he served as a member of the Supervisory Board of the Development Bank of North Macedonia, where for 10 months acted as Chief Operating Officer (COO), as well. In 2021, in a study conducted by Stanford University (USA), he was ranked among the Top 2% of the most influential scientists in the world.

DAMAC Group: Symbol of Successful Development

Sara Omar Aljaberi and Khaula Alkaabi

Abstract

Several world's most well-known organizations originated in family businesses. For instance, JP Morgan Chase, Ford Motor Company, and Walmart are a few family enterprises that have grown into huge corporations in the United States. Likewise, family businesses are the backbone of the UAE's economy, creating jobs, adding economic value to the country, and pioneers in entrepreneurship and innovation. DAMAC Group is a well-known family-based enterprise. Since its inception in 1982 in catering and logistics, the company has developed tremendously to an excellent and broad portfolio in various industries such as property and real estate, retail and fashion, data centers, hospitality, logistics, and investment. In this chapter, we will discuss several insights into the history of DAMAC Group since its inception and the locations of the spread of branches around the Emirates. In addition, a detailed overview of its market segments and corporate social responsibility-related activities is summarized and discussed.

1 Introduction

The United Arab Emirates (UAE) has been highlighted as a unique organizational environment that offers exciting prospects to improve the management field in a steadily developing conversation on how laws, conventions, and values rooted

---

S. O. Aljaberi (✉)
College of Humanities and Social Sciences, United Arab Emirates University, Abu Dhabi, UAE
e-mail: 202020041@uaeu.ac.ae

K. Alkaabi
Geography and Urban Sustainability Department, United Arab Emirates University, Al Ain City, United Arab Emirates
e-mail: khaula.alkaabi@uaeu.ac.ae

within indigenous contexts impact the way enterprises are managed and directed (Alkaabi, 2020, 2021; Alkaabi et al., 2023; Aloulou, 2023; Oudah et al., 2018; Ramadani et al., 2023). Understanding the family business phenomena in the UAE is particularly relevant and pertinent for at least two reasons. First, family firms account for up to 90% of all companies in the UAE, employ 80% of the workforce, and contribute 60% of the region's GDP (Al-ansaari et al., 2015; Family Business in Abu Dhabi, 2019). These findings reflect the ability of family enterprises to influence regional development in an environment of expanding economic and geopolitical relevance. Second, the UAE is distinguished by a unique set of institutional characteristics, including collectivism, patriarchy, a high level of religiosity among the population, Islam is the dominant, but not the only, religion, and deep institutional voids, all of which can have a significant impact on family business behavior and outcomes (Dayan et al., 2019).

For the reasons above, the last two decades have seen a proliferation of research activities focused on investigating the governance, behavior, prosperity, and growth of family companies in the middle east (Al-Dajani & Marlow, 2010; Samara, 2021). Despite this growing interest, research on family companies in the UAE remains fragmented. The real estate market contributes 6% of the UAE's GDP and is the most transparent property market in the Middle East and North African region, gaining the "Transparent" tier (Thomas & Potluri, 2020). The community development of DAMAC is thoughtfully designed to promote healthy lifestyles and well-integrated, eco-friendly sustainable communities for its residents, to attain healthy well-being and social life through the "National Policy of Residentials Communities" six principles of urban design and launching sustainability program focusing on fitting environmental and sustainable guidelines to their operations and maintenance of project development. Therefore, this chapter provides several insights into the history of DAMAC Group since its inception and the locations of the spread of branches around the Emirates. In addition, a detailed overview of its market segments and corporate social responsibility-related activities is summarized and discussed (DAMAC Group, n.d.).

Hussain Sajwani, a Dubai-based billionaire, owns and manages the DAMAC Group, a private corporate empire. Since its inception in 1982 in catering and logistics, the company has developed tremendously to an impressive and broad portfolio in various industries, such as data centers, property development and real estate, hospitality, retail and fashion, and logistics, as illustrated in Fig. 1. In the next sections, we provide a brief overview of DAMAC Group, a well-known family business-based enterprise in UAE, and highlight several attributes that are playing a key role in their tremendous growth over the past years.

2 Business Overview

DAMAC Group is a well-known Emirati family enterprise participating in the development of the UAE. A detailed overview of its several market segments is given below (DAMAC Group, n.d.).

DAMAC Group: Symbol of Successful Development

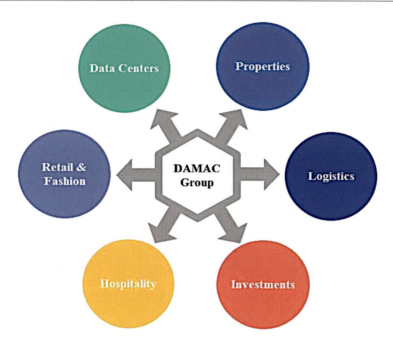

Fig. 1 Overview of several market segments of DAMAC Group (DAMAC Group, n.d.). Source: DAMAC Group. Published with the company's permission

2.1 Property

With the launch of DAMAC Properties in 2002, the DAMAC Group formed its property development division, which has evolved and expanded to become a widely recognized brand name worldwide. DAMAC properties envision itself as a leading Middle Eastern luxury real estate developer, delivering residential, leisure, and commercial properties across MENA and afar. Their mission is to cater to eccentric dream houses with a luxurious transformative lifestyle to global customers and challenge the market. DAMAC's values are innate to the company, valuing customers' preferences and requirements to deliver memorable moments, leading in the real estate industry, empowering team flourishment, encouraging creativity, and acting on these four values. They have collaborated with several well-known national and international organizations, including Rotana, Zuhair Murad, Cavali, and so on, and have completed several projects. An overview of a few key projects of DAMAC properties is illustrated below (DAMAC Group, n.d.).

2.1.1 DAMAC Hills

DAMAC Hills is a luxury residential community along Umm Suqeim Road, Dubai. The gated community surrounds nearly four million square feet of parkland and the Trump International Golf club. The community design follows six principles of the "National Policy for Residential Community," which is its prime location in

Fig. 2 Overview of DAMAC hills (DAMAC Group, n.d.). Source: DAMAC Group. Published with the company's permission

reasonable proximity to other destinations outside the community, a connected community, an integrated community, and a place for social life and cultural expression. Figure 2 illustrates the overview of DAMAC hills, which is iconic project of DAMC properties.

The community consists of 3008 townhouses and villas, 4335 residential apartments, 163 hotel villas, 4317 hotel apartments, hotel apartments, and hotel rooms overlooking either the golf course or park view (Propsearch.ae, n.d.).

The community's strategic location has a good road network, connecting it with Sheikh Zayed bin Hamdan al Nahyan street and reducing travel time. Most of Dubai's landmarks are just 15–25 min away from the community, such as Global village, Burj Khalifa, JBR walk, Dubai Marina, and Dubai Mall. The community is categorized into 25 subcommunities surrounding the parkland and golf course, each with its eccentric design. Figure 3 illustrates the geographical overview of DAMAC hills.

DAMAC hills create a community with everything within reach for the people living within, such as essential services varying from retail, clinics, markets, and schools. Amenities like the golf course, basketball court, fruit garden, artificial

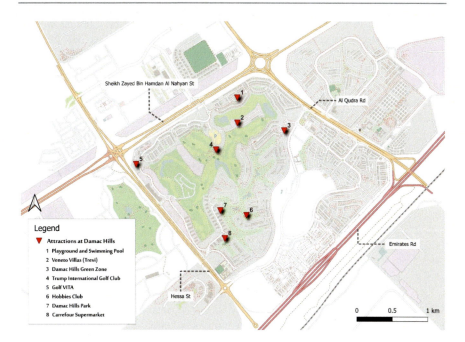

Fig. 3 Geographical illustration of DAMAC hills (DAMAC Group, n.d.). Source: DAMAC Group. Published with the company's permission

beach, horse stables, skate parks, gyms, football field, cricket ground, kids play area, jogging track, swim pools, and pet farm. Most commercial regions are located in Calero (Figs. 1 and 2) with a community center, supermarket, salon, and barber, which is excellent for people to gather and socialize.

2.1.2 DAMAC Hills 2

DAMAC Hills 2, formerly known as "Akoya Oxygen," is a new eco-friendly and sustainable community located on the outskirts of Dubai in Dubai land, away from the crowded, bustling city. DAMAC Hills 2 is the second most popular area in Dubai for affordable villas, with an average of 77,000 yearly rent for 5-bedroom villas.

The area of the community is spread over 42 million square feet, promoting a lifestyle of tranquility around a championship golf course with features of landscaped gardens, parks, and leafy boulevards, as well as offering a road connectivity framework with spaces devoted to hybrid and cycles.

DAMAC Hills 2 offers 10,000 private villas and townhouses with private parking and outdoor spaces, over 2000 hotel rooms and 650 serviced villas, and around 1200 apartments, built using energy-efficient materials, environmentally friendly lighting, and solar water heating systems (Bayut, n.d.). The community focuses on the improvement of people's well-being and being sustainably eco-friendly, offering various eco-friendly amenities such as jogging tracks, a horse stable, a farmers' market, Zen Garden, a fishing lake, paintball, a karting circuit, and more, as well as various community services such as clinics, supermarkets, restaurants, and schools.

2.1.3 DAMAC Towers Nine Elms

DAMAC Towers Nine Elms is the first project in Europe and a major international project out of the Middle East, spanning 4 million square feet, located in Nine Elms in London, England, south of the river Thames. The 50-story tower is one of the tallest residential buildings in London, in partnership with Versace home, with up to 450 units compromising studios and 1–3 bedroom apartments at the starting price of 712,000 GBP (3,248,022 AED) and exclusive penthouse suites (Oxborrow, 2022).

The ultramodern designed tower has a range of amenities that includes a roof garden, private cinema, swimming pool, and state-of-the-art gymnasium, and creating the ultimate luxurious lifestyle. The tower's location is also strategic, located near a few of London's major landmarks, such as the London Eye, Buckingham Palace, London Bridge, Hyde Park, and a few significant universities, within 10–30 min walking distance.

2.1.4 Mandarin Oriental Resort

The partnership between DAMAC and Mandarin Oriental Resort has set forth to develop a resort stretching out to three private islands in South Male Atoll, Bolidhuffaru, Maldives, taking up 34 hectares that are scheduled to open in 2025.

The resort comprises 64 overwater villas, 130 stand-alone villas, 66 beachfront villas, and exclusive private residences with private pools (Gulf News, 2022). The serene luxury resort offers various amenities such as specialty restaurants, sunset bars, and dining outlets, as well as event space for any occasion such as weddings or meetings, resorts, a tropical garden, salons, pools, sauna, and steam rooms. Leisurely activities available vary from tennis courts, water sports, clubs, diving centers, and large coves and beaches.

2.2 Data Center

After identifying a demand for such centers in emerging and neglected countries worldwide, DAMAC saw the potential to invest in technological infrastructure and hubs in 2021. DAMAC regarded data center construction as a natural sector expansion opportunity where it could leverage its experience and expertise in the development industry to deliver efficient and creative data center projects to market. The mission of the DAMAC data center segment is *"We are committed to the data center market in the long-term and have dedicated resources to serve the needs of hyperscalers, cloud service providers, content companies, over-the-top (OTT) players, and enterprises. We enable local digital innovation by delivering new levels of application performance, service performance and user experience, while keeping data in-country* (DAMAC Group, n.d.)."

2.3 Retail and Fashion

DAMAC entered the luxury retail and fashion sectors to diversify its holdings further in 2019 with the acquisition of the globally recognized Italian fashion business Roberto Cavalli and the Swiss jewelry brand de GRISOGONO. The acquisitions are part of DAMAC's goal to diversify its portfolio by acquiring luxury assets with growth potential. The company is always on the lookout for new luxury brands to develop (DAMAC Group, n.d.).

2.4 Hospitality

DAMAC Hotels and Resorts is an extension of the company's well-known property development expertise, adhering to DAMAC Properties' highest quality standards and giving the ultimate luxury living experience and investment opportunity. DAMAC Hotels & Resorts, founded in 2012, manages over 1000 serviced hotel apartments, separate stand-alone 5-star hotels, and a tropical beach resort as part of its hospitality portfolio (DAMAC Group, n.d.).

2.5 Investments

DAMAC considers itself a long-term investor in the dynamic markets that influence modern society. Thus, they have invested in cybersecurity, cloud computing, climate technology, and life sciences innovation. The Company provides investors the chance to take part in the future expansion of one of the region's top luxury real estate developers, and thereby offering a high return on equity due to better project management, land acquisition at good cost, active capital management, speedy execution, proactive sales, and management team (DAMAC Group, n.d.).

2.6 Logistics

Global Logistics Company, founded in 1982, served as the DAMAC Group's first foray into the catering and logistics industry. Later, this spread to the CIS, GCC, Middle East, and Africa. The company's vision is *"To create long-term relationships with our customers by remaining committed to quality management systems, food safety guidelines of local authorities, and relevant industry codes of practice. We strive to deliver the most efficient services to clients while seeking opportunities to expand our business and service offering*s (DAMAC Group, n.d.)."

3 Project and Awards

As a significant subsidiary, DAMAC Properties has developed several communities and projects, contributing significantly to the UAE's economy. The recent significant projects developed by the DAMAC Properties are summarized in Table 1.

DAMAC has one of Dubai's happiest communities as a result of its strong dedication to quality and innovation. In December 2022, at the International Real Estate Community Management Summit, the Luxury Owners Association Management Company LLC of DAMAC Properties took home two major awards. The organization received a Gold Award for the best crisis management initiative of the year 2022 and a Silver Medal for the year's happiest residential community. The Dubai Land Department (DLD), through its Real Estate Regulatory Agency (RERA), has recognized DAMAC Properties' community management division, LOAMS, for its exceptional initiatives in managing its communities and buildings. The company has also previously taken home significant industry honors from the Gulf Real Estate Awards, including "Winner—Best Owners Association Management Firm Y2017," "Finalist—Best Owners Association Management Y2018," and "Runner Up Best Owners Association Management Initiative Y2019 (Damac Properties, 2022)." Figure 4 summarizes a few significant awards received by DAMAC Properties over the years.

4 CSR-Related Initiatives

The Hussain Sajwani—DAMAC Foundation was established out of a deep-seated commitment to youth empowerment and giving back to the communities. The foundation's mission is to significantly improve the lives of the underprivileged in the region by empowering youth and providing them with the knowledge and skill set they need to secure future jobs.

Table 1 Overview of the recent vital projects by DAMAC Properties

No.	Project	Description
1.	DAMAC Lagoons (Ibiza)	It offers Mediterranean-inspired townhouses
2.	CAVALLI COUTURE	Designer apartments overlooking Dubai Canal
3.	Monte Carlo	Mediterranean-inspired townhouses
4.	Elegance Tower	Luxury apartments
5.	Marbella	Townhouses
6.	Chic Tower	Designer apartments
7.	Gems Estates	Luxury villas and mansions
8.	Beverly Hills Drive	Luxury mansions
9.	Safa Two de GRISOGONO	Luxury apartments
10.	Malta	Townhouses

Source: DAMAC Group. Published with the company's permission

Fig. 4 Several awards, achieved by DAMAC properties over the past years. Source: DAMAC Group. Published with the company's permission

As a locally based business, DAMAC believes it is crucial to give back to the communities where it operates and which have so generously supported it. The foundation is committed to helping young people reach their greatest potential via work and education. The foundation strives to empower the larger community of youth in the Arab area as it works to create sustainable futures for future generations. Over the years, DAMAC has consistently participated in philanthropic initiatives, collaborating with various international and regional organizations like the Red Crescent, Dubai Cares, Dar Al Ber Society, and the Dubai Executive offices.

Following the CSR initiatives, DAMAC Group gave AED 5.0 million to the UAE's 1.0 billion initiative launched by Sheikh Muhammad. Likewise, the foundation also gave AED 3.0 million to the Arab hope makers initiative.

5 Sustainability-Related Initiatives

A sustainable approach is important when it comes to preserving resources and protecting the environment and our social and economic development, both in the long and short term. DAMAC has launched a "Sustainability Program," focusing on project development operation and maintenance, aiming to augment their developments by following environmental and sustainable entities guidelines and policies. A few of their achievements include:

As a part of DEWA's strategy, they have installed a free green charging vehicle station in collaboration with DEWA in DAMAC Hills 2 and are targeting more DAMAC communities. The company uses low-flow water fixtures to reduce water consumption in DAMAC Hills and has implemented a water reclamation system processed at a sewage treatment plant. DAMAC communities also include energy recovery ventilation, eco-responsible interiors, sustainable building materials, solar-powered heating systems, and installation of environmentally friendly lighting and led solar street lighting.

DAMAC Suburbia, located in Jebel Ali Dubai, has illustrated adherence to the environment, health, and safety sustainable criteria for the built environment by the Department of Planning and development Trakhees, achieving a "Green Building Certification." They have shown that 30% of its material is recycled, sourced more than 22% regionally, and saves 22% and 33% on using fresh water.

The Group, recently recognized for "Smart Innovation" at the Future Workspace Summit and Awards 2022, is still committed to advancing the adoption of technology throughout construction, sales and post-sales, and support services. Moreover, DAMAC recently entered the metaverse as the first real estate company. It helped to pioneer the digital asset market in the area. To construct digital cities, improve the Group's sales prospects, and increase consumer involvement, the corporation has committed $100 million under the umbrella of D-Labs.

In addition, DAMAC also rose to the top of the list of developers who made it easier for people to use cryptocurrencies to buy real estate. The organization has changed from a traditional sales technique to a more digital sales approach by collaborating with businesses specializing in machine learning, improving and expanding its digital channels.

6 Summary

The DAMAC Group, a private corporate empire since its inception in 1982 in catering and logistics, has developed tremendously to an impressive and broad portfolio in various industries, such as data centers, property development and real estate, hospitality, retail and fashion, and so forth.

The company has developed several state-of-the-art projects, such as DAMAC Hills, DAMAC Towers, and so on. Due to their commitment to quality and innovation, at the International Real Estate Community Management Summit, the Luxury Owners Association Management Company LLC of DAMAC Properties took home two major awards in December 2022. The company has also previously taken home significant industry honors from the Gulf Real Estate Awards, including "Winner—Best Owners Association Management Firm Y2017" "Finalist—Best Owners Association Management Y2018" and "Runner Up Best Owners Association Management Initiative Y2019."

DAMAC is strongly associated with CSR activities. Therefore, the Hussain Sajwani—DAMAC Foundation was established out of a deep-seated commitment to youth empowerment and giving back to the communities. The foundation's mission is to significantly improve the lives of the underprivileged in the region by empowering youth and providing them with the knowledge and skill set they need to secure future jobs. Moreover, by understanding corporate social responsibility of following sustainable development goals, DAMAC has launched a "Sustainability Program," focusing on project development operation and maintenance, aiming to augment their developments by following environmental and sustainable entities guidelines and policies. Overall, DAMAC Group is one of the largest companies in the Emirates and contributes significantly to shaping the country's future.

7 Questions for Discussion

1. DAMAC has launched a sustainability program focusing on project operations and maintenance; how have they contributed to that?
2. How do DAMAC communities create a social and interconnected community?
3. How do DAMAC and the National Policy for Residential Communities 6 principles align?

References

Al-ansaari, Y., Bederr, H., & Chen, C. (2015). Strategic orientation and business performance an empirical study in the UAE context. *Management Decision, 53*(10), 2287–2302. https://doi.org/10.1108/MD-01-2015-0034

Al-Dajani, H., & Marlow, S. (2010). Impact of women's home-based enterprise on family dynamics: Evidence from Jordan. *International Small Business Journal, 28*(5), 470–486. https://doi.org/10.1177/0266242610370392

Alkaabi, K. (2021). Customers' purchasing behavior toward home-based SME products: Evidence from UAE community. *Journal of Enterprising Communities: People and Places in the Global Economy.*. https://www.emerald.com/insight/content/doi/10.1108/JEC-11-2020-0187/full/html, *16*, 472. https://doi.org/10.1108/JEC-11-2020-0187

Alkaabi, K. (2020). Effects of geographic distribution of small and medium-size enterprises on growth, innovation, and economic contributions: A case study of UAE. *International Journal of Applied Geospatial Research (IJAGR)., 11*(4), 23–41. https://doi.org/10.4018/IJAGR.2020100102

Alkaabi, K., Ramadani, V., & Zeqiri, J. (2023). Universities, entrepreneurial ecosystem and family business performance: Evidence from The United Arab Emirates. *Journal of the Knowledge Economy.* https://doi.org/10.1007/s13132-023-01384-9

Aloulou, W. J. (2023). *Family business in gulf cooperation council countries (GCC): Toward the future.* https://doi.org/10.1007/978-3-031-17262-5_8.

Bayut. (n.d.). *Damac Hills.* Retrieved from https://www.bayut.com/area-guides/damac-hills-2/

DAMAC. (n.d.). *Group.* Retrieved from https://www.damacgroup.com/en/

Damac Properties. (2022, December 23). *Damac has one of Dubai's happiest communities.* Retrieved from https://www.damacproperties.com/en/media-centre/press-releases/damac-has-one-dubais-happiest-communities#:~:text= The company has also previously, the Gulf Real Estate Awards.

Dayan, M., Ng, P. Y., & Ndubisi, N. O. (2019). Mindfulness, socioemotional wealth, and environmental strategy of family businesses. *Business Strategy and the Environment, 28*(3), 466–481. https://doi.org/10.1002/bse.2222

Family Business in Abu Dhabi. (2019, November). Retrieved from https://abudhabichamber.ae/-/media/Project/ADCCI/ADCCI/Media-Center%2D%2D-Publications/Research-and-Reports/2019/Family-business-sector-report_December-English.pdf

Gulf News. (2022, December 7). *Dubai's Damac Group signs contract with Mandarin Oriental to manage luxurious resort in Maldives.* Retrieved from https://gulfnews.com/business/tourism/

dubai-damac-group-signs-contract-with-mandarin-oriental-to-manage-luxurious-resort-in-maldives-1.1670391992486.

Oudah, M., Jabeen, F., & Dixon, C. (2018). Determinants linked to family business sustainability in the UAE: An AHP approach. *Sustainability (Switzerland), 10*(1). https://doi.org/10.3390/su10010246

Oxborrow, I. (2022, June 30). Damac Towers Nine Elms in London: Dubai developer completes first European project. *The National*. Retrieved from https://www.thenationalnews.com/business/property/2022/06/30/damac-towers-nine-elms-in-london-dubai-developer-completes-first-european-project/

Propsearch.ae. (n.d.). *Damac Hills*. Retrieved from https://propsearch.ae/dubai/damac-hills

Ramadani, V., Aloulou, W., & Zainal, M. (2023). *Family business in gulf cooperation council countries*. Springer.

Samara, G. (2021). Family businesses in the Arab Middle East: What do we know and where should we go? *Journal of Family Business Strategy, 12*(3), 100359. https://doi.org/10.1016/j.jfbs.2020.100359

Thomas, S. S., & Potluri, R. M. (2020). An exploratory research on the implementation of corporate social responsibility (CSR) in the real estate sector of UAE: A dyadic perspective. *Journal of Distribution Science, 18*(10), 101–110. https://doi.org/10.15722/jds.18.10.202010.101

Sara Omar Aljaberi studied Urban planning at the Geography and Urban Sustainability Department and German language at UAE University. Sarah is currently partaking in UAE University Summer Undergraduate Research Experience program grant on "School layout design and children experiences" and tutors at the UAE University tutorial center. She presented at the 26th McGill International Entrepreneurship Conference. Her research interests include urban design, sustainable cities, urban sociology, transport & mobility, and happiness & well-being.

Khaula Alkaabi is a Professor in the Geography and Urban Sustainability Department at the UAEU. She holds a BA degree from UAEU; an MA and a PhD in Geography from UNCG in the USA; and a Public Sector Innovation Diploma from the University of Cambridge, UK. Her research interests include transportation, land use planning, spatial analysis and geostatistics, GIS, drone applications, economic geography, smart cities, entrepreneurship, and innovation. She was the Chair of the Geography Department from 2013 to 2017, and the Chief Innovation Officer for UAEU from 2015 to 2022. She has published several academic articles in scientific international journals like *Journal of Transport Geography, Frontiers*, and *Journal of Enterprising Communities, Geomatics Natural Hazards and Risk, Journal of Cleaner Production*, and *Transportation Research Part F*. She has published several book chapters with Ashgate, Routledge, and Springer. She has received several research grants and rewards including UAEU's "University Excellence Award for Service Excellence" in 2022, "Outstanding Leadership Awards in Education" in 2022, "Feminine Monitoring for Sustainable Environment Award" in 2019, and the "Best Academic Research at Sustainable Transport Competition" by RTA in 2018.

Pronto Carwash Company: Your Ride to the Mobility Car Wash

Asma Mohammed Al Madhaani and Mahra Al-Ali

Abstract

This chapter introduces Mr. Mohammed Al Hammadi, the Co-Founder of Pronto Carwash, a growing small to medium-sized company. After experiencing a setback with his laundry business, Mr. Al Hammadi devised the concept of a mobile cloud carwash services business to compensate for the losses. Pronto Carwash offers a range of services, including car washing, waxing, and house cleaning. Following its initial success, the company launched its first fully equipped vehicle and aims to rapidly expand its fleet. Pronto Carwash has also made notable contributions to social activities and secured governmental agreements, making its presence felt in various spheres.

1 Introduction

Starting a car service business can be a lucrative venture for those interested in the automotive industry. Nowadays, mobile car wash services can be a great business idea for those interested in the automotive industry. Furthermore, the most successful companies are those that are moving in the direction of technological development by constructing cloud and mobile companies to make the lives of their customers easier. The introduction discusses the steps and inspiration of carwash companies.

Firstly, there are some steps to consider when starting a car wash service business that are explained in this chapter, which are researching the market, selecting a

A. M. Al Madhaani (✉) · M. Al-Ali
College of Humanities and Social Sciences, Department of Geography and Urban Sustainability, United Arab Emirates University, Al Ain, UAE
e-mail: 201310934@uaeu.ac.ae; 201505401@uaeu.ac.ae

location, choosing company services, purchasing needed equipment, hiring employees, marketing the business, and providing excellent customer service.

By explaining those steps, Research the market: Conduct market research to identify the demand for car wash services in the area. It has three goals, which will allow you to determine whether there is an unmet need in the location where you want to build your car wash to assist you in developing a solid company plan to satisfy this need. Lastly, to help you gather the information needed to calculate the potential sales of your car wash (The Business Plan Shop, n.d.). This will help to determine the potential size of the customer base, as well as the competition that might be faced, choose a location: Select a location that is easily accessible to customers and has a high traffic volume. Consider whether want to purchase or lease a property for the company car wash, and choose company services: Decide which types of car wash services will be offered, such as exterior washes, interior detailing, waxing, or additional services such as tire and rim cleaning or engine cleaning, Purchase equipment needed: Purchase or lease the necessary equipment for the car wash business, such as car wash machines, pressure washers, vacuum cleaners, and other necessary tools and supplies, Hire employees: Hire employees to help the company to run the business, such as customer service representatives, car wash attendants, and detailers. Make sure to provide proper training to ensure quality services, Market business: Promote the company car wash business through advertising and social media. Consider offering promotions or discounts to attract customers and provide excellent customer service: Provide excellent customer service to ensure customer satisfaction and repeat business as it is summarized in Fig. 1.

Consider offering loyalty programs to reward frequent customers, starting a car wash service business requires a significant investment of time and money, but with careful planning and attention to detail, it can be a successful and profitable venture.

Secondly, there are some sources of inspiration for incorporating a mobile car wash service into the business that will be explained such as convenience, customization, environmental friendliness, timesaving, targeting businesses, personalized customer service, and flexibility.

In more detail, one of the biggest advantages of a mobile car wash service is that it offers convenience to customers. They can have their car washed at their home or workplace, without having to go to a car wash facility (convenience). With a mobile car wash service, the company can offer customized services to customers, such as exterior washes, interior detailing, waxing, and more (customization). The company can also offer additional services such as tire and rim cleaning, engine cleaning, and more. A mobile car wash service can be a more environmentally friendly option as it saves water and reduces the number of chemicals used in the washing process (environmental friendliness). A mobile car wash service can save customers time as they do not have to spend time driving to a car wash facility, waiting in line, or having to wait for their car to be washed (timesaving). Mobile car wash services can also target businesses, such as car dealerships or rental companies, to offer their services on a regular basis (targeting businesses). A mobile car wash service can offer a more personalized customer service experience. The company can get to

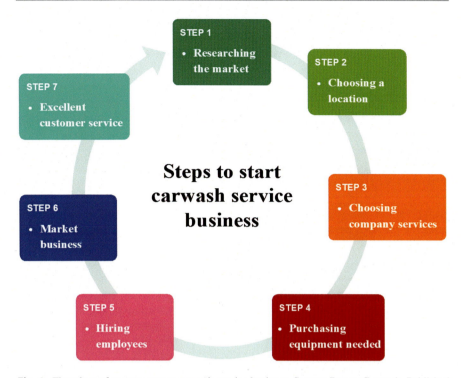

Fig. 1 Flowchart of steps to start a carwash service business. Source: Pronto Carwash. Published with the company's permission

know its customers and their preferences and offer tailored services to them (personalized customer service). A mobile car wash service allows for greater flexibility as the owner can adjust the company schedule to accommodate the customers' needs (flexibility).

Starting a mobile car wash service can offer many benefits to customers and be a successful business venture. It is important to do proper market research, invest in high-quality equipment, and offer excellent customer service to succeed in this industry.

To sum up everything that has been stated so far of summarizing the steps and inspiration of the car wash services business. Starting a car wash service business can be a profitable venture for those interested in the automotive industry. The business requires careful planning, investment in equipment and supplies, and proper training of employees. With the right approach and attention to detail, a car wash service business can be a successful and rewarding enterprise.

2 Inspiration Overview of Pronto Carwash Company

2.1 The Story Behind Pronto Carwash Company

Pronto Carwash Company is considered a cloud company that uses mobility. The inspiring story behind raising the idea of Pronto Carwash Company is that Mr. Mohammed Al-Hammadi started his business in the cleaning field by owning a laundry. Afterward, in 2018, his laundry business was declining so he decided to think about a new business that is low-cost and with on-hand equipment and monthly invoices. Here was Pronto's carwash business idea pop-up to him. Moreover, Mr. Al-Hammadi started his company by searching for the right global equipment, especially from German companies, because they are the best in the market for car care solutions. Therefore, Mr. Al-Hammadi started his company by using the cars that are already there from the laundry business, so Mr. Al-Hammadi prepared the first car with vacuum machines, car shampoo care, and chemical solution. However, the first car was highly costed but after getting experience with the market the next cars were well prepared. Nowadays, Pronto Carwash has seven prepared-ready vehicles distributed around the Emirate of Abu Dhabi. Mr. Al-Hammadi referred his thanks to the support of his family and brothers, and their trust in him to establish the company from scratch. Fortunately, Pronto Carwash Company was the first development of this kind of business on the market.

2.2 The Vision of Pronto Carwash Company

A company vision statement is an essential component of any successful organization (Hisrich & Ramadani, 2017). It serves as a guiding light for the company's future, defining its purpose and direction. Here are some reasons why a company vision statement is important for instants to clarify direction with clear vision statement helps to define the direction of the company. It provides a sense of purpose and a common goal that everyone can work toward, sets priorities the vision statement helps to set priorities for the company. It helps to prioritize the company's goals and objectives, which in turn helps to focus resources and efforts and inspires employees with a strong vision statement that can inspire employees and create a sense of purpose. It can help to motivate employees to work towards a common goal and can provide a sense of pride in the work they are doing, also, it attracts customers. A clear and compelling vision statement can attract customers who share the company's values and beliefs. It can help to create a strong brand identity and differentiate the company from its competitors and drives innovation through a well-crafted vision statement that can encourage innovation and creativity. It can inspire employees to think outside the box and come up with new ideas and solutions to achieve the company's goals. A company vision statement is crucial for setting the direction, priorities, and purpose of an organization. It inspires employees, attracts customers, and drives innovation, ultimately leading to the success of the company. Every company has their vision that helps the company to be continually working in a stable mood. The vision of Pronto Carwash says: "We strive to contribute to the preservation of the environment in civilized ways, we aim to continue the innovation and development of the service provided in line with our changing lifestyle. we work to build fruitful relationships, between government and private institutions and individuals and gain confidence in the excellence and quality of service provided" (AlHammadi, 2023).

2.3 Pronto Mobile Carwash Company

A mobile car wash service is a type of car washing service that comes to the customer's location to clean their vehicle, rather than the customer driving to a fixed location such as a car wash facility. Mobile car wash services are popular because they offer convenience and flexibility to customers who want their cars cleaned without the hassle of driving to a car wash or detailing facility.

Mobile car wash services are particularly useful for people who are too busy to visit a car wash or detailing facility, or who want their cars cleaned while they are at work or at home. Furthermore, mobile car wash services can benefit people with mobility issues or those who are unable to drive to a car wash due to vehicle issues or other reasons.

Pronto mobile carwash company is designed to meet the specification of mobile technologies. "It provides a mobile service specialized in washing and cleaning cars from inside and outside in a comprehensive and high quality, mobile service Car wash and professional staff, provided with advanced washing and cleaning equipment and, just there when and where the client does exist" (AlHammadi, 2023).

3 The Journey of Successes

The journey of success is unique to each individual and may require overcoming obstacles, taking chances, and pursuing objectives tenaciously and persistently. Although each person's road to success may be unique, there are a few recurring themes.

Having a clear vision of what you want to accomplish is one of the most important aspects of success. It may be necessary to set specific goals and create a plan to achieve them. Successful people frequently have a strong sense of purpose and remain committed to their goals in the face of adversity.

Overall, the path to success is marked by a combination of vision, action, perseverance, and support. You can achieve success and great things in your life by staying focused on your goals and working hard to overcome obstacles.

Pronto Carwash Company started its success by following the standard successful plans. The workflow of the company depends on the customer order assigned, the location of the order, and the vehicle assigned, using the vehicle to reach with shortest route and time, and then taking the customer's opinion about the requested services, as shown in Fig. 2. For the service to be done there are seven vehicles

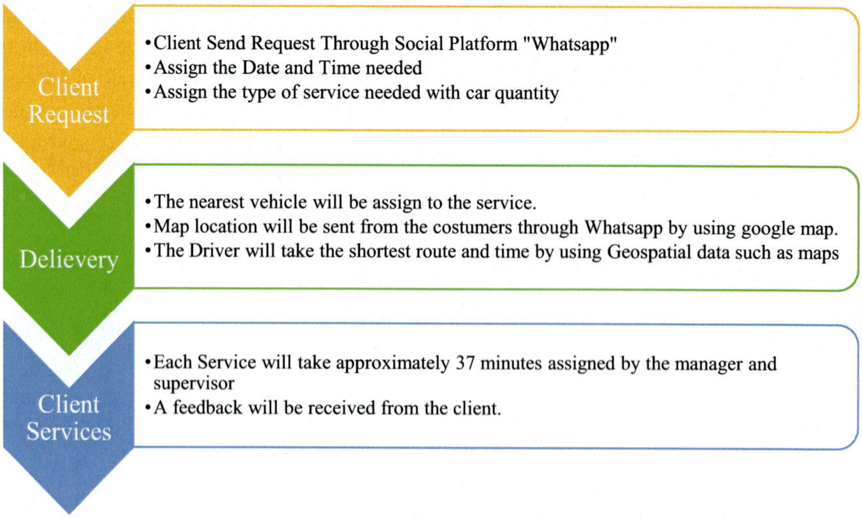

Client Request
- Client Send Request Through Social Platform "Whatsapp"
- Assign the Date and Time needed
- Assign the type of service needed with car quantity

Delievery
- The nearest vehicle will be assign to the service.
- Map location will be sent from the costumers through Whatsapp by using google map.
- The Driver will take the shortest route and time by using Geospatial data such as maps

Client Services
- Each Service will take approximately 37 minutes assigned by the manager and supervisor
- A feedback will be received from the client.

Fig. 2 Pronto carwash workflow. Source: Pronto Carwash. Published with the company's permission

distributed in the Emirate of Abu Dhabi. Each vehicle is assigned to do the services needed by the client with a minimum of 10 services per day. There are 13 employees in the company with different roles of supervision, drivers, cleaners, and customer service. Furthermore, the plans that kept Pronto Carwash Company to stay successful in the market is at the beginning of the company one vehicle occurred to do the job but fourthly and surprisal that the next vehicle was prepared for the service due to the success Mr. Al-Hammadi started his business with low purchased cost from the customers with less than half of the regular price. Also, the spread of the company was through new technologies such as using social media platforms such as WhatsApp and Instagram which recently considered the greater marketing and running business platforms because they are open free to use, and easily reachable by all types of customers that even the high branded companies rely on due to its popularity.

The services that Pronto Carwash Company provides are interior and exterior car wash, depending on the customer's request for the levels of washing, as the company provided four levels normal service, silver service, gold service, and diamond services which are detailed and highlighted in Fig. 3. Another service is waxing and polishing cars. However, Pronto Carwash Company provided loyalty packages for regular customers.

Fig. 3 Pronto carwash level of services and packages. Source: Pronto Carwash. Published with the company's permission

4 Financial Management and Strategy

4.1 Expenses and Revenue

Financial management is an important part of running a successful business. While doing financial management, we must be conscious of the original acquisition of the land, building, and turnkey car wash systems (Harakh, 2018). One of the most important aspects of financial management is tracking and managing the company's revenue and expenses. Wages, rent, utilities, and supplies are examples of expenses incurred by a business to carry out its operations. Revenues, on the other hand, represent the money earned by the company from the sale of its goods or services. Proper expense and revenue management is critical for the company's financial health and sustainability.

Understanding your company's financial performance depends on your ability to measure revenue. (Freedman, n.d.) Tracking and analyzing expenses and revenues enable the company to identify areas where it can reduce costs, increase profits, and improve efficiency. This information helps in making informed decisions about budgeting, investment, and pricing strategies. It also helps in creating financial statements that are crucial for investors, stakeholders, and financial institutions.

Pronto Carwash was established with the money of the owner and assets of the previously failed business, by using its vehicles and renewing them to meet the new business needs. Moreover, the monthly expenses of the Pronto car wash company vary from month to month by about 22,000 dirhams per month, including salaries, patrol, and equipment as shown in Fig. 4. Expenses may vary according to the company's needs for cleaning equipment, supplies, and necessary developments to meet the market demands. The company is expanding in terms of increasing workers, materials, and vehicles for the cleaning service. As all these costs are

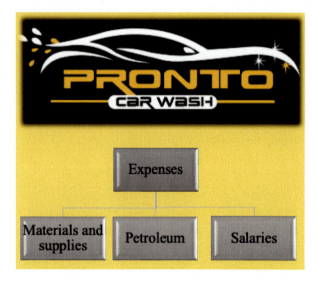

Fig. 4 Pronto carwash expenses. Source: Pronto Carwash. Published with the company's permission

covered by the company's income, including the company's revenues ranging from 45,000 to 60,000 dirhams per month. To sum that up, Pronto Carwash get the revenues almost doubled from the expenses which makes it successful, to meet this a priority has been the number one focus with experiences the good customer service and it also helps in maintaining the label of being the first who start up this kind of business and continually running since 2019.

Effective management of expenses and revenues requires a comprehensive understanding of financial principles and accounting practices. It also involves regular monitoring of financial data and adjusting the company's operations accordingly. With sound financial management practices, a company can achieve financial stability and success in the long run.

4.2 Profitable Development

Growth is challenging in and of itself, but achieving steady profitable growth is even more challenging (Crane, 2021). The profitable growth of a company can be accomplished through a combination of strategic planning, effective management, and innovation. To stay ahead of the competition, businesses must focus on providing value to their customers, optimizing their operations, and investing in research and development.

The profitable development of Pronto company has been since its inception of the establishment, from the operation of the first vehicle for cleaning that has been prepared by the best equipment, vacuums, and solutions brands from internationally with respect to the hygiene of the client's car, workers, and the equipment used such as towels, brushes and extra.

5 The Power of Open Sources Geospatial and Costumer Outreaching

The geospatial analysis involves the gathering, visualizing, and modifying of imagery, GPS, satellite photos, and historical data that are either explicitly specified as geographic coordinates or street addresses, postal codes, or characterized as a forest stand when applied to geographic models (Campbell & Shin, 2012). Geospatial analysis is an effective tool that helps businesses better understand and target their customers. Businesses can learn more about the behavior, preferences, and needs of their customers by analyzing location-based data. By creating more individualized experiences for customers, this information may be utilized to create more targeted marketing campaigns, new goods, and services suited to particular markets or consumer segments, and increase customer satisfaction. Geospatial research may also help companies find new markets and growth prospects, as well as improve the efficiency of their logistics and supply chains. In general, geospatial analysis is a useful tool for companies looking to better understand their clients and promote growth. However, nowadays most small to medium companies use open sources freely to aid their geospatial purposes for spatial needs they can use Google Maps for navigation, Google Earth for exploring, and QGIS for creating maps, while for attribute needs a database management system will take a place to accommodate the need of storing the costumers' details information and records, for instance, Excel, Access, and Oracle.

One of Pronto's most important strengths is the location for the service, where cleaning vehicles and workers are distributed in the most densely populated areas, and they are distributed every 2 hours in different areas, which increases the demand for the service and as an advertisement for the company at the same time.

Pronto keeps pace with modern technology with the customer to track the service, by providing the customer with a live map through Google Maps and sending it using the WhatsApp program, where the customer can track the arrival time by using the live location of Pronto vehicle that will be sent by the customer service agent to represents the adjusted time of arrival to the customer. While on the other hand, the manager also can use this location service to monitor the arrival and departure time for the vehicle to elaborate on the limit of the service time with each customer.

5.1 The Use of Hotspot Maps

A hotspot map, often called a heat map, is a graphical display of data that employs color to illustrate the relative density or intensity of a phenomenon over a certain area. To display vast volumes of data in an understandable way, it is frequently used in data visualization.

Hotspot maps are useful in various industries, such as marketing, and business intelligence. It is an excellent method for determining where data is and is not present, giving the company crucial information (Fragapane, 2021).

In marketing, hotspot maps can show the locations where customers are most concentrated, allowing businesses to target their marketing efforts more effectively.

Pronto Carwash Company uses the hotspot map to assure the spread of the current customers along the Emirate of Abu Dhabi as is shown in the map in Fig. 5. The most density of customers is outside of the Abu Dhabi Islands and that is because of the increase in the carwash spots. While outside the Island there are new regions that lack carwash services, such as Khalifa City, AL Falah City, Shakhbout City, and Al Shamkha City. They are considered highly residential areas where mostly the locals occur the cities are color coded as red color in the map. This gives an indication of the manager and supervisor to distribute the most vehicles around these cities to assure fast reaching to the client and this aid the power of using hotspot maps regularly by collecting the locations from the data.

5.2 The Most Requested Categories for the Service

Pronto is considered one of the most companies requested in demand for carwash services competitiveness company. Moreover, the good average of service costs and

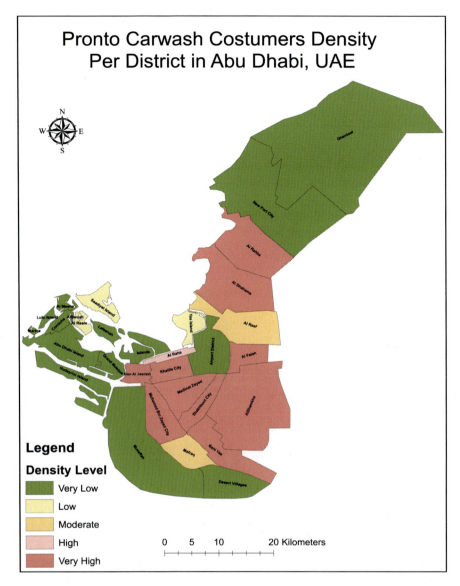

Fig. 5 Pronto carwash customer's density. Source: Pronto Carwash. Published with the company's permission

taking into consideration all the loyalty and discount cards made the spread of Pronto Carwash Company among the people in society through their recommendations and that is on behalf of the suggestion from one client to another.

The gender distribution of the usage of these beneficial services, from 2019 to 2023, shows that 60% of females and 40% of males use them (Fig. 6). There are many reasons for attracting female customers, such as the easiness of reach,

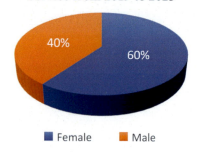

Fig. 6 Demography of the customers. Source: Pronto Carwash. Published with the company's permission

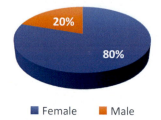

Fig. 7 Demography of the customers during COVID-19. Source: Pronto Carwash. Published with the company's permission

reduction of females going to the carwash spots which are considered as unfamiliar because of stereotyping in the emirate society, and to maintain the time loss for the trip to the spots which might be far from the accommodation place.

During the COVID-19 Pandemic, Pronto Carwash showed a significant change in the increments of female customers by 80% in 2020 and 2021 (Fig. 7), which contributed to the company's revenues during that period and was considered one of the companies that had a successful duration in the pandemic, unlike the other companies with different market stratifications such low, medium, and even large competitors.

6 Toward the Future

The future of a car wash company should consider the changing demands of customers and the competitive landscape of the industry. An important aspect of the plan could be investing in environmentally friendly and sustainable practices, such as the use of water-saving technologies and biodegradable cleaning products. Another key area to consider is the growing demand for convenience and speed in car wash services, which can be addressed by offering mobile or on-demand car wash services. In addition, the company can expand its services beyond the traditional car wash and provide other services in the field of washing and cleaning in several fields. The plan may include developing the equipment used and diversifying the equipment used. Collaborating with motor insurance providers to increase customer reach and generate additional revenue streams.

Pronto's plans are to expand in the field of home washing, increase the number of cars for cleaning cars to more than 60 cars, and diversify the used high-quality equipment that keeps pace with the new types used in the field of washing, and increase the number of workers, due to the high demand for the service.

Among the other services that the company would like to add is also the creation of a dashboard (graphs), to study the percentage of demand for the service per day, month, and year, and this enables an understanding of the company's position to provide the best solutions and services better and faster. In addition to making a map on which customers are distributed and clear ways to locate them, and clarifying the methods used to facilitate the provision of service.

7 The Spread of Social Participation

Participation in social activities and events is the term used to describe how people and groups engage with one another. Social participation maintains social cohesion and promotes economic development (Xie et al., 2022). Also, it aids in creating and maintaining social bonds and a sense of community. It also contributes to the development of social capital, which is a network of connections between people that fosters collaboration and support among them.

To sum up, everything that has been stated so far Pronto Carwash Company plays an important role in being part of many governmental authorities as contracted to clean their vehicle. Also, the company participates in major events to clean the events' vehicles.

8 Questions for Discussion

1. Behind what business failure was Pronto Carwash Company introduced?
2. What type of social media platform does Pronto Carwash Company use?
3. What are the main three expenses of the Pronto Carwash Company?
4. What are the most gender-requested services during COVID-19?
5. What kind of social participation does Pronto Carwash Company provide?

References

AlHammadi, M. (2023, February 19). *Personal communication.*

Crane, A. (2021, March 7). How to achieve consistent profitable growth. *Sales focus advisory.* Retrieved from https://salesfocusadvisory.com/consistent-profitable-growth/

Fragapane, R. (2021, June 15). How heat maps are used for business mapping. *Maptive.* Retrieved from maptive.com/heat-maps-for-business/

Freedman, J. (n.d.). Importance of measuring revenue. *Small Business–Chron.com.* Retrieved from https://smallbusiness.chron.com/importance-measuring-revenue-67227.html

Harakh, D. (2018). *Dream clean car wash business plan.* (Master thesis). Retrieved from https://scholarworks.calstate.edu/downloads/sf268602w

Hisrich, R., & Ramadani, V. (2017). *Effective entrepreneurial management.* Springer.

The Business Plan Shop. (n.d.). *How to write the business plan for a car wash.* Retrieved from https://www.thebusinessplanshop.com/en/blog/business-plan-car-wash

Campbell, J. E., & Shin, M. (2012). *Geographic information system basics v.1.0.* Retrieved from https://2012books.lardbucket.org/pdfs/geographic-information-system-basics.pdf

Xie, P., Cao, Q., Li, X., Yang, Y., & Yu, L. (2022, September 2). The effects of social participation on social integration. *Front Psychol, 13.* https://doi.org/10.3389/fpsyg.2022.919592

Asma Al Madhaani is a master's student in remote sensing and geographic information systems and holds a bachelor's degree in geographic information systems from the United Arab Emirates University in 2019. She has many projects related to the environment and how and importance of geographic information systems in studying this field.

Mahra Al-Ali , a committed and determined person, is now studying for a master's degree in remote sensing and geographic information systems at the United Arab Emirates University that is expected to graduate in 2023. Mahra Al-Ali is dedicated to obtaining academic success and making significant contributions to her profession. She has a solid academic background and a great desire to learn new things. During her undergraduate studies, Mahra Al-Ali completed research projects and internships, which provided her with valuable skills and a thorough understanding of her field. Mahra Al-Ali graduated with BA in 2021 with a grade of very good. Mahra Al-Ali is keen to advance her education as a master's student and learn more about her field of concentration.

CADD Emirates Computers: Providing Cutting-Edge Technology Solutions and Services for a Digital-First World

Mariam Slayem Alblooshi and Abeer Alyammahi

Abstract

CADD Emirates Computers is a leading provider of CAD and engineering solutions, as well as ICT infrastructure, networking and security, hardware maintenance, and hospitality solutions. Despite facing challenges with maintaining face-to-face interactions with customers, the company has overcome this by strategically locating offices in different Emirates and centralizing project planning and procurement. With a commitment to quality and 100% customer satisfaction, CADD Emirates is well-positioned for continued success by expanding into new areas and empowering clients through IT and technology solutions. The company's strong leadership team, focus on innovation, and strategic planning have helped it stay ahead of competitors and adapt to evolving business and technological landscapes. Additionally, by utilizing location-based analytics tools, CADD Emirates can effectively transport goods and services to its clients, enabling it to reach customers and move goods across the country efficiently.

M. S. Alblooshi (✉)
Department of Geography and Urban Sustainability, United Arab Emirates University, Abu Dhabi, UAE
e-mail: 201609566@uaeu.ac.ae

A. Alyammahi
National Water and Energy Center, United Arab Emirates University, Abu Dhabi, Al Ain City, UAE
e-mail: Abeeralyammahi@uaeu.ac.ae

1 Introduction

In today's world, technology has become an integral part of our daily lives, exerting a significant influence on individuals, communities, businesses, and even nations (Brooke, 2022; Nikoloski, 2012; Reyes & Castillo, 2019; White, 2023). This impact is particularly evident in the business sector, where technology has brought about substantial changes in management practices, manufacturing processes, communication methods, and overall operational efficiency. Information and Communication Technology (ICT) encompasses the diverse range of digital tools and systems that facilitate effective information usage by individuals, businesses, and organizations. It encompasses electronic devices that manipulate and transmit data in digital formats.

CADD Emirates is one of the leading Enterprise Solutions Provider and ICT Integrator in UAE, delivering an extensive array of solutions and services to clients not only within the United Arab Emirates but also internationally (CADD Emirates, n.d.-a). The company has a rich history of providing CAD and engineering solutions to the architecture, engineering, and construction (AEC) industry. Since its inception, CADD Emirates has continuously transformed to meet the evolving needs of its clients and to stay ahead of technological advancements.

In addition to CAD and engineering solutions, CADD Emirates has expanded its portfolio to include ICT infrastructure, networking and security, backup and disaster recovery, and hardware maintenance. The company has also ventured into hospitality solutions, offering a comprehensive range of enterprise business solutions such as ERP, CRM, BI, FM, and more (CADD Emirates, n.d.-a).

CADD Emirates has faced its fair share of challenges over the years. One of the biggest challenges has been maintaining face-to-face interactions with customers across all Emirates due to the need for frequent travel. To overcome this challenge, the company has established branches in Abu Dhabi and the northern Emirates, while centralizing project planning and procurement. This approach ensures efficient services, optimum prices, and on-time project delivery while meeting local needs.

CADD Emirates is committed to upholding high standards of quality and delivery, as evidenced by its ISO certification. This commitment to quality has set the company apart from its competitors in the industry. Furthermore, CADD Emirates has won major orders and turnkey projects from reputable clients such as Gems Group, One Zabeel, Etisalat, RTA Dubai, ENOC, and Emirates Global Aluminium.

As CADD Emirates continues to grow and expand, the company is positioning itself for continued success. The company plans to foray into new areas to meet the growing needs of its clients. Its commitment to empowering clients through IT and technology solutions will continue to drive its growth and success in the years to come.

The purpose of this chapter is to provide readers with a comprehensive overview of CADD Emirates, including its history, challenges, use of GIS, competitive advantages, notable achievements, and future outlook. By the end of this chapter, readers will have a better understanding of CADD Emirates and its position as a leading provider of technology solutions and services in the UAE.

2 History and Background

CADD Emirates was founded in 1997 as a provider of CAD and engineering solutions. The company quickly established itself as a pioneer in the proliferation of CAD and engineering solutions in the AEC vertical. Since then, CADD Emirates has been providing state-of-the-art solutions to its clients across various industries, including architecture, engineering, construction, and more.

Over the years, CADD Emirates has undergone significant transformation to stay ahead of the ever-evolving needs of its clients. The company has expanded its portfolio to include a wide range of solutions and services, including ICT infrastructure, networking and security, backup and disaster recovery, hardware maintenance, and more. CADD Emirates has also made a name for itself in the hospitality industry, offering a comprehensive range of enterprise business solutions such as ERP, CRM, BI, FM, and more.

Despite facing challenges such as maintaining face-to-face interactions with customers across all Emirates, CADD Emirates has continued to grow and expand its operations. The company has established branches in Abu Dhabi and the northern Emirates, and centralized project planning and procurement to ensure efficient services, optimum prices, and on-time project delivery while meeting local needs.

CADD Emirates' commitment to quality has set it apart from its competitors in the industry. The company is one of the very few ICT companies in the UAE to be ISO certified. Its ISO certification is a testament to its belief in quality-first and its commitment to delivering on its promises consistently.

Today, CADD Emirates stands as a leading provider of technology solutions and services in the UAE. The company offers a comprehensive range of solutions and services for ICT Infrastructure, Networking and Security, Backup and Disaster Recovery, and Hardware Maintenance, among others. Table 1 provides a breakdown of the services offered by CADD Emirates.

2.1 CADD Emirates Vision and Mission

CADD Emirates is committed to becoming a trusted and reliable provider of IT solutions that enable its clients to achieve their business objectives. The company aims to accomplish this by offering innovative and tailored technology solutions that

Table 1 CADD Emirates services

Service category	Services
Engineering Solutions	CAD, BIM, CAE, CAM, PLM, PDM, 3D Printing
ICT Infrastructure	Networking, Storage, Virtualization, Cloud, Backup & DR
Security Solutions	Endpoint Protection, Firewall, VPN, Email and Web Security
Hospitality Solutions	IP Telephony, IPTV, Guest Wi-Fi, Digital Signage, IPTV Streaming
Enterprise Solutions	ERP, CRM, HRM, FM, BI, Retail POS

Source: CADD. Published with the company's permission

are focused on delivering exceptional service and upholding the highest ethical and quality standards, ultimately resulting in 100% client satisfaction. CADD Emirates believes in building long-term relationships with its clients by staying ahead of the curve in a rapidly evolving technology landscape.

CADD Emirates envisions to be the foremost provider of cutting-edge and sustainable IT solutions that enable businesses to succeed in a digital-first world. The company strives to achieve this by fostering a culture of innovation, agility, and excellence that encourages collaboration, creativity, and continuous improvement. CADD Emirates aims to empower its clients to leverage technology to its fullest potential and drive growth, profitability, and sustainability for their organizations.

2.2 Values Culture at CADD Emirates

CADD Emirates is a values-driven organization that is committed to building strong and successful relationships with its customers, employees, and partners. Their core values are centred around a customer-centric approach, ethical and moral standards, teamwork, individual career growth, and a commitment to creating a safe and healthy work environment. Some of the core values observed at CADD Emirates are listed in Table 2.

3 Leadership and Management

CADD Emirates, a leading provider of engineering software solutions and services, boasts of a top management team that comprises some of the most respected and accomplished individuals in the industry. Their rich experience and expertise have been instrumental in shaping the company's growth and success over the years. The top management team at CADD Emirates consists of illustrious and distinguished personalities who bring with them a wealth of knowledge and skills (CADD

Table 2 Core values

Values	Description
Excellence	CADD Emirates pursue excellence in everything they do by delivering quality products and services that meet or exceed expectations.
Integrity	CADD Emirates uphold honesty, transparency, and ethical standards in all their dealings with clients, partners, and employees.
Innovation	CADD Emirates foster a culture of innovation by encouraging creativity, learning, and improvement among their team members.
Collaboration	CADD Emirates work as one team with their clients, partners, and employees by sharing knowledge, ideas, and resources.
Customer Satisfaction	CADD Emirates aim to achieve 100% customer satisfaction by understanding their needs, providing solutions that add value and ensuring timely delivery.

Source: CADD. Published with the company's permission

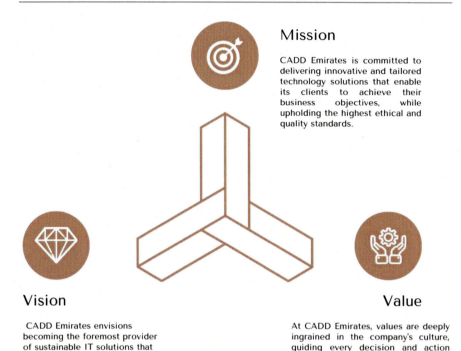

Fig. 1 CADD Emirates vision, mission, and values. Source: CADD. Published with the company's permission

Emirates, n.d.-b). Their visionary leadership and strategic planning have enabled the company to stay ahead of the competition and constantly innovate to meet the evolving needs of their clients. Figure 1 shows the top-down structure of CAAD Emirates management. With a focus on excellence, innovation, and customer satisfaction, the top management team at CADD Emirates continues to drive the company's growth and success in the highly competitive engineering software solutions and services market.

3.1 Chairman: Sheikh Salem Sultan Saqr Al Qasimi

Sheikh Salem Sultan Saqr Al Qasimi, the Chairman of CADD Emirates, is a well-respected business leader and entrepreneur in the UAE (CADD Emirates, n.d.-b). He is an engineer by profession and a visionary leader who guides the company with his expertise and experience. He is also a board member of several other organizations and a prominent figure in the UAE society. With a deep understanding of the region's economic landscape and a commitment to driving innovation and growth,

Sheikh Salem has been instrumental in the success of CADD Emirates over the years. Under his visionary leadership, the company has evolved to become a leading provider of enterprise solutions and ICT integration services in the UAE, with a reputation for excellence and customer-first philosophy. Sheikh Salem's passion for empowering businesses through IT and his dedication to delivering high-quality solutions and services have earned him the respect and admiration of his peers and clients alike.

3.2 Vice Chairman: Sheikh Majed Sultan Saqr Al Qasimi

Sheikh Majed Sultan Saqr Al Qasimi, the Vice Chairman of CADD Emirates, is a highly experienced and accomplished business leader in the UAE (CADD Emirates, n.d.-b). He is a dynamic and innovative leader who oversees the strategic direction and growth of the company. He is also involved in various social and charitable initiatives and a respected member of the UAE. Having a solid foundation in finance and a profound comprehension of the business environment in the UAE, Sheikh Majed has played a crucial role in the progress and achievements of CADD Emirates throughout the years. He has played a key role in developing the company's strategic vision, driving innovation and growth, and ensuring that it remains at the forefront of the rapidly evolving IT landscape. Sheikh Majed's commitment to excellence, his customer-first philosophy, and his unwavering dedication to quality have earned him the respect and trust of his peers, clients, and employees alike.

3.3 Board Member: Sheikh Nasser Sultan Saqr Al Qasimi

Sheikh Nasser Sultan Saqr Al Qasimi is a distinguished board member of CADD Emirates (CADD Emirates, n.d.-b). He is a seasoned and accomplished professional who contributes to the company's success with his knowledge and skills. He is also active in various cultural and educational activities. With extensive experience in business and finance, Sheikh Nasser brings valuable insights and perspectives to the company's strategic direction and operations. His leadership and guidance have been invaluable in establishing CADD Emirates as a trusted ICT integrator and a leading provider of enterprise solutions in the region (Fig. 2).

4 Transportation and Strategic Locations for Business Success

Efficient transportation is of utmost importance for the success of businesses, as it enables them to effectively deliver goods and services to their customers (Goldsby et al., 2017). The connectivity and transportation capabilities of a business are significantly influenced by its strategic positioning. By locating business operations in close proximity to transportation nodes, such as ports, airports, or highways,

CADD Emirates Computers: Providing Cutting-Edge Technology Solutions... 143

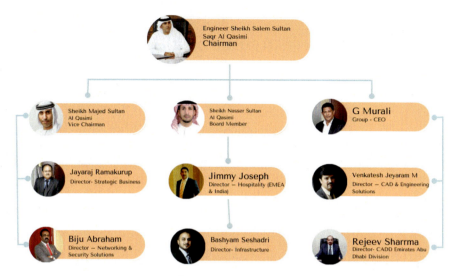

Fig. 2 Organizational structure. Source: (CADD Emirates, n.d.-b). Published with the company's permission

businesses can enjoy improved connectivity and lower transportation costs (Esri, n. d.).

CADD Emirates, a company with offices in Abu Dhabi, Dubai, Ras Al-Khaimah, and Fujairah (Fig. 3), has strategically chosen the locations of its offices to ensure efficient transportation links to serve its clients effectively. The Abu Dhabi office is situated on Khalifa Street (CADD Emirates, n.d.-c), an important transportation hub in the capital city. This strategic location enables the company to deliver goods and services to clients in Abu Dhabi and neighboring areas seamlessly, capitalizing on the accessibility provided by the transportation network.

In Dubai, CADD Emirates has its corporate office located in the Prism Tower at Business Bay (CADD Emirates, n.d.-c). This prime location offers easy access to major highways and roads, facilitating the smooth transportation of goods and services. The strategic placement of the office allows the company to leverage the transportation network, connecting with customers and suppliers efficiently.

The Ras Al-Khaimah office is situated in the well-connected Aluraiby Building B Block (CADD Emirates, n.d.-c), ensuring excellent transportation links to the northern region of the UAE. Recognizing the critical role of transportation networks in the movement of goods and people, this location enables CADD Emirates to efficiently transport goods and services to its clients in the area.

Lastly, CADD Emirates' Fujairah office is strategically positioned on Al Hail Industrial Street, providing excellent transportation links to the eastern region of the UAE. This advantageous location enables the company to effectively cater to its clients in the area by utilizing the efficient transportation network for seamless connections with customers and suppliers. Through strategic placement of offices

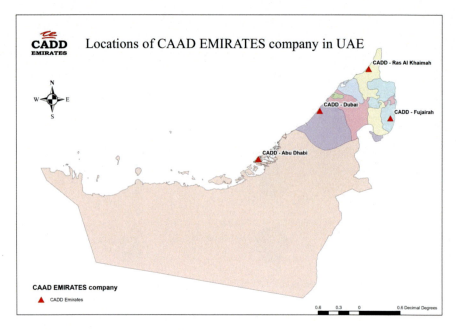

Fig. 3 CADD Emirates company location. Source: CADD Emirates (n.d.-c). Published with the company's permission

across various regions in the UAE, CADD Emirates maximizes the benefits of efficient transportation links, ensuring efficient service delivery to its clients.

The Company's strategic location of its offices in different regions of the UAE provides it with efficient transportation links to its clients. By utilizing location-based analytics tools, businesses like CADD Emirates can effectively transport goods and services to their clients, enabling them to reach their customers and move goods across the country efficiently.

5 Major Challenges Faced and Overcome

CADD Emirates has faced several challenges over the years that have tested its resilience and ability to adapt to changing circumstances. One of the major challenges faced by the company was the difficulty in maintaining face-to-face interactions with customers across all Emirates due to travel restrictions. This resulted in losing touch with some accounts, leading to a decline in business.

To overcome this challenge, CADD Emirates established branch offices in Abu Dhabi and northern Emirates, allowing for better communication and collaboration with customers in these areas. Additionally, the company centralized its project planning and procurement while executing projects through local offices. This approach ensured efficient services and optimum prices for customers, while also meeting their local needs.

Another significant challenge faced by CADD Emirates was the need to keep pace with changing technology and evolving customer needs. The company overcame this challenge by investing in training and development programs to ensure that its employees had the necessary skills and expertise to provide cutting-edge solutions to customers. Furthermore, the company has expanded its offerings to include a wide range of solutions and services for ICT Infrastructure, Networking and Security, Backup and Disaster Recovery, and Hardware Maintenance, among others.

Despite these challenges, CADD Emirates has remained steadfast in its commitment to providing high-quality solutions and services to its customers. The company's ability to adapt and evolve has been key to its success over the years, and it continues to explore new areas to meet the growing needs of its customers.

Transportation is a crucial aspect of businesses, facilitating the delivery of goods and services to customers (Goldsby et al., 2017). Upon examining the locations of CADD Emirates Company offices, it is apparent that the company has strategically placed its offices in various regions of the UAE to cater to its clients' needs efficiently.

6 CADD Emirates Successful Previous Projects

CADD Emirates offers a wide range of business solutions and services for computing infrastructure, networking and security, CAD and engineering, hospitality technologies, and business automation.

6.1 Business Solutions and Infrastructure

CADD Emirates has a deep understanding of business processes and practices and provides consulting services coupled with deployment and support for organizations ready to invest in business automation. It has partnered with IBM to offer IBM Cloud Pak for Data, a platform that helps businesses collect, organize, and analyze data. Besides IBM, several other giants have also been partnered with CADD Emirates such as Lenovo to offer Lenovo ThinkSystem servers and storage solutions, which are designed to deliver high performance, reliability, and scalability for various workloads as well as Microsoft, to offer Microsoft Azure, a cloud computing platform that helps businesses build, deploy and manage applications and services. Some of the projects that CADD Emirates has done related to business solutions and infrastructure include:

- Providing enterprise resource planning (ERP) solutions for a leading manufacturing company in UAE.
- Implementing document management systems (DMS) for a large oil and gas company in Kuwait.

- Deploying customer relationship management (CRM) solutions for a renowned retail chain in Oman.
- Installing business intelligence (BI) and analytics solutions for a government entity in Bahrain.
- Providing cloud computing and virtualization solutions for a hospitality group in Qatar.

These are some examples of how CADD Emirates has delivered successful business solutions and infrastructure projects for its clients across the Middle East.

6.2 CAD and Engineering

CADD Emirates has played a pioneering role in ushering in design automation software and tools in the Middle East through its decade-long partnership with Autodesk USA. It has been providing design solutions to large and medium enterprises in UAE, Qatar, Kuwait, Bahrain, and Saudi Arabia since 1998. CADD Emirates has also partnered with Oracle to offer Oracle Cloud, a cloud computing platform that helps businesses run their applications and workloads on a secure and scalable infrastructure. Besides this, there is another alliance with Adobe to offer Adobe Sign, a cloud-based e-signature service that helps businesses streamline document workflows and reduce paper costs. Some of the projects that CADD Emirates has done related to CAD and Engineering include:

- Providing Autodesk software and training for a leading architectural firm in UAE.
- Implementing building information modeling (BIM) solutions for a large construction company in Kuwait.
- Deploying 3D modeling and simulation solutions for a renowned engineering consultancy in Oman.
- Installing digital prototyping and product lifecycle management (PLM) solutions for a manufacturing company in Bahrain.
- Providing GIS and mapping solutions for a government entity in Qatar.

6.3 Hospitality

CADD Emirates provides operations, leisure, communication systems, display system, and guest services solutions to the hotel industry. It uses state-of-the-art technologies and has many properties in the UAE as its clients. CADD Emirates has partnered with Guestware, Shiji, and Ariane, three companies that offer innovative technology solutions for the hospitality industry. Guestware provides a cloud-based guest experience management software that helps hotels improve guest satisfaction and loyalty. Shiji provides a platform that connects hotels with multiple distribution channels and data sources. Ariane provides self-service check-in/out technology that helps hotels reduce operational costs and enhance guest convenience. Some of the projects that CADD Emirates has done related to hospitality include:

- Providing interactive TV and digital signage solutions for a luxury hotel in Dubai.
- Implementing property management systems (PMS) and point of sale (POS) solutions for a resort in Abu Dhabi.
- Deploying IP telephony and wireless Internet solutions for a hotel chain in Sharjah.
- Installing CCTV and access control solutions for a boutique hotel in Ajman.
- Providing smart room and energy management solutions for a hotel apartment in Ras Al Khaimah.

These are some examples of how CADD Emirates has delivered successful hospitality projects for its clients across the UAE.

6.4 Networking and Security

CADD Emirates provides networking and security solutions that can maintain a perfect balance between information accessibility and data security for various organizations. It has a team of certified networking and security experts along with products from leading OEMs. CADD Emirates has partnered with Cisco, Hewlett Packard Enterprise, and Fortinet, three companies that offer advanced technologies for networking and security (Fig. 4). Cisco provides a range of products and services that help businesses connect, communicate, and collaborate more efficiently. Hewlett Packard Enterprise provides a platform that helps businesses transform their IT operations and accelerate innovation. Fortinet provides a broad portfolio of security solutions that protect businesses from cyber threats. Some of the projects that CADD Emirates has done related to networking and security include:

- Designing and implementing a secure network infrastructure for a leading bank in UAE.
- Providing network optimization and performance management solutions for a large telecom operator in Saudi Arabia.
- Deploying wireless LAN solutions for a prestigious university in Oman.
- Installing IP telephony and unified communications systems for a government entity in Bahrain.
- Implementing network access control and firewall solutions for a hospitality group in Qatar.

These are some examples of how CADD Emirates has delivered successful network projects for its clients across the Middle East.

Fig. 4 CADD Emirates partners. Source: CADD Emirates (n.d.-d). Published with the company's permission

7 Adapting to the Changing Business Landscape

As technology continues to evolve, companies must adapt to remain competitive. CADD Emirates has been at the forefront of adapting to the changing business landscape, continuously enhancing its services and solutions to meet the needs of its clients.

7.1 Technological Advancements and Adaptation

Over the years, CADD Emirates has adapted to numerous technological advancements. The company began as a provider of CAD software and services but has since transformed to stay in step with evolving customer needs and the changing IT landscape. Today, CADD Emirates offers a single-point reference for a wide range of solutions and services for ICT Infrastructure, Networking and Security, Backup and Disaster Recovery, and Hardware Maintenance.

7.2 Services and Solutions Offered

CADD Emirates offers a wide range of services and solutions that cater to the needs of various industries. The company has found widespread acceptance for its Hospitality solutions and has recently augmented its portfolio with a comprehensive range of Enterprise Business Solutions including ERP, CRM, BI, FM, and more. The company has a centralized project planning and procurement process to ensure customers receive efficient services and optimum prices, while local execution ensures projects are on time and meet local needs.

CADD Emirates has always prioritized quality and upholding standards in its services, and the company is one of the very few ICT companies in the country to be ISO certified. CADD Emirates strives to deliver on commitments consistently, and this commitment to quality sets it apart from other companies in the industry.

Overall, CADD Emirates has adapted to technological advancements and changing customer needs to remain at the forefront of the engineering solutions and IT industries. The company continues to foray into new areas encouraged by the trust of its customers and their growing needs. The future for CADD Emirates is bright as it holds promises of a multinational company ready to tread the untrodden paths in its quest for Empowerment through IT.

7.3 Competitive Advantage

CADD Emirates prides itself on its commitment to delivering high-quality solutions and services, which has been a cornerstone of the company's success. Unlike many other companies in the industry, CADD Emirates places a "Quality-First" belief at the forefront of all its operations. This belief ensures that every project is approached with a focus on delivering the best possible quality, while also meeting deadlines and staying within budget. The Company is one of the very few ICT companies in the UAE to be ISO certified, which further solidifies its commitment to upholding standards and delivering on commitments consistently. This certification is a testament to the company's dedication to quality management, continuous improvement, and customer satisfaction. The combination of these factors has enabled CADD Emirates to stand out in the industry and establish itself as a trusted partner for customers across the UAE.

8 Notable Success Stories and Achievements

CADD Emirates has achieved several notable successes and milestones in its journey. Some of these include:

- Major Orders and Turnkey Projects: CADD Emirates has successfully won several major orders and turnkey projects in the region. These include:
  - Complete Wi-Fi and networking solutions for Gems Group, One Zabeel, Etisalat, RTA Dubai, ENOC, and Emirates Global Aluminium.
- Successful Implementation of Solutions: CADD Emirates has a proven track record of successfully implementing solutions for its clients. Some of the notable examples include:
  - Implementation of a comprehensive ICT infrastructure and network solution for a leading hotel chain in the UAE, resulting in improved guest experience and increased operational efficiency.
  - Implementation of a customized ERP solution for a major construction company, resulting in improved project management and cost control.
  - Implementation of a cutting-edge security and surveillance solution for a large industrial facility, resulting in improved safety and security measures.

These success stories are a testament to the CADD Emirates' commitment to quality and customer satisfaction. The company's expertise in engineering and technology, coupled with its customer-centric approach, has enabled it to deliver innovative and effective solutions that meet the evolving needs of its clients.

9 CADD Emirates Future Plans

CADD Emirates is positioning itself for continued success by expanding its portfolio of services and solutions and leveraging technological advancements to meet the evolving needs of its customers. The company plans to foray into new areas to keep up with changing trends and customer demands.

The company has always been committed to quality and efficiency, and it plans to continue upholding these values in the future. The company will continue to focus on delivering high-quality solutions and services to its clients while keeping pace with the latest technological advancements.

To facilitate future growth, CADD Emirates has established a strong presence across various locations in the UAE, including Abu Dhabi and the northern Emirates. This enables the company to provide localized services while ensuring consistency in quality and service delivery.

CADD Emirates also plans to leverage its extensive experience and expertise in the engineering and construction industry to further expand its presence in the market. The company will continue to work closely with its clients to understand their needs and deliver customized solutions that meet their unique requirements. Overall, CADD Emirates is well-positioned to continue its growth and success in the future by leveraging its expertise, commitment to quality, and focus on customer satisfaction.

10 Conclusion

In conclusion, CADD Emirates is a leading engineering solutions company that has successfully adapted to the changing business landscape and technological advancements over the years. The company has faced several challenges but has overcome them with strategic planning and effective implementation. CADD Emirates' commitment to quality and ISO certification has set it apart from other companies in the industry. With a strong leadership team and a focus on innovation and growth, CADD Emirates is well-positioned for continued success in the future.

11 Questions for Discussion

1. What is the importance of transportation and strategic locations for the success of businesses, and how has CADD Emirates utilized location-based analytics tools to enhance its transportation efficiency?
2. What sets CADD Emirates apart from other engineering solutions companies in the industry, and what are some of its key success factors?
3. What do you think are some potential areas for further expansion and growth for CADD Emirates in the future, and why?
4. What impact has the COVID-19 pandemic had on CADD Emirates' operations, and how has the company responded to these challenges?
5. What is the role of leadership in CADD Emirates' success, and what qualities do you think are important for effective leadership in the technology solutions industry?

References

Brooke, C. (2022). The importance of information technology in business today. *Business 2 community*. Retrieved from https://www.business2community.com/tech-gadgets/importance-information-technology-business-today-01393380

CADD Emirates. (n.d.-a). *Corporate profile*. Retrieved from https://www.caddemirates.com/about-us/profile/

CADD Emirates. (n.d.-b). *Management team*. Retrieved from https://www.caddemirates.com/about-us/management-team/

CADD Emirates. (n.d.-c). *Locations*. Retrieved from https://www.caddemirates.com/contact-us/dubai/

CADD Emirates. (n.d.-d). *Alliances*. Retrieved from https://www.caddemirates.com/alliances/

Esri. (n.d.). *Transportation*. Retrieved from https://www.esri.com/en-us/industries/transportation/overview

Goldsby, T. J., Iyengar, D., Rao, S., & Council of supply chain management professionals. (2017). *The definitive guide to transportation: Principles, strategies, and decisions for the effective flow of goods and services*. Pearson Education.

Nikoloski, K. (2012). The role of information technology in the business sector. *International Journal of Science and Research*. Retrieved from https://www.ijsr.net/archive/v3i12/U1VCMTQzMjA=.pdf

Reyes, J. R., & Castillo, D. (2019). Importance of ICT's use in business management and its contribution to the improvement of university processes. In book: *Information and communication Technologies of Ecuador (TIC.EC)*. Retrieved from https://www.researchgate.net/publication/328367833_Importance_of_ICT's_Use_in_Business_Management_and_Its_Contribution_to_the_Improvement_of_University_Processes

White, D. (2023, February 2). 5 advantages of information and communication technology in business. *TechFunnel*. Retrieved from https://www.techfunnel.com/information-technology/5-advantages-of-information-and-communication-technology-in-business/

Mariam Slayem Alblooshi is a dedicated graduate student in the Department of Geography and Urban Sustainability at UAE University (UAEU), United Arab Emirates. She earned her Bachelor's degree in Geoinformatics from UAEU in 2021 and is now pursuing a Master's degree in Remote Sensing and Geographic Information System. Mariam's research interests include environmental monitoring, innovative technology, and spatial analysis. Specifically, she is passionate about using machine learning to monitor animal behavior and protect coastal ecosystems.

Abeer Alyammahi is a research assistant at NWEC, UAEU, with a focus on water quality, hydrology, environmental modeling, and Geographic Information Systems (GIS). She graduated with a Bachelor of Geographic Information Systems from United Arab Emirates University in Spring 2021 and completed a 4-month internship at Fujairah GIS Center. Currently, she is pursuing her Master of Science in Remote Sensing and Geographic Information Systems at United Arab Emirates University, where she continues to expand her knowledge and expertise in GIS and related fields.

Bin Ham Group: Building a Legacy of Excellence in United Arab Emirates Investments

Aysha Nadheer, Fatima S. Alawani, and Ramo Palalić

Abstract

Bin Ham Group, an esteemed commercial conglomerate headquartered in the United Arab Emirates (UAE), has established itself as a prominent player with a diversified portfolio spanning various industries. The company's unwavering commitment to excellence is evident in its impressive track record of accomplishments and its significant contributions to the UAE's economy and society. Bin Ham Group has been the recipient of numerous prestigious awards and accolades in recognition of its valuable services to the UAE's economy and society.

Each division within Bin Ham Group is dedicated to specific Sustainable Development Goals (SDGs), actively implementing sustainable business practices and fostering a culture of sustainability among its employees. The company has introduced effective SDG goals, placing particular emphasis on enhancing real estate management across both administrative and commercial units. Additionally, Bin Ham Group has undertaken various projects to improve pumping station implementation, while also addressing the development of critical civil projects, including roadways, wastewater treatment facilities, and road lighting.

As a prominent business group in the UAE, Bin Ham Group places utmost importance on philanthropy, innovation, and sustainability. By prioritizing these core values, the group actively contributes to the betterment of society and

---

A. Nadheer (✉) · F. S. Alawani
United Arab Emirates University, Al Ain City, UAE
e-mail: 201612064@uaeu.ac.ae; 201302502@uaeu.ac.ae

R. Palalić
Sultan Qaboos University, Al-khod, Oman
e-mail: r.palalic@squ.edu.om

© The Author(s), under exclusive license to Springer Nature Switzerland AG 2023
K. Alkaabi, V. Ramadani (eds.), *Family Business Cases*, Springer Business Cases,
https://doi.org/10.1007/978-3-031-39252-8_11

reinforces its commitment to building a prosperous and sustainable future for the UAE.

1 Introduction

The Bin Ham Group has been a leader in the UAE economy for more than three decades, during which time it has also established itself as one of the country's most recognizable brands (Bin Ham Group, n.d.-a). Bin Ham Group is a prominent business conglomerate based in the United Arab Emirates (UAE), with a diverse portfolio of companies operating in various industries. Family businesses in the UAE have been fostering the nation's economy for a long time. The United Arab Emirates is promoting a unique organizational environment that could help advance the management field. Families own more than 90% of businesses in the UAE (KPMG, 2022). The United Arab Emirates (UAE)-based Bin Ham Group is a major business conglomerate that owns many companies in different sectors. Sheik Musallam established the Group in 1979, and it has since become one of the most influential corporations in the area. Forex International, Agriculture, Education, Oil and Gas, Travel and Tourism, Real Estate, Hospitality, General contractor, printing and publishing, and Electromechanical are the businesses of the Group. This work intends to reflect the history of the company, sectors associated with it, achievements, and projects associated with the company. Additionally, it sheds light on the latest projects and developments associated with the Group. Finally, it focuses on sustainability measures and the CSR activities related to the company.

2 History of the Bin Ham's Company

The company was involved in the development of several commercial and residential properties across the UAE, including hotels, resorts, and high-rise buildings. In the 1980s, Bin Ham Group expanded into the hospitality industry, opening several hotels and restaurants across the UAE (Bin Ham Group, n.d.-a). Throughout the 1990s and 2000s, Bin Ham Group continued to diversify its portfolio, expanding into other industries including healthcare and retail. The company has established several hospitals and clinics, and also opened several retail outlets across the UAE. In addition to its business ventures, Bin Ham Group is also involved in several philanthropic initiatives, including supporting various charitable organizations and causes. Such, profiled business activities were enabled by the corporate culture, which preceded the following organizational structure shown in Fig. 1. Bin Ham Group is a diversified conglomerate based in the United Arab Emirates with operations across various sectors as shown in Fig. 2.

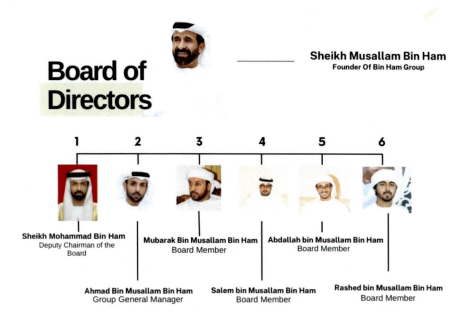

Fig. 1 The figure shows the board directors of Bin Ham's Group. Source: Bin Ham Group (n.d.-b). Published with the company's permission

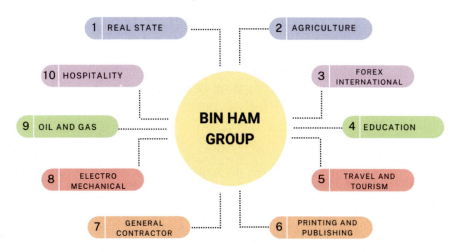

Fig. 2 Sectors associated with Bin Ham Group. Source: Bin Ham Group (n.d.-a). Published with the company's permission

3 Business Overview

Bin Ham Group operates in several industries, as is described below.

3.1 Real Estate

In 2007, Bin Ham Group established "Bin Ham Real Estate" as the real estate arm of the group to manage its residential, administrative, and commercial units in Al Ain, Abu Dhabi, Dubai, and Sharjah using the most up-to-date scientific methods recognized in the industry and to maximize economic return (Bin Ham Group, n. d.-c). Among them, especially in light of recent developments that have introduced new mechanisms into the work of real estate developers and increased competition in the field of real estate investment.

Bin Ham Group has made significant contributions to the real estate sector in the UAE by developing several iconic commercial and residential projects. Some of its prominent real estate projects include Ajman China Mall, Bin Ham Residence in Sharjah, and Hamriyah Free Zone in Sharjah. The UAE's real estate market generates approximately 5.5% in 2020 of the UAE's overall GDP (Statista Research Department, 2023). After reaching a plateau, real estate prices in the UAE have begun to show an upward trend (Turak, 2023). Also, the UAE eased some of its rules, which is excellent news for the travel and hospitality, transportation and logistics, construction, and real estate markets. In the heart of the Middle East, the UAE has emerged as a thriving economic and cultural hub. Real estate professionals from all around the world have come to the conclusion that the market is once again starting to completely reopen its doors to visitors and investors. Bin Ham Group's community development is meant to encourage healthy lifestyles and well-integrated, eco-friendly, and sustainable communities for its residents (Bin Ham Group, n.d.-c).

3.2 Agriculture

Bin Ham Group UAE has a significant presence in the agriculture industry, and they have established a strong reputation for providing high-quality agricultural products to the local market. They work with leading international companies to import and distribute fresh fruits, vegetables, and other agricultural products. In addition, they also invest in local farming operations and promote sustainable agriculture practices to support the growth of the industry in the UAE. Their agriculture business is part of their larger vision of promoting food security and sustainable development in the region. They prioritize providing nutritious and safe food to the local population while minimizing the environmental impact of their operations. The group's commitment to innovation and sustainability has made them a trusted partner in the UAE's agriculture industry.

3.3 Forex International (Trading)

Bin Ham Group has a well-established trading business, with a focus on importing and exporting a wide range of products, including electronics, building materials, and food items. The Group is comprised of more than 30 different companies and foundations, and it is involved in a wide variety of business sectors, such as oil drilling, well drilling, general contracting, engineering, general trading, publishing, education, financial services, travel, and investment in real estate, hotel management, and media. The Group is changing its attention worldwide by focusing foreign investments in several Arab and other nations.

Sheikh Musallum Salem bin Ham is a prominent corporate figure in the United Arab Emirates and serves as the Chairman of the Group (Bin Ham Group, n.d.-b). He has been a trailblazer in the development of several investment projects and national leaders who have left an indelible impact on public life due to their contributions. The company is working to absorb the incredible transformations taking place internally and externally by entering into new areas of investment offered by the growing economic activity for the UAE and the ever-increasing interest in foreign investments, particularly in Arab countries such as Yemen, Oman, Sudan, Morocco, and Egypt.

3.4 Education

Bin Ham Group is contributing to the education sector by establishing United School, Bin Khaldoon Private School in Al Yahar, Dar Al Uloum Private School in AlAin and Baniyas, which offer high-quality education in the UAE (Bin Ham Group, n.d.-d). The school's administration team aims to create an atmosphere at school that will improve how parents may communicate with the rest of the school community to strengthen the bond between the two groups. They intend to encourage the children's general growth and development as their primary focus. In addition to academics, they strongly emphasize developing the children's interests in extracurricular activities. Also, the educational establishment offers financial assistance through scholarships and incentives to exceptional students who have performed very well.

3.5 Travel and Tourism

Bin Ham Group has built several hotels and resorts in the UAE, providing world-class hospitality services to both domestic and international tourists. Some of its prominent hospitality projects include the Al Salam Hotel in Dubai and Bin Ham Resort in Ajman (Bin Ham Group, n.d.-e).

3.6 Printing and Publishing

Bin Ham Group UAE has a strong presence in the printing and publishing industry. They offer a wide range of printing services, including commercial printing, digital printing, and offset printing. They also provide publishing services, such as book publishing and printing, magazine printing, and brochure printing. The company uses advanced printing technologies and state-of-the-art equipment to ensure high-quality output and timely delivery.

Their printing and publishing business is driven by their commitment to innovation, quality, and customer satisfaction. They work closely with their clients to understand their printing needs and provide customized solutions that meet their requirements. The company's focus on quality and customer service has made them a preferred partner for many businesses in the UAE and abroad. With their expertise in printing and publishing, they help businesses to create a strong brand identity and communicate their message effectively to their target audience.

3.7 General Contractor

Bin Ham Group's construction businesses are known for their focus on quality, innovation, and sustainability. The group uses advanced construction technologies and methods to deliver projects efficiently and with minimal environmental impact. Its construction projects have won several awards and recognition for their quality and sustainability practices. Bin Ham Group's construction businesses play a significant role in the UAE's real estate and construction sector, contributing to the country's economic growth and development.

3.8 Electromechanical Industry

Bin Ham Group UAE has a strong presence in the electromechanical industry. They provide a wide range of services related to the design, installation, and maintenance of electrical and mechanical systems in residential, commercial, and industrial buildings. The company offers solutions for electrical systems, HVAC (heating, ventilation, and air conditioning) systems, plumbing, fire protection, and security systems. Their electromechanical business is driven by their commitment to quality, safety, and sustainability (Bin Ham Group, n.d.-f). They leverage their expertise and experience to provide innovative solutions that meet the needs of their clients while ensuring the efficient use of resources and minimizing the environmental impact of their operations. The company's focus on quality and customer service has made them a trusted partner in the UAE's electromechanical industry.

3.9 Oil and Gas

Bin Ham Group UAE is actively involved in the oil and gas industry. Senergy Wave, a subsidiary of Bin Ham Group, is dedicated to providing a wide range of specialized services for onshore and offshore oil and gas fields and facilities. Through strategic collaborations with renowned international oil and gas companies, Senergy Wave actively engages in exploration, development, and production activities to harness oil and gas reserves in the UAE and various other countries (Bin Ham Group, n.d.-g). Senergy Wave General Trading Company prioritizes sustainability and innovation as the driving forces behind their oil and gas business. With their deep expertise and extensive experience, they continuously strive to develop groundbreaking solutions that enhance resource efficiency and mitigate the environmental footprint of their operations. Their unwavering commitment to sustainability and innovation has solidified their reputation as a trusted partner within the UAE's oil and gas industry.

3.10 Hospitality

Bin Ham Group has made a notable impact in the hospitality industry since 2005 when they established City Seasons Hotels (Bin Ham Group, n.d.-h). The founders envisioned creating hotels that exuded style, modernity, and comfort, while placing a strong emphasis on delivering exceptional quality, luxury, and value. Over the years, they have successfully operated and managed eight exceptional facilities in the United Arab Emirates and Oman. Among their esteemed properties is the renowned Royal Rose Hotel, a property they own and operate with meticulous attention to detail, offering guests an unparalleled level of luxury and service. The company also provides a range of services to support the hospitality industry, such as event management, catering, and facility management. Their hospitality business is driven by their commitment to providing exceptional service and creating memorable experiences for their guests (Bin Ham Group, n.d.-a). They prioritize innovation, quality, and sustainability in all their operations. The company's focus on innovation and quality has made them a preferred choice for business and leisure travelers in the UAE.

4 Bin Ham Group: CSR Commitment and Prestigious Awards

Bin Ham Group demonstrates its commitment to corporate social responsibility (CSR) through various initiatives, including its annual Iftar gathering held during the holy month of Ramadan (Bin Ham Group, n.d.-j). The event aims to foster communication and strengthen the social bond among employees at all levels within the organization. The iftar took place at the Salem Bin Ham Cultural Center and was attended by esteemed members of the company's leadership. Moreover, Bin Ham Group has supported several community development initiatives, including organizing various events to celebrate national and cultural festivals, promoting community sports events, and contributing to the country's social welfare sector.

Bin Ham Group prioritizes the well-being and safety of its employees and the broader community. With a strong dedication to maintaining high standards, the company has established stringent safety guidelines and protocols across its construction sites. These measures aim to create a secure working environment and minimize risks associated with construction activities. By implementing robust safety practices, Bin Ham Group demonstrates its commitment to safeguarding the health and welfare of all individuals involved in its operations.

The Bin Ham family has received several prestigious awards, recognizing their outstanding contributions in various fields. Sheikh Dr. Mohammed bin Muslim bin Ham Al Ameri, Deputy Secretary-General of the Intergovernmental Institution for the Use of Micro-Algae Spirulina Against Malnutrition (IIMSAM), was honored as the Arab Cultural Personality in 2019. This prestigious title is awarded to influential individuals in the Arab world who have made significant contributions to culture and knowledge (Bin Ham, n.d.-a). Additionally, Sheikh Dr. Mohammed bin Muslim bin Hamri Al Ameri was recognized by the Kingdom of Bahrain with the prestigious award of His Highness Shaikh Khalifa bin Ali Al Khalifa for charitable work in 2018. This distinguished award acknowledges Sheikh Dr. Mohammed's philanthropic and humanitarian endeavors, as well as his international charitable contributions (Bin Ham, n.d.-b). Furthermore, Sheikh Dr. Mohammed Musallem bin Ham Al Ameri was presented with the Mahatma Gandhi Seva Medal of Humanity by the Gandhi Global Family (GGF) in 2018. This highly regarded accolade, conferred by an UN-affiliated organization, is the second highest award bestowed by the GGF. It highlights Sheikh Dr. Al Ameri's significant contributions to community development, support for world peace, and efforts to combat malnutrition and hunger. His instrumental role in addressing global malnutrition and hunger, particularly through his involvement with IIMSAM, played a pivotal role in earning him this esteemed recognition. Notably, his contributions include initiatives like the Sheikh Zayed Centre for Free Distribution of Spirulina in Kenya, which has been providing vital support since its establishment in 2009 (Bin Ham, n.d.-c).

5 Projects Associated with Bin Ham Group

Bin Ham Towers

Bin Ham Towers (Fig. 3) is a residential building complex, which contains three towers in Taawun Sharjah, close to the border between Sharjah and Dubai. The development features studio and one-and three-bedroom apartment layouts, as well as a fitness center, elevators, a swimming pool, and a tennis court. Additionally, the development is located in close proximity to several well-known destinations, including Ansar Mall, Al Arab Mall, and Al Mamzar Park (Bayut, n.d.). Taawun Sharjah is a highly sought-after neighborhood for renters looking for a home in the Sharjah region close to the Dubai border. Numerous conveniences enrich the lives of

Fig. 3 Bin Ham Towers Group. Source: Bin Ham Group (n.d.-a, n.d.-b, n.d.-c). Published with the company's permission

locals in this convenient area. Schools, medical facilities, food services, shops, and more can all be found here. One-bedroom apartments in Bin Ham Towers start at around AED 25 k annually and have a total area of about 1270 square feet (Bayut, n. d.). Each unit comprises bedrooms, kitchens, living rooms, bathrooms, and other essential spaces. The kitchens are equipped with built-in cabinetry, providing a convenient and functional amenity for residents.

Al Wahda Building

The Al Wahda apartment complex, situated in the heart of Deira, offers a unique and convenient living experience. The unit encompasses 13 elegant floors, thoughtfully divided into 6 commercial floors and 7 residential floors, situated on Al Ittihad Road (Bin Ham Group, n.d.-c). The apartments consist of well-designed 2-bedroom units, and residents can benefit from the convenience of parking facilities available in the building's underground garage. The Al Wahda complex is highly sought-after, promising a life of luxury to its residents. Its prime location provides easy access to both commercial and residential areas, offering a high standard of living. Moreover, the apartments are equipped with cutting-edge double-glazed windows, ensuring optimal sunlight control and privacy. In order to ensure adequate ventilation and space, the ceilings are purposefully kept high.

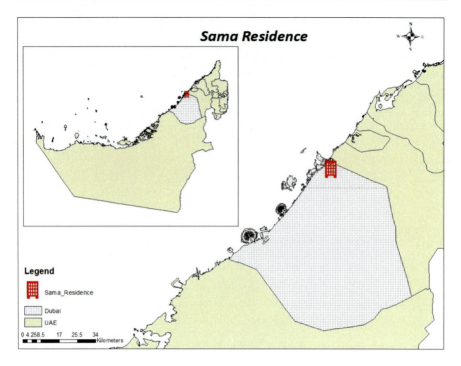

Fig. 4 Geographical illustration of the Sama Residence location in Dubai, UAE. Source: Bin Ham Group (n.d.-c). Published with the company's permission

Sama Residence

Sama Residence presents an ideal setting for family living, with its range of thoughtful amenities and features. Each apartment is complemented by a swimming pool, a modern health club, and a relaxing pool deck, providing ample opportunities for recreation and leisure. The safety and security of residents are prioritized with round-the-clock security surveillance, ensuring peace of mind. Ample parking facilities are also available for residents' convenience. These residences are thoughtfully designed to accommodate various lifestyle needs, offering a harmonious living environment. With its prime location, luxurious amenities, stylish finishes, and exceptional services, Sama Residence provides great value, particularly for families seeking a remarkable living experience. Figure 4 provides a visual representation of the geographical location of Sama Residence in Dubai, UAE. The geographical location of Sama Residence in Dubai holds significant importance for several reasons:

1. *Attracting and Retaining Employees*: A favorable location can attract and retain top talent. Many individuals consider the proximity of their workplace to their residence to optimize their work-life balance. Sama Residence's location in

Table 1 Overview of selected properties associated with Bin Ham Group

No.	Project	Location	Description
1	The Bay Residence project on Yas Island in Abu Dhabi	Abu Dhabi	Luxury apartments
2.	Al Aman House	Dubai	Luxury complex
3.	Al Wahda Building	Dubai	Luxury apartments
4.	Bin Ham Towers	Sharjah	Residential complex

Source: Bin Ham Group (n.d.-c. and n.d.-i) and Baraka Real Estate Development (2023). Published with the company's permission

Dubai provides accessibility and convenience for employees, making it an appealing choice.

2. *Work-Life Balance*: The geographical location influences the overall quality of life for residents. Dubai offers a vibrant and dynamic environment with a multitude of amenities, entertainment options, and cultural attractions. Sama Residence's location in Dubai provides residents with access to these offerings, contributing to a well-rounded lifestyle.
3. *Business Opportunities*: Dubai is a thriving hub for business and commerce, attracting numerous local and international companies. Being situated in Dubai provides Sama Residence with proximity to potential business opportunities, networking events, and a favorable business environment.
4. *Infrastructure and Connectivity*: Dubai boasts excellent infrastructure, including modern transportation systems, international airports, and well-developed road networks. The geographical location of Sama Residence ensures residents have convenient access to these essential facilities, facilitating ease of travel and connectivity.

Overall, the geographical location of Sama Residence in Dubai is crucial for attracting employees, providing a desirable work-life balance, accessing business opportunities, benefiting from robust infrastructure, and capitalizing on the market potential of the city.

Al Aman House
The Al Aman House (Al Aman House) is a mixed-use complex in the middle of town—a one-of-a-kind vacation spot tailored to active families. Central air conditioning (chiller), a fully equipped gym, sauna, steam rooms, an adult and children's pool, ample underground parking, and state-of-the-art security features like 24-h automatic surveillance, CCTV, and access control systems can all be found at Al Aman House (Bin Ham Group, n.d.-c).

City Gate
Located in the heart of the city, the residential building, known as City Gate, offers a wide variety of attractive, modern apartments for rent at very reasonable prices (Bin Ham Group, n.d.-c). Apartments with three bedrooms are available and are ideal for

families. City Gate's security and maintenance services are available 24/7, making it a convenient option. Situated close to Deira City Center on Airport Road, the project aims to create a sustainable, community-oriented lifestyle for its residents by drawing inspiration from sustainable residential developments around the world.

Real Estate Business
The company's real estate division is one of its most prominent, with a portfolio of commercial and residential properties across the UAE (Table 1). Bin Ham Group's hospitality arm also owns and manages several luxury hotels and resorts in the country, including City Seasons Hotels.

Tourism and Hotels
City Seasons Hotels, which has locations in Abu Dhabi, Dubai, Al Ain, and Muscat, is benefiting from strong demand from locals. The occupancy rates in the chain's properties experienced a notable growth, reaching 88% by the end of 2022 (Bin Ham Group, n.d.-i).

6   Sustainable Development Goals and Bin Ham Group

Bin Ham Group recognizes the importance of the 17 Sustainable Development Goals (SDGs) for long-term sustainability (United Nations, n.d.). As a result, each sector of the company is dedicated to focusing on specific SDGs through the implementation of sustainable business practices and empowering their workforce to embrace sustainable approaches. Notably, the company has placed a strong emphasis on real estate management in both administrative and commercial units, contributing to the attainment of effective SDG goals. The company has also embarked on projects aimed at improving pumping stations and has undertaken initiatives to develop various civil projects, including the construction of roadways, wastewater treatment facilities, and road lighting. Each sector of Bin Ham Group has made significant progress in attaining the following SDGs:

SDG1: No poverty Bin Ham Group contributes to poverty reduction through its focus on providing better education and creating employment opportunities. The company recognizes the significance of education in advancing societal development and plays a role in offering quality education at an advanced level. Bin Ham Company for General Contracting, a prominent entity within Bin Ham Group, actively engages in construction projects that support poverty reduction efforts. They have successfully undertaken significant projects such as the construction of primary schools for girls in Alsamha and the development of 106 public houses (Bin Ham Group, n.d.-d). By building essential infrastructure and housing, the company contributes to improving living conditions. Additionally, the company's commitment to hiring specialized and highly qualified staff ensures job creation and provides employment opportunities to individuals, further addressing the issue of poverty.

SDG2: Zero hunger Bin Ham Group company aligns with SDG 2, which aims to end hunger, achieve food security, improve nutrition, and promote sustainable agriculture. Since its establishment in 1974, Bin Ham Agricultural Company has played a pioneering role in the agricultural renaissance in Al Ain and Abu Dhabi. Through its megaprojects, the company has contributed significantly to expanding the green landscape and promoting sustainable agriculture in the early history of the UAE. Bin Ham Agricultural Company has been involved in various projects that have enhanced agricultural development. Their initiatives include the creation of prominent parks, forestation projects, and the establishment of recreational areas such as Hili Fun City and Ain Al Faydha Resort. Moreover, the company has showcased its strong presence in diverse development projects. They have successfully implemented pumping stations, water networks, and wastewater purification plants, which are vital for supporting sustainable agricultural practices.

SDG3: Good health and well-being Bin Ham Group company aligns with SDG 3, which focuses on ensuring healthy lives and promoting well-being for all at all ages. Bin Ham Group recognizes the importance of healthcare and infrastructure development in promoting a healthy society. The company has actively contributed to the implementation of housing projects, public schools, hospitals, mosques, and residential compounds, which are essential elements for supporting the well-being and health of communities. By undertaking housing projects, Bin Ham Group addresses the need for safe and adequate shelter, which is a fundamental requirement for maintaining good health and well-being. Access to affordable and quality housing contributes to improved living conditions and enhances the overall health and happiness of individuals and families.

In addition to housing, Bin Ham Group has been involved in the construction of public schools, hospitals, and mosques. These facilities play a crucial role in providing essential services to the community and promoting access to education, healthcare, and spiritual well-being. Accessible and well-equipped schools and hospitals contribute to better education outcomes, improved healthcare services, and enhanced overall quality of life. Through its involvement in these projects, Bin Ham Group demonstrates its commitment to promoting SDG 3 by creating environments that support healthy lives, access to healthcare and education, and the overall well-being of individuals and communities.

SDG4: Quality education in Ham Group company aligns with SDG 4, which focuses on ensuring inclusive and equitable quality education and promoting lifelong learning opportunities for all. Bin Ham Group recognizes the importance of education as a fundamental right and a key driver of personal and societal development. The company's commitment to SDG 4 is reflected in its education initiatives and investments (e.g., Dar Al Uloum Private Schools in Baniyas and Al Ain, and Bin Khaldoon Private School in Al Yahar) aimed at providing quality education to individuals of all ages.

SDG5: Gender equality Bin Ham Group company aligns with SDG 5, which focuses on achieving gender equality and empowering all women and girls. The education department of Bin Ham Group plays a crucial role in fostering gender equality by providing education opportunities to children without any gender differences. Through its education initiatives, Bin Ham Group ensures that both girls and boys have equal access to education and are encouraged to pursue their academic and personal development. Furthermore, Bin Ham Group actively employs both genders across its sectors, demonstrating its commitment to gender equality in the workplace. By fostering gender equality in education and employment, Bin Ham Group contributes to the broader goals of SDG 5.

SDG6: Clean water and sanitation Bin Ham Group company aligns with SDG 6, which focuses on ensuring access to clean water and sanitation for all. Bin Ham EM, a subsidiary of the company, has played a significant role in projects related to water and wastewater management, thereby contributing to the achievement of SDG 6 targets. Bin Ham EM's establishment of the Infrastructure and Civil Division signifies its commitment to developing water-related infrastructure, including wastewater treatment plants, wastewater networks, drainage networks, and irrigation systems. These projects contribute to the sustainable management and conservation of water resources. Furthermore, the company's engagement in landscaping projects demonstrates its holistic approach to water management. Creating sustainable landscapes that utilize water efficiently and promote biodiversity aligns with SDG 6's objectives.

SDG7: Affordable and clean energy Bin Ham Group's subsidiary, Bin Ham EM, aligns with SDG 7 by contributing to the goal of ensuring access to affordable, reliable, sustainable, and modern energy for all. Through its Infrastructure & Civil Division, Electrical, Mechanical, & Instrumentation Division, and Trading Division, Bin Ham EM undertakes projects related to infrastructure development, electrical and mechanical works, and landscaping. These divisions are instrumental in implementing energy-efficient solutions and promoting sustainable practices in the construction and maintenance of various facilities.

SDG8: Decent work and economic growth Bin Ham Group is strongly aligned with SDG 8, which focuses on promoting sustained, inclusive, and sustainable economic growth, full and productive employment, and decent work for all. The company plays a significant role in creating employment opportunities by employing over 2000 qualified individuals across various sectors. Bin Ham Group actively contributes to economic growth through its diverse portfolio of businesses, including hospitality, construction, agriculture, electrical and mechanical engineering, and more. By providing quality job opportunities and fostering a supportive work environment, the company promotes decent work and economic empowerment. Additionally, Bin Ham Group's commitment to sustainable business practices and innovation contributes to the development of a resilient and inclusive economy.

Through its operations, the company actively supports the objectives of SDG 8 by promoting productive employment, economic growth, and sustainable development.

SDG9: Industry, innovation, and infrastructure Bin Ham Group is closely aligned with SDG 9, which aims to build resilient infrastructure, promote inclusive and sustainable industrialization, and foster innovation. The company actively invests in technological advancements and innovation to enhance its operations and improve efficiency across various sectors. Bin Ham Group contributes to the development of sustainable infrastructure projects, including construction, electrical and mechanical engineering, and civil works. By promoting the growth of industries and supporting technological advancements, the company plays a vital role in advancing economic diversification and supporting sustainable industrialization.

SDG10: Reduced inequality Bin Ham Group is actively aligned with SDG 10, which focuses on reducing inequalities within and among countries. The company emphasizes inclusivity and diversity in its workforce, providing equal opportunities for employees and promoting a supportive work environment. Bin Ham Group also engages in corporate social responsibility initiatives that aim to uplift marginalized communities and promote social inclusiveness. By fostering a culture of fairness and equality, the company contributes to creating a more equitable society, in line with the objectives of SDG 10.

SDG11: Sustainable cities and communities Bin Ham Electrical and Mechanical Company, established in 1988, has emerged as a prominent player in the fields of electrical, mechanical engineering, and civil projects, making significant contributions to sustainable development goals, particularly SDG-11: Sustainable Cities and Communities. As part of its ongoing development, the company has recently set up fully equipped workshops in Abu Dhabi, AL Mufrag, Suihan, and Liwa. These workshops include facilities for electromechanical works, mechanisms, and vehicle maintenance, equipped with state-of-the-art machinery and equipment. With a workforce of over 2000 skilled employees and a fleet of 300 vehicles, the workshops aim to cater to the diverse needs of the company's activities, expedite project completion, enhance performance, and ensure the delivery of high-quality products and services (Bin Ham Group, n.d.-f).

The company places great emphasis on implementing robust health and environmental protection policies and procedures, adhering to both local and international standards. It remains committed to fulfilling legal and regulatory requirements to safeguard public health and preserve the environment. Bin Ham Electrical and Mechanical Company has been the recipient of numerous accolades and certifications, including ISO 9001, ISO 14001 (2008 Quality Certification and 2004 Environmental Certification), Health and Safety Certificate 2007, and OHSAS 18001, further highlighting its commitment to excellence and adherence to industry standards (Bin Ham Group, n.d.-f).

SDG12: Responsible consumption and production Bin Ham Group is committed to aligning with SDG 12, which emphasizes responsible consumption and production. The company promotes sustainable practices throughout its operations to ensure efficient use of resources and minimize waste. By implementing measures such as recycling and waste reduction, they strive to reduce their environmental footprint. Bin Ham Group also focuses on producing high-quality products that meet international standards, ensuring responsible consumption by customers.

SDG13: Climate action Bin Ham Group's Electromechanical division aligns with SDG 13, which focuses on climate action. By formulating sewage treatment plants and implementing strong policies for health and environmental protection, the company contributes to mitigating the impacts of climate change. Their commitment to ensuring the quality of products and services further demonstrates their dedication to sustainable practices in line with SDG 13.

SDG16: Peace, justice, and strong institutions Bin Ham Group's subsidiary, Forex International Company, aligns with SDG 16. Forex International Company plays a vital role in developing financial services and fostering strong institutional relationships with major banks operating within the UAE. By facilitating international transactions and formulating arrangements for various financial services, Forex International contributes to the establishment of robust institutions that promote transparency, accountability, and fairness in global financial transactions (Bin Ham Group, n.d.-k).

SDG17: Partnerships to achieve the goals Bin Ham Group has announced its intention to establish economic partnerships with several countries in the region as part of its strategic plan to enhance its local, regional, and global presence (Bin Ham Group, n.d.-l). This aligns with the UAE's vision of economic diversification and increasing investments in industries and tourism both within the region and internationally. Bin Ham Group is currently exploring various development and tourism projects in collaboration with Arab and international companies. Through these partnerships, the UAE aims to invest in diverse economic sectors and seize new global opportunities, establishing itself as a secure and attractive destination for investors and prominent entrepreneurs. This approach exemplifies the spirit of SDG 17 by fostering collaboration between countries and promoting sustainable development on a global scale.

7   Conclusion

In conclusion, Bin Ham Group emerges as a highly respected and esteemed family business conglomerate in the UAE. With a strong focus on innovation, sustainability, and philanthropy, the company has garnered a remarkable reputation and achieved significant success across various industries and fields. The commitment to excellence and the substantial contributions made by Bin Ham Group to the UAE's economy and society are evident from its impressive track record.

The company's Corporate Social Responsibility (CSR) initiatives further highlight its dedication to being a responsible corporate citizen. By aligning with established Sustainable Development Goals (SDGs), Bin Ham Group actively contributes to the sustainable development of society and the environment. The organization's dedicated team of experts ensures the implementation of unique quality measures tailored to each project, surpassing client expectations.

Bin Ham Group upholds stringent quality management standards for every project, reflecting its unwavering commitment to excellence. Additionally, the company's sustainability-related actions demonstrate a profound dedication to minimizing environmental impact and advancing a sustainable future. Notably, the Group's energy business was recognized with the prestigious "Energy Management Project of the Year" award at the 2019 Middle East Energy Awards. This accolade acknowledged Bin Ham Group's commitment to sustainability through the reduction of its carbon footprint and adoption of renewable energy solutions.

Overall, Bin Ham Group stands as a leading example of an Emirati family business entity that excels in its commitment to innovation, sustainability, and social responsibility. Its outstanding achievements and dedication to creating a positive impact on society and the environment reinforce its prominent position in the UAE's business landscape.

8   Questions for Discussion

1. Who serves on the board of directors of Bin Ham Group?
2. In which sectors does Bin Ham operate?
3. Can you provide examples of popular projects undertaken by Bin Ham?
4. What is Bin Ham Group's commitment or mission?
5. Based on the information provided, how do you envision the future of Bin Ham Group in the next 10 years?
6. Analyze the business portfolio of Bin Ham Group, highlighting its strengths and weaknesses. Offer suggestions for improving the current portfolio.
7. Is Bin Ham Group equipped to compete on a global scale?
8. Examine Bin Ham Group's alignment with the Sustainable Development Goals (SDGs) and provide objective justifications for their implementation. What challenges might arise, and what potential solutions could be considered?

References

Baraka Real Estate Development. (2023). *The bay residence*. https://www.barakadevelopment.ae/wp-content/uploads/2023/03/The-Bay-Residence-Brochure.pdf

Bayut. (n.d.). *Bin ham towers*. Retrieved from https://www.bayut.com/buildings/bin-ham-towers/

Bin Ham, M. (n.d.-a). *Awards*. Bin Ham Group. Retrieved from https://mohamedbinham.com/en/archives/2432

Bin Ham, M. (n.d.-b). *Bahrain honors Dr. Mohammed Bin Musallem Bin Ham with "the charity work" award*. Retrieved from https://mohamedbinham.com/en/archives/2099

Bin Ham, M. (n.d.-c). *Mohammed Bin Ham" the first Arab wins the medal "Gandhi world of humanity*. Retrieved from https://mohamedbinham.com/en/archives/2098

Bin Ham Group. (n.d.-a). *About us*. Retrieved from https://binhamgroup.com/en/about-us/

Bin Ham Group. (n.d.-b). *Board of directors*. Retrieved from https://binhamgroup.com/en/board-of-directors/

Bin Ham Group. (n.d.-c). *Real Estate*. Retrieved from https://binhamgroup.com/en/real-estate-2/

Bin Ham Group. (n.d.-d). *Education*. Retrieved from https://binhamgroup.com/en/education-2/

Bin Ham Group. (n.d.-e). *Travel & tourism*. Retrieved from https://binhamgroup.com/en/travel-tourism/

Bin Ham Group. (n.d.-f). *Electro-mechanical*. Retrieved from https://binhamgroup.com/en/electro-mechanical/

Bin Ham Group. (n.d.-g). *Senergy wave general trading company*. Retrieved from https://binhamgroup.com/en/senergy-wave-general-trading-company/

Bin Ham Group. (n.d.-h). *Hospitality*. Retrieved from https://binhamgroup.com/en/hospitality/

Bin Ham Group. (n.d.-i). *Bin Ham group records outstanding performance during 9 months of 2022*. Retrieved from https://binhamgroup.com/en/bin-ham-group-records-outstanding-performance-during-9-months-of-2022/

Bin Ham Group. (n.d.-j). *Bin Ham group hosts Iftar for employees*. Retrieved from https://binhamgroup.com/en/bin-ham-group-hosts-iftar-for-employees/

Bin Ham Group. (n.d.-k). *Forex international*. Retrieved from https://binhamgroup.com/en/forex-international/

Bin Ham Group (n.d.-l). *Bin ham group partnerships in the countries of the region*. Retrieved from https://binhamgroup.com/en/bin-ham-group-partnerships-in-the-countries-of-the-region/

KPMG. (2022). *The regenerative power of family businesses: United Arab Emirates edition*. Retrieved from https://assets.kpmg.com/content/dam/kpmg/ae/pdf-2022/11/the-regenerative-power-of-family-businesses.pdf

United Nations. (n.d.). *Sustainable development goals*. Retrieved from https://sdgs.un.org/goals

Statista Research Department. (2023, January 2). *Real estate in the UAE–statistics & facts*. Statista. Retrieved from https://www.statista.com/topics/9139/real-estate-in-the-uae/#topicOverview

Turak, N. (2023, March 10). *Dubai's record property demand is creating a nightmare for some residents*. CNBC. Retrieved from https://www.cnbc.com/2023/03/10/dubais-record-property-demand-is-creating-a-nightmare-for-some-residents.html

Aysha Nadheer, is a Master's student of Science in Remote Sensing and Geographic Information Systems at UAEU, Al Ain City. Aysha Nadheer had been interning in Al Ain Municipality at the Department of Town Planning, also she worked as Research Assistant with Dr. Naeema AlHosani, Chair of the Geography and Urban Sustainability Department, which took place during 2020–2021. Nonetheless, she worked on several projects in 2023, including Selecting suitable sites for new petrol stations and Roles of grocery stores during the COVID-19 pandemic: GIS Application with Dr. Mohamed Yagoub.

Fatima S. Alawani is a Master's student of Science in Remote Sensing and Geographic Information Systems at UAEU. Between 2019 and 2022, she worked as an Environmental Monitoring Specialist at the Environment Protection and Development Authority in Ras Al-Khaimah. From 2022 to 2023, she served as the Acting Head of the Evaluation and Inspection Section at the Monitoring Department.

Ramo Palalić is an Assistant Professor of Entrepreneurship and Family Business Management, at the College of Economics and Political Science (EQUIS accredited), Sultan Qaboos University (SQU), Oman. His research is in the area of entrepreneurship, leadership, and family businesses. Dr. Palalić has authored and co-authored many articles in globally recognized journals like *Management Decision, International Journal of Entrepreneurial Behavior & Research, International Entrepreneurship and Management Journal*, and alike. Additionally, he has co-authored/co-edited several books and many book chapters in the field of business and entrepreneurship published with internationally prominent publishers (Springer, Routledge, World Scientific). Moreover, Dr. Palalić is serving as the Associate Editor of *Journal of Enterprising Communities*, Co-EiC of *Gestion 2000*, Associate Editor of *Heritage and Sustainable Development (HSD)*, as well as board member in several well-established international journals.

iSpatial Tech: GEO-AI-Enabled Solutions for Smart Cities

Reda Maroufi, Jaber Mohammed Alketbi, and Marco Valeri

Abstract Companies that use AI and machine learning can reap numerous benefits, including increased efficiency, better decision-making, and the ability to automate repetitive or time-consuming tasks. Companies can also use these technologies to gain insights from large amounts of data and make more accurate predictions about future trends or events. This paper describes iSpatial Tech, an AI company that knew how to seize the moment. The study includes an introduction, company information, leadership, business overview, products, projects, and rewards. The company information document identifies its history, size, and location, while the introduction emphasizes its role in smart city business. iSpatial Tech's executive chapter defines their roles and positions. The business highlights the company's mission, goals, and strategies, while the products section characterizes its AI solutions. iSpatial tech's AI projects demonstrate success both with UAE and international awards.

R. Maroufi (✉)
Department of Municipalities and Transportation, Al Ain, Abu Dhabi, UAE
e-mail: Reda.maroufi@aam.gov.ae

J. M. Alketbi
Government Official, Al Ain, Abu Dhabi, UAE
e-mail: 201016548@uaeu.ac.ae

M. Valeri
Niccolò Cusano University, Rome, Italy
e-mail: marco.valeri@unicusano.it

© The Author(s), under exclusive license to Springer Nature Switzerland AG 2023
K. Alkaabi, V. Ramadani (eds.), *Family Business Cases*, Springer Business Cases,
https://doi.org/10.1007/978-3-031-39252-8_12

1 Introduction

Deep learning, 3D technologies, automation, augmented reality, virtual reality, and big data analytics are essential technologies that are changing many sectors and elements of daily life. Self-driving cars, fraud detection, picture and speech recognition, and targeted marketing all use artificial intelligence (AI). AI can boost productivity, cut expenses, and make smarter decisions (Haleem et al., 2022; Tuner, 2023). Deep learning is a branch of AI that trains artificial neural networks to recognize patterns in big data sets (Goodfellow et al., 2016). This technology is utilized in picture, audio, and natural language processing (LeCun et al., 2015; West & Allen, 2018). By letting robots learn and adapt, deep learning could transform numerous sectors. Augmented reality (AR) adds digital information to the actual environment. Gaming, education, and healthcare employ AR to create interactive experiences. AR could boost customer satisfaction and efficiency. Machines do human activities in automation. Manufacturing, transportation, and finance use automation to boost productivity and cut costs. Automation could boost productivity and create new jobs. Analyzing enormous data sets to gain insights and better decision-making is called big data analytics. Big data analytics improves efficiency and lowers costs in healthcare, finance, and marketing (Kelleher & Tierney, 2018). Big data analytics can improve decision-making and provide new business prospects. These technologies are crucial and can change many elements of society. In the next years, they will be used in many sectors and applications. iSpatial Techno Solutions is a Geo smart consultancy and solutions firm that integrates enterprise business processes into a results-driven approach that enables communication and interaction between various business and IT environments, streamlining operations (iSpatial Techno Solutions, n.d.-a). Their area of expertise is developing scalable Geo-enabled rapid solution platforms employing ESRI and Microsoft technologies to provide high-quality, reasonably priced solutions. Their cutting-edge solutions are used by smart cities, government sectors, oil and gas, utilities, transportation, insurance, banking, property development, environmental, educational, and healthcare verticals.

iSpatial Techno Solutions develops GIS solutions for location intelligence (web and mobile) that integrate transformative technologies using AI, Deep learning, AR/VR, 3d solutions, IoT, and big data analytics. It is a certified ISO 9001-2015 company, has made 6 successful products, sold them to over 100 customers globally in all 5 continents, stated links with 20 strong business partners in the likes of ESRI, Microsoft, and IBM and won 6 international awards and Quality certifications-ISO 9001:2015, ISO 14001:2015 (EMS), and ISO 45001:2018 (OHSMS) (iSpatial Techno Solutions, n.d.-a).

2   Company Information

Mr. Ibrahim Al Obaidly, an Emirati technology entrepreneur, and his business partner, Narendra Babu Vattem, founded the company in 2009 and relocated it in 2017. He is also the proprietor of ARDHIYAT ALIBDAA, a technology-focused company that develops and supports sophisticated solutions based on emerging and disruptive technologies. He is referred to as a technology fanatic dating from his days at Bayanat (a Geospatial institution specializing in remote sensing and GIS).

iSpatial Techno Solutions has successfully implemented 20+ major projects for USA and UAE clients using the latest innovative technologies like ESRI, Microsoft. NET, SharePoint, IBM Watson, Google Dialog Flow (Voice BOT solution), Google AI, IOT Data Analytics, ESRI Live Dashboards and Analytics, and Web.

The team consists of a mix of domain and technically skilled professionals: SMEs with more than 30 years of experience and GIS specialists with more than 15 years of experience with in-depth experience in implementing various enterprise GIS solutions using ESRI and Microsoft technologies, as follows below:

- Solution Architects
- Data Scientist/ Data Analysts/Data Architect
- Statistics Analyst, Statistics Specialists/Expert
- Statistics Advisors & SM
- Data Scientist
- Functional Consultants (SME) /Project Managers
- Business Analysts
- System Administrators
- Specialists (Data Management, migration, QA/QC)
- Web/Mobile Application Developers
- UI/UX Developers
- Cloud Infrastructure Specialists

iSpatial Techno Solutions has branches in the UAE, India, and San Diego, California. They have a total of 50 employees, 20 of whom are located in Abu Dhabi branches. The company's headquarters are located in the UAE, where consultancy, professional services, support, sales, and marketing are handled alongside the US branch. India houses the backend development team and human resources. The maps in Figs. 1 and 2 demonstrate the locations of the branches of the company worldwide and locally.

3   Company Leadership

In 2009, Mr. Ibrahim established the company as its owner and founder. Later, in 2017, he, along with his business partner and co-founder, Mr. Narendra Babu Vattem, relocated the company to the UAE. Mr. Ibrahim possesses over 30 years of experience in geospatial services and IT (Table 1). His leadership is characterized

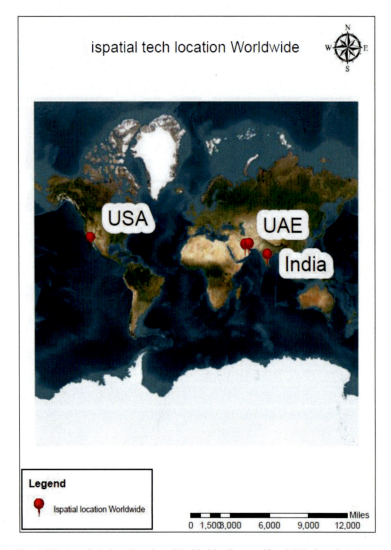

Fig. 1 iSpatial Techno Solutions locations Worldwide. Source: iSpatial Techno Solutions (n.d.-b). Published with the company's permission

by determination and technical expertise, which have greatly benefited the organization. Mr. Babu has successfully managed over 30 large-volume projects throughout his 22-year career in diverse sectors including oil and gas, utilities (electric and gas), infrastructure development, telecom, smart cities, and government. These projects span various regions such as the USA, India, Singapore, UAE, Saudi Arabia, and the Middle East. Mr. Rajanjkanth, a self-starter and results-driven IT consultant, brings 22+ years of experience in enterprise architecture, information

iSpatial Tech: GEO-AI-Enabled Solutions for Smart Cities 177

Fig. 2 iSpatial Techno Solutions location in Abu Dhabi, UAE. Source: iSpatial Techno Solutions (n.d.-b). Published with the company's permission

management, artificial intelligence, business analysis, data management, software development, and systems administration.

With a specialized focus on GIS, Mr. Shanmukha has accumulated over 18 years of experience in the field. Mr. V. Sai has a decade of experience in digital transformation, business analysis, scenario assessment, and software implementation. For a comprehensive overview of the leadership team, please refer to Table 1, which provides additional details.

Table 1 Company leadership

Ibrahim Al Obaidly	Owner	30+ years of experience in geospatial services and information technology. Mr. Ibrahim is a tenacious leader with broad technical expertise. His extensive knowledge of geospatial services and expertise in information technology were a huge advantage to our entire organization
Narendra Babu Vattem	CEO	Narendra is an energetic professional with 22+ years of expertise in business development, strategic planning, consulting, business process implementation into various IT solutions, and operations.
Rajanikanth Thouta	Executive Director	Self-starter and results-driven IT consultant with 22+ years of expertise in enterprise architecture, information management, AI, business analysis, data management, software development, systems administration, oil and gas, engineering, utilities, telecom, and government experience.
Shanmukha Kumari	CTO	A dynamic IT professional with 18+ years of experience in enterprise GIS systems, data process automation, data analysis, and business process management. Good experience with ESRI products: Portal for ArcGIS, Operations Dashboard, Collector, Servers, Python, Desktop, ArcSDE, and Extensions.
V Sai Phaneendra	Director	10+ years of digital transformation, business analysis, scenario assessment, and software implementation experience. Expertise in implementing digital technologies and processes to improve operational efficiency, customer engagement, and business performance.

Source: iSpatial Techno Solutions. (n.d.-a). Published with the company's permission

4 Business Overview

iSpatial Techno Solutions was established with the goal of offering the most sophisticated solutions to business and social problems. Rapid solution development platforms that would accelerate the delivery of high-quality, affordable solutions have been successfully created by them. They offer their clients a value proposition in the fields of web and mobile solutions, business analytics, business process automation, and enterprise integration solutions. Location-based Geo Enabled Solutions (GIS—3D and 2D). The team of innovators is hard at work creating solutions using cutting-edge technologies including automation, deep learning, augmented reality, virtual reality, 3D solutions, and artificial intelligence. Their ability to successfully complete projects for clients while reducing costs and timeliness by at least 50% without compromising quality is one of their key success factors. Their tasks include identifying the best opportunities, locating suitable individuals, designing the framework for solutions, and meeting project deadlines. The solutions adopted by the company's clients were recognized with numerous important international awards.

The creation of geospatial information technology smart solutions for smart cities, smart villages, and the private and public sectors to manage the spatial data infrastructure (SDI), ICT4D, building integrated platforms, e-services, and business process automation for improved planning, execution, and maintenance is one of iSpatial Techno Solutions' specialized areas of expertise. The company's core values, philosophy, goals, strength, and plans are listed as follow.

4.1 Philosophy

Every company has a unique philosophy that is a road map of their goals and the insets for achieving those goals with that mentality in mind. iSpatial Techno's philosophy is "Our core competency lies in building a scalable Geo-enabled rapid solution development platform using ESRI, artificial intelligence, and Microsoft technologies."

4.2 Business Goals

To achieve greatness in what you most desire, you should have goals that make the end of your journey and hard work as clear as possible. With iSpatial Techno, they established that they have "to be a customer-focused, quality-driven, and innovative company that is committed to helping their clients succeed in a rapidly changing technological landscape."

4.3 Future Plan

iSpatial Techno knows that the survival of their company depends on preparing for the future of technology, and a future plan is essential, so their target is to build innovative Geo-enabled artificial intelligence solutions, live data analytics, and digital innovations for smart cities, sustainability, oil and gas, utilities, and local government.

4.4 Strengths

By combining processes, controls, and programs, iSpatial Techno Solutions has been delivering worldwide technology solutions that promote efficiency, higher productivity, performance, transparency, and online workflows. By analyzing various data sources and business logic rules, their solutions enable quick decision-making, increasing productivity, and efficiency across the board.

4.5 Company Values

- *One Stop Customer Experience*: Creating a positive customer experience through the implementation of cutting-edge solutions and cutting-edge technologies.
- *Professional Approach with Cutting Edge Technologies*: Experience with enterprise-level Web, Mobile, and Desktop IT solutions using Microsoft, iOS, Android, ERP, AI Data Science, SAP, and GIS applications.
- *Scalable and Configurable Solutions*: BrAeInTM—AI framework, Smart PermitTM, Smart Geo AppsTM, eCube SoftwareTM, eCube AppsTM, and Smart Field GeoTM are highly scalable and configurable flagship products.
- *Sustainable Global Delivery*: "Following the Sun" global delivery models to optimize time, cost, and resources when designing and implementing solutions.

4.6 Quality, Environment, Health, and Safety Policy

At iSpatial Techno Solutions, they strive to achieve enhanced customer satisfaction by delivering quality products through project completion within a safe and healthy working environment through effective implementation of quality, environment, and occupational health and safety management systems.

4.7 iSpatial Techno Solutions Diversity and Inclusiveness Policy

iSpatial Techno Solutions strongly believes that valuing diversity and inclusiveness is a competitive advantage that helps us reach our vision of creating unmatched value for our clients, customers, employees, business partners, and shareholders. Figure 3 gives an overview of the products and services of the company.

5 Products

BrAeIn is an intelligent IoT analytics and AI-based solution that enables the development of real-time monitoring intelligence dashboards and predictive analytics. It connects to optimize corporate operations and connect all live systems to the centralized big data environment for condition monitoring, warnings, and notifications. This technology consists of dialog flow, tensor flow, predictive analytics, IOT integration, ESRI location analytics, BI reporting, content management, big

Fig. 3 Overview of Products and services of iSpatial Techno Solutions. Source: iSpatial Techno Solutions. (n.d.-a). Published with the company's permission

data, system integration, and robotics API. Predictive analytics using AI and location analytics is used to aid in operational decisions.

Smart GeoApp is a framework that helps to build web and mobile geo-enabled applications with full spatial analysis, reporting, and location-based services. It also supports KPI dashboards and analytical reports and provides real-time monitoring and a value proposition for web-based and mobile 2D/3D GIS application frameworks. Additionally, it supports ESRI, Microsoft, NET Framework, and reporting tools.

ESmart Permit is a web-based application that automates the approval process for work permits. It focuses on reducing conflict and energizing work as communities grow. Business drivers are responsible for motivating work, while ESRI, Microsoft, the NET Framework, DMS, and reporting tools are used to manage the process.

Smartfield Geo, business driver, mobile GIS application, SAP and GIS systems, Geolocation and decision support, KPI dashboards, SSO and role-based security system integration, and Smart Field Geo are all important ideas in the tech industry. Smartfield Geo is a mobile field application that collects field data and analyses spatial mapping offline and online, while Bussiness Driver provides efficient location-based work order management. GIS applications also help plan work order allocation and execution based on zones, while ESLOG is a time system that integrates with SAP.

ECube Apps is a cloud-based SaaS data collection and analysis platform for customer satisfaction surveys, field data collection, online registrations, opinion polls, and online examinations. It helps plan work order allocation and execution based on zones, such as SAP and GIS systems, and provides business efficiency, openness, print less, accessibility, helping customers save time and money, and analytics data history. It also uses Microsoft's Net Framework and Reporting Components.

ECube Software is a platform for quickly developing business applications for the web and mobile devices at a reduced cost, enabled by Microsoft's Net Framework and Reporting Components. It allows users to configure business entities (forms), application security, reports, business rules, and validation.

iSpatial Tech: GEO-AI-Enabled Solutions for Smart Cities   183

6   Projects

iSpatial Techno Solutions runs projects around the USA, India, and the UAE. The most successful projects have gained their clients some of the most prestigious accreditations and honors. The company is known to be very versatile in its execution, and the following are some of their unprecedented works supporting that statement.

6.1   Type of Projects Described by Owner Interview

"We serve our clients by combining technology and emotion and tackling modern problems at iSpatial Techno Solutions. Our team is dedicated to creating smart solutions for multiple sectors to deliver unique, long-term results. Smart city solutions for local governments include public safety, urban planning, assets, risk prediction analysis, and 5G network development. We improve utility operational efficiency, risk mitigation planning, asset monitoring, business analytics, and smart field inspections. In the oil and gas business, we deliver real-time air, marine, and soil quality monitoring solutions for leak detection, well planning, HSE compliance, and environmental insights. We monitor animals, agriculture, and food. Advantages are crucial, and we check food safety, storage, and establishment to assist agricultural expansion. In educational institutions, the company we offer field inspections and AI-based online smart learning management systems. I S T provides healthcare COVID response dashboards and information. State-of-the-art cloud infrastructures, geo-enabled artificial intelligence, data science, analytics, and information technology are used to deliver the most pleasing and trustworthy outcomes across all sectors. Managed services to optimize corporate productivity with modern technologies."

6.2   Summary Types of Projects

- Artificial Intelligence Solutions
- Geospatial Solutions
- IoT and BI
- Big Data Analytics
- Application Integration Services
- Web and Mobile Applications
- Professional Services
- Cloud Infrastructure Services

6.3 Federal Geographic Information Centre: UAE National Atlas (50 Years of Success for UAE)

The National Atlas reflects the country's success story during the past 50 years, and future prospects and strategic initiatives to continue and enhance that success during the next 50 years.

Interactive maps, indicators, geographical statistics, satellite images, and visual media have been utilized to show the country's achievements in time series over the past 50 years in the fields of health, education, infrastructure, economy, energy, and water, culture and heritage, population, women's empowerment, youth empowerment, environment, future horizon, regional and international context, and geospatial information. The design adopted is interactive and interconnected in order to form a storyline that enables the user to identify the extent of development in the target areas.

The development of the National Atlas comes within the framework of the center's responsibilities and competencies as it is the official reference at the federal level regarding geographic information, its collection, and provision of related services, and within its efforts to achieve its strategic objectives aimed for building and developing the spatial data infrastructure system at the level of the UAE, which would support the achievement of the various objectives of the strategy national decision-making process. Figure 4 demonstrates the context of work of iSpatial.

6.4 ADNOC: Methane Detection

Satelytics conducted methane liquid, hydrocarbon leak, and water leak analyses at nine ADNOC areas of interest using high-resolution imagery. Supplementary coarse-resolution methane analyses were also provided across the entire United Arab Emirates. The project workflow is listed in Fig. 5.

Fig. 4 iSpatial Techno Solutions context of work. Source: iSpatial Techno Solutions. (n.d.-c). Published with the company's permission

iSpatial Tech: GEO-AI-Enabled Solutions for Smart Cities   185

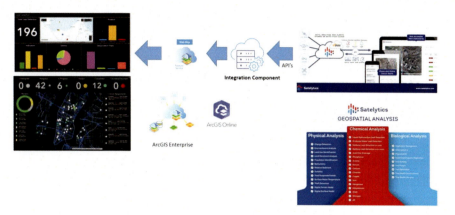

Fig. 5 Methadone project flow. Source: iSpatial Techno Solutions. (n.d.-c). Published with the company's permission

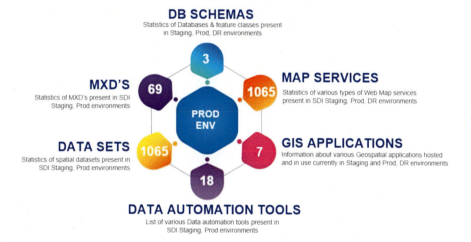

Fig. 6 ADDA schema of work. Source: iSpatial Techno Solutions. (n.d.-c). Published with the company's permission

6.5 AD SDI–G42 Cloud Migration and Upgrade for ADDA

Migration of Abu Dhabi Spatial Data Infrastructure (AD-SDI) from ADDA's internal data center (on-premises) to the G42 Cloud platform and enhancement of its functionalities by upgrading software infrastructure to make SDI systems available 24*7. The schema of work is given in Fig. 6.

6.6 Environment Agency, Abu Dhabi Azure Cloud Migration/Upgrade

The team has achieved successful migration of the EAD Environment Portal to the Microsoft Cloud environment and implemented the latest ArcGIS platform upgrade. They have seamlessly provided ongoing operational support, ensuring smooth functioning of data, applications, user access, and integration.

Over the past 3 years, they have successfully completed multiple GIS and IoT data analytics projects. These include the delivery of a live bird tracking solution (www.adbirdathon.ae), a live air quality data analytics platform (https://enviroportal.ead.ae/map/), and a fisheries management system for a client of the Environmental Agency-Abu Dhabi (EAD).

6.7 ADNOC: OnGIS Migration/Upgrade to Azure Cloud

ADNOC OneGIS is a centralized deployment of the ESRI GIS suite of applications at ADNOC, aiming to unify the user experience, enable data governance, and streamline application management. The application is currently hosted on premises via ADNOC's private data centers. The IST Team implemented a cloud-based infrastructure for the ADNOC OneGIS solution, aiming to further enhance application management and the provisioning of services to business users. The latest ESRI ArcGIS Enterprise environment was deployed in the existing ADNOC's Azure Landing Zone. It will follow the hub-and-spoke model, where the ESRI solution will have its own Vnet, and these or this Vnet will be peered to the ADNOC core Vnet. The solution will reuse shared services like firewalls and domain controllers for Active Directory.

6.8 Dubai Municipality Smart Data Acquisition Using Geo-AI

The project will develop an automated workflow based on machine learning and artificial intelligence (ML/AI) technologies in order to extract objects of interest using an OBIA classification (Object-Based Image Analysis) method. The features (or objects) are defined as, but are not limited to, buildings, roads, agricultural areas, forestry plantations, green urban areas, disturbed ground, sand dunes, gravel plains, and sabkhas. Extracted objects will be accompanied by individual detection accuracy. It will be necessary to take these detections from archives and newly acquired satellite images calibrated to the base map. From these extractions, the most up-to-date land cover and land use maps of Dubai will be created. These updated maps will be used as a base map for analysis and future iterations. Changes in the area of interest can be monitored at selected intervals, where suitable satellite data capture allows. The algorithm will be tailored and therefore requires training for maximum efficiency and highest accuracy in the Middle East. It is likely to take several months to reach this level of accuracy. Some of the outputs are listed in Fig. 7.

Fig. 7 iSpatial Techno Solutions project overview for Dubai municipality. Source: iSpatial Techno Solutions. (n.d.-c). Published with the company's permission

6.9 ADSDI (Abu Dhabi Spatial Data Infrastructure): ADDA

Offering GIS and AI services from 2016 to date, Development of GeoHub (www.rawy.abudhabi), SDI Consulting Services, SOPs, SDI Operations Dashboard, Special Olympics location analytics dashboards, Data Automation, Data QA/QC Rules Engine, ETL data migration, General Map Viewer, AI-based Voice Activated NLP platform for ADDA Policies and Governance using IBM Watson and ESRI API's, building an AI-enabled Azure cloud-based platform called Digital Reach Environment (DRE) by closely collaborating with the Microsoft team.

6.10 Abu Dhabi Municipality, UAE (GIS Professional Services)

Web GIS Applications and Geo-Enabled Reporting Dashboards Development Services for ESRI ArcGIS Server JavaScript API, ASP.NET, JavaScript, HTML-5, and Spatial Data Management, GIS System Administration, and Operational Support Web GIS Applications and Geo Enabled Reporting Dashboards Development Services for ESRI ArcGIS Server JavaScript API, ASP.NET, JavaScript, HTML-5 and spatial data management, GIS System administration, and operational support. An internal dashboard is developed to show each project's KPI and compare plots in ELMS and GIS. A dashboard is designed for viewing the community facilities; it shows all community facility counts for each zone, sector, and plot. It identifies the areas that do not have community facilities like mosques, schools, etc. The Property Management Dashboard shows area-wise how many properties are constructed, not constructed, and under construction. By seeing this dashboard, users can know how many units are sold, not sold, etc.

6.11 Abu Dhabi Food Control Authority, UAE

Develop an enterprise-level Geographic Information System (GIS) solution encompassing various components such as data model design, migration, quality assurance and quality control (QA/QC), integration with the ArcGIS Data Standard for Infrastructure (ADSDI), and seamless data exchange. Furthermore, create a user-friendly portal for ArcGIS, enabling efficient access and utilization of geospatial data.

In addition, construct ten geo-enabled applications catering to different needs, including a facility finder, a general map viewer, an irrigation network management tool, agricultural forms automation, a mobile application for field inspection, an operations dashboard for food storage, and a planning and completion status tracker for inspection activities. These applications are seamlessly integrated with existing business systems.

To ensure a robust and reliable GIS system, the company commits to providing a comprehensive warranty and operational support for a duration of 4 years. This support includes regular system health checks, efficient data management, continuous application enhancements, and user training. The company also focuses on capacity-building initiatives to empower your team with the necessary skills and knowledge for effective system utilization.

6.12 Majid Al Futtaim Properties, UAE

Implemented enterprise GIS systems include enterprise asset management, utility network data migration (water, sewer network, and stormwater), urban planning, land development, sales and lease management, and geo-enabled KPI dashboards. Build an enterprise-class, highly available GIS system in AWS that could include a platform, spatial data management and web applications, dashboards, and GIS integration with CRM.

6.13 ADNOC Sour Gas

Enterprise GIS system upgrades to 10.8 environments, data migration, application migration, and configured operational dashboards.

6.14 Geo AI Models for City of the Palo Alto, CA, USA

For tree canopy mapping, iSpatial Techno Solutions created algorithms that combine sophisticated automatic feature extraction methods with in-depth interactive evaluations and editing. The region of interest's tree canopy can now be mapped more precisely and in greater detail than before thanks to this combination of sensor and mapping technologies, enabling city planners to assess the tree density over a

iSpatial Tech: GEO-AI-Enabled Solutions for Smart Cities   189

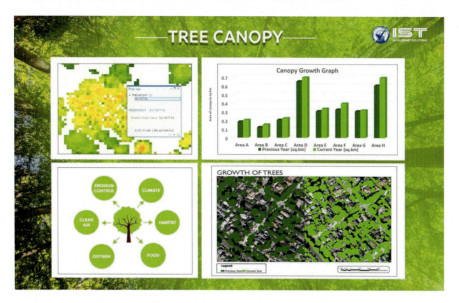

Fig. 8 iSpatial Techno Solutions tree canopy for US projects. Source: iSpatial Techno Solutions (n.d.-c). Published with the company's permission

certain time period. These analytics can determine property-specific improvement goals and predict the amount of tree loss in a planned development. In Fig. 8, the study's statistics are presented.

6.15 Al Ain Municipality Project

iSpatial Techno Solutions is currently working with AAM on a big project that can put both parties on a bigger screen. The AI from iSpatial Techno Solutions engine's capabilities must meet the minimum standards listed below.

The AI engine should aid in the daily operations of the GIS by incorporating many analytics and AI use cases and a technological solution. The solution must reliably recognize and identify numerous features (municipal and city assets) from images and videos using computer vision. All acquired data must be linked to the GIS system and databases of Al Ain Municipality. The collected data must be rendered visually on the GIS platform through dashboards and reports powered by AI. The engine must be accessible on-premises within the AAM network. The use of cloud features must be based on necessity. In addition, the engine should be capable of deep learning or self-learning, depending on the use case.

Mainly, the requirements of AAM are as follows.

6.16 AI and Deep Learning Models to Be Delivered for Feature Detection and Base Map Update

- Detection of Ezba (animal farms), boundary walls, fences, buildings, palm trees, and green areas from satellite or aerial imagery.
- The requirement is to train a model to identify Ezba, boundary walls, fences, buildings, palm trees, and green areas from satellite or aerial imagery whenever a new set of imagery is available and to validate the possibility of automatically detecting the edges of the farm boundaries.
- Do edge detection on the identified features and transfer the detected vector features to the GIS database.
- The model should be extendable to include any additional features if required in the future.
- To classify the Terrestrial LIDAR data to identify the different classes in the LAS file and extract the features to vector GIS format with minimum user input.
- Road sign board, Shop Names, Speed Limits detection and read the signboards automatically from geo-referenced 360 imagery (Both English and Arabic).
- To be able to detect, classify and read the sign boards and catalogue the information in a GIS database so that queries like "How many signboards are available" can be performed.

iSpatial has already deployed the required platform libraries to support building the Geo AI machine learning algorithms and models. Table 2 lists of the libraries.

Table 2 Platform libraries

Category	Tools/Libraries
Classification	• Maximum Likelihood
	• Random Trees
	• Support Vector Machine
Prediction	• Empirical Bayesian Kriging
	• Areal Interpolation
	• EBK Regression Prediction
	• Ordinary Least Squares
	• Regression and Exploratory Regression
	• Geographically Weighted Regression
	• Forest-based Prediction
Clustering	• Spatially Constrained Multivariate Clustering
	• Multivariate Clustering
	• Density-based Clustering
	• Image Segmentation
	• Hot Spot Analysis
	• Cluster and Outlier Analysis
	• Space Time Pattern Mining

Source: iSpatial Techno Solutions. (n.d.-c). Published with the company's permission

6.17 Deep Learning Model Execution in the Al Ain Region

iSpatial Techno Solutions has performed the below-mentioned models on the demo data:

- Building Footprints
- Tree Detection
- Road Extraction
- Land Use and Land Cover Classification
- Parcel Extraction

6.18 Building Footprints Model

Often accomplished by manually digitizing elements. Deep learning models are very capable of learning these intricate semantics and are able to generate superior results. Use this deep learning model to automate the laborious manual process of obtaining building footprints, thereby drastically lowering the time and effort needed. Figure 9 shows some of the buildings extracted by the AI from the company.

iSpatial Techno Solutions has successfully achieved optimal accuracy for our building extraction model by changing a few parameters such as batch size, threshold value, padding value, and true prediction value. Here, the building count is 1000, and the accuracy is more than 98%.

6.19 Tree Detection Model

Tree identification identifies all satellite image pixels that relate to trees. This deep learning algorithm is designed to recognize trees in aerial or drone imagery with great resolution. Applications for tree detection include vegetation management, forestry, and urban planning. Due to their extensive spatial and temporal coverage, high-resolution aerial and drone imagery can be used for tree detection. Here, the tree count is 2500, which is less than 75% in terms of accuracy. Figure 10 shows the extracted trees.

6.20 Road Extraction Model

This deep learning model is used to extract roads from high-resolution (30–50 cm) satellite or aerial data. In producing base maps and analysis procedures for urban planning and development, change detection, and infrastructure planning, road layers are useful. Digitizing roads from photos is a time-consuming task that is often accomplished by manually scanning features. Deep learning models are very capable of learning these intricate semantics and are able to generate superior results. Use this approach to deep learning to automate and expedite the process of gathering

Fig. 9 AI building extraction for Al Ain project. Source: iSpatial Techno Solutions. (n.d.-d). Published with the company's permission

road layers. Here, the total road extracted is around 88,984 m (which is 2000 m more than the original), and the accuracy is more than 80% with noise and outliers. A small sample of the extracted roads is shown in Fig. 11.

6.21 Land Cover Extraction Model

The earth's surface is described by its land cover. Urban planning, resource management, change detection, agriculture, and a number of other uses that call for

iSpatial Tech: GEO-AI-Enabled Solutions for Smart Cities

Fig. 10 AI tree canopy for Al Ain project. Source: iSpatial Techno Solutions. (n.d.-d). Published with the company's permission

information on the earth's surface can all benefit from land-cover maps. The classification of land cover is a challenging task that is difficult to complete with conventional techniques. Deep learning models can learn these complex interpretations quite well and produce better results as a result. There are a few publicly available datasets for land cover, but their spatial and temporal coverage may not always suit the user's needs. Creating datasets for a certain time period is equally tough, as it involves knowledge and time. Use this technique of deep learning to automate the manual procedure and drastically minimize the time and effort necessary. The result of area segmentation is demonstrated in Fig. 12.

Fig. 11 AI road extraction for Al Ain project. Source: iSpatial Techno Solutions (n.d.-d). Published with the company's permission

6.22 Parcel Extraction Model

Parcels are land units that specify property borders and are important for creating base maps and managing land. Historically, parcel mapping has been performed using highly precise surveying techniques, but this may be costly and time consuming. Increasingly, high-resolution photography is employed for plot delineation, and the application of deep learning models can automate and accelerate the process.

Residential parcels are frequently associated with visible bounds, but because legally recognized parcels can be formed without a clearly delimited boundary, this model simply deduces feasible approximations of their limits. This model can be

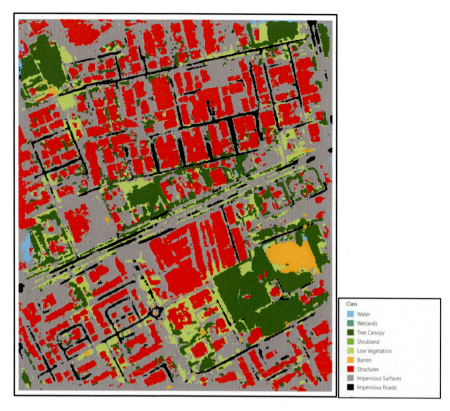

Fig. 12 AI image segmentation for Al Ain project. Source: iSpatial Techno Solutions. (n.d.-d). Published with the company's permission

used to generate base maps, which can then be manually edited for additional refinement. A sample area of the parcel output from AI is listed in Fig. 13.

6.23 Other Projects

The company has several clients in the public sector (Abu Dhabi Digital Authority, Statistic Center, Department of Education Council, Department for Urban Planning and Municipalities, ADNOC, RAK Police GHQ, The City of Palo Alto, The City of San Diego, Sempra Energy, Nakheel, Saudi Aramco, Picarro, etc.). Other projects and services completed by iSpatial Techno Solutions in the UAE include the following:

- Smart Permit
- UAE national atlas
- Birdathon

Fig. 13 AI road parcel for Al Ain project. Source: iSpatial Techno Solutions. (n.d.-d). Published with the company's permission

- Special Olympics dashboards
- AD government SDI cloud
- Food Control Authority Enterprise GIS
- Automation of Oil Lab Analysis: Build a Web/Mobile Application
- Air quality monitoring for the Environment Agency
- Geo Analytics: Animal Holding Inspection Management
- Property Development Client in the UAE

7 Awards and Recognitions

7.1 Special Appreciation from the Environmental Agency Department Abu Dhabi EAD Innovation Week 2020

iSpatial Techno Solutions presented AI-based solutions as a part of EAD Innovation Week (Fig. 14).

7.2 Technology Sponsor for the Abu Dhabi Special Olympics 2019

The 2019 Special Olympics World Games have featured iSpatial Techno Solutions as an official supporter. The Special Olympics (#specialolympics2019) is the world's largest humanitarian sporting event, empowering people of determination with intellectual disabilities through the power of sport. iSpatial Techno Solutions, in conjunction with ADDA, is pleased to support this initiative by developing a GIS-integrated web design utilizing ESRI technology that showcases Special Olympics story maps, athlete information and analytics, sporting venues in 3D, and real-time torch run and medal information.

Fig. 14 Award during EAD 2020. Source: iSpatial Techno Solutions. (n.d.-e). Published with the company's permission

7.3 ESRI Partner Conference 2020

iSpatial Techno Solutions was thrilled to see two of their best customer stories at the plenary. The Environment Agency, Abu Dhabi (EAD) Birdathon, a web-based GIS application to track the migratory pattern of Flamingos for biodiversity, and Abu Dhabi Digital Data Authority (ADDA) Smart and Innovative Story Maps on Special Olympics World Games 2019.

7.4 For Their Successful Implementations, Their Clients Received Awards

- Enterprise GIS System for Abu Dhabi Food Control Authority: Received Multiple Awards from ESRI UC, GISTEC, UAE, and UAE local government
- SAG Award 2015 ESRI UC for Oil & Gas client
- ESRI SAG Award from ESRI UC 2018-Sempra Energy USA
- EGI Award 2018-MAFP UAE

8 Conclusion

In conclusion, iSpatial Techno Solutions has become one of the leaders in the UAE when it comes to smart cities. The company has made a number of cutting-edge AI products and services by using machine learning, deep learning, and natural language processing in new ways. These products and services could change industries like healthcare, finance, and retail. iSpatial Techno Solutions' team of talented data scientists, engineers, and developers is committed to staying at the forefront of AI research and development, and the company has made big investments in its infrastructure and technology to support its growth.

9 Questions for Discussion

1. How is iSpatial technology dealing with the current technological boom?
2. Managing multiple companies, do you find it difficult to invest your time in one of them?
3. Do you think that AI might one day be a possible threat to professions?
4. What is the most challenging part when it comes to AI and your long-standing experience?

Acknowledgments The authors express deep gratitude to Mr. Ibrahim Yousif Al Obaidly, the founder of iSpatial Techno Solutions, for providing the necessary information for this chapter.

References

Goodfellow, I., Bengio, Y., & Courville, A. (2016). *Deep learning*. MIT press. https://www.deeplearningbook.org/

Haleem, A., Javaid, M., Qadri, M. A., Singh, R. P., & Suman, R. (2022). Artificial intelligence (AI) applications for marketing: A literature-based study. International journal of intelligent. *Networks, 3*, 119–132. Retrieved from. https://doi.org/10.1016/j.ijin.2022.08.005

iSpatial Techno Solutions. (n.d.-a). *Overview*. Retrieved from https://www.ispatialtec.com/

iSpatial Techno Solutions. (n.d.-b). *Contact*. Retrieved from https://www.ispatialtec.com/contact.html

iSpatial Techno Solutions. (n.d.-c). *Geospatial solutions*. Retrieved from https://www.ispatialtec.com/contact.html

iSpatial Techno Solutions. (n.d.-d). *Artificial intelligence solutions*. Retrieved from https://www.ispatialtec.com/contact.html

iSpatial Techno Solutions. (n.d.-e). *Events*. Retrieved from https://www.ispatialtec.com/events.html

Kelleher, J. D., & Tierney, B. (2018). *Data science: An introduction*. CRC Press.

LeCun, Y., Bengio, Y., & Hinton, G. (2015). Deep learning. *Nature, 521*(7553), 436–444. https://doi.org/10.1038/nature14539

Tuner, J. (2023, March 29). *How managers can adopt AI in the workplace to improve productivity and reduce costs*. Beautiful.ai. Retrieved from https://www.beautiful.ai/blog/how-managers-can-adopt-ai-in-the-workplace-to-improve-productivity-and-reduce-costs

West, D. M., & Allen, J. R (2018, April 24). *How artificial intelligence is transforming the world*. Brookings Institution. Retrieved from https://www.brookings.edu/research/how-artificial-intelligence-is-transforming-the-world/.

Reda Maroufi is a geospatial specialist who worked at Bayanat for almost a decade, specializing in remote sensing and photogrammetry. During his time there, he worked extensively on high-resolution images, including triangulation, ortho-rectified images, and DEM. He transitioned to working with LiDAR technology and currently manages various projects at Al Ain Municipalities.

Jaber Mohammed Alketbi is a government official who has experience working with and managing various GIS departments. He has also contributed to the development of multiple geospatial projects in collaboration with these departments.

Marco Valeri is Senior Lecturer in Organizational Behavior at Niccolò Cusano University, Italy. He is a Lecturer in Applied Organizational Behaviour at Xenophon College, London. He is an Adjunct Professor at the Faculty of Social Sciences and Leisure Management, School of Hospitality, Tourism and Events, Taylor's University, Malaysia. He is an Associate Researcher in Strategy, Magellan Research Center, School of Management, Iaelyon Business School, Jean Monet University, France. His teaching and consultancy fields include strategic management, leadership development, cross-cultural management, and international hospitality management. His research areas include sustainability and green practices, strategy implementation, knowledge management, family business, crisis management, information technology, and network analysis. He has a long and extensive international academic experience and has taken visiting positions at several universities. He is a member of several Editorial Boards of international tourism journals, reviewer and editor of several handbooks on entrepreneurship, tourism, and hospitality management.

Juma Al Majid Holding Group: Story of Success and Achievement

Esra Qasemi, Hafsah Alderei, and Grisna Anggadwita

Abstract

Family businesses are the cornerstone of the United Arab Emirates economy, accounting for over 90% of the nation's economic activity. Many businesses play a crucial role in achieving the nation's vision to develop sustainable urban communities by implementing and developing several state-of-the-art real estate projects. Juma Almajid is one of these businesses that have a long history in shaping the urban land escape across the Gulf region and are deemed essential to every economy. Empirical evidence reveals that they contribute to a massive chunk of the region's non-oil gross domestic product. The Forbes magazine recognized it as one of the "Top 100 Arab family businesses in 2020 in the Middle East." Guided by the significance of family businesses in the UAE's economy, this chapter provides a brief overview of the Juma Al Majid Holding group. A brief insight into its history, organizational structure, work culture, success factors, and significance in the Gulf region is identified and summarized.

1 Introduction

The economy of the United Arab Emirates (UAE) has multiplied over the past few years positioning it on the global map as one of the fastest-rising emerging markets. Becoming one of the World Trade Organization members enabled the government to spur its development and open its economy to multinational corporations (Al-Ali,

---

E. Qasemi (✉) · H. Alderei
College of Humanities and Social Sciences, United Arab Emirates University, Abu Dhabi, UAE
e-mail: 201801621@uaeu.ac.ae; 201703837@uaeu.ac.ae

G. Anggadwita
School of Economics and Business, Telkom University, Bandung, Indonesia
e-mail: grisnaanggadwita@telkomuniversity.ac.id

© The Author(s), under exclusive license to Springer Nature Switzerland AG 2023
K. Alkaabi, V. Ramadani (eds.), *Family Business Cases*, Springer Business Cases,
https://doi.org/10.1007/978-3-031-39252-8_13

Fig. 1 The leadership team of the Juma Al Majid group. *Source:* Juma Al Majid Holding Group LLC. (n.d.-a). Published with the company's permission

2008; Toledo, 2013). Nonetheless, it brought a significant challenge to local companies as international organizations would conduct trade freely and efficiently perform business in the region (Chabrak et al., 2017; Krarti & Dubey, 2018).

Therefore, local firms must be configured to accommodate and deal with fierce competition from international firms. It ensures that they take advantage of new technologies, benefit from economies of scale, and are more competitive locally and internationally (Stevenson & Jarillo, 2007; Koelemaij, 2022). Being an imperative part of the nation's economy, family businesses must comply with international standards such as the International Financial Reporting Standards as dictated by the UAE Commercial Companies law No. 2 of 2015 (Communication Legal Translation, 2015).

Family businesses have contributed significantly to economic growth (Alkaabi et al., 2023; Dana & Ramadani, 2015; Ramadani et al., 2017; Anggadwita et al., 2017) because they are an essential source of job creation in many countries, including the UAE (Ramadani et al., 2015; Rexhepi et al., 2017). According to Chrisman et al. (2011), family businesses are better equipped to respond to disruptions than non-family businesses, so they tend to be more resilient.

Juma Al Majid Holding Group is a leading Emirati Family business established in 1950 (Fig. 1). During its formative years, the company was primarily involved in trading activities. The company began to diversify as the Emirate entrenched itself as a single country. Diversification began in the construction sector but later shifted to other fields such as travel, general trading, food imports, and other industries. Juma Al Majid is also, locally and globally, an active player in the financial investment and portfolio management sector (Juma Al Majid Holding Group LLC., n.d.-a). In 2022, Forbes ranked Al Majid position 34 in the list of the top 100 Arab family enterprises in the Arab region (Forbes Middle East, 2022).

Juma Al Majid's philosophical ideology drives the organization to satisfy and surpass the expectation of all consumers through social awareness, integrity, honesty, and service excellence. This perspective is entrenched in the firm's business aspects and is credited for its unrivaled success (Juma Al Majid Holding Group LLC., n.d.-a). Figure 1 summarizes the leadership team of the Juma Al Majid group (Juma Al Majid Group, n.d.-a).

This chapter briefly overviews Juma Al Majid group and its market segments. Besides, a brief insight into its history, organizational structure, work culture, success factors, and significance in the Gulf region is identified and summarized.

2   Business Overview

The Juma Al Majid Holding Group is a conglomerate with its main office in Dubai, UAE, and was established by H.E. Juma Al Majid in 1950 (RocketReach, n.d.). The group now extends across the GCC and beyond, as well as the entire UAE. It is driven by ethics, leadership, service excellence, and teamwork. Figure 2 illustrates the overview of its significant market segments, which are summarized in the following section.

Fig. 2 Overview of the significant market segments of the Juma Al Majid group. *Source:* Juma Al Majid Holding Group LLC (n.d.-b). Published with the company's permission

2.1 Commercial

The Group's Commercial divisions have introduced several well-known brands to the UAE and beyond, supported by solid alliances with the greatest firms across a wide range of industry verticals. They engage in businesses related to consumer and office solutions, fast-moving consumer goods, and automotive and heavy equipment. The group's business activities include Fast Moving Consumer Goods (FMCG), Automotive and Heavy Equipment, and Consumer and Office Solutions.

The Automotive and Heavy Equipment division markets commercial vehicles, SUVs, passenger cars, lubricants, heavy equipment, spare parts, and tires to fulfill the need of every market segment in the UAE (MENAFN, 2022). Juma Al Majid FMCG division can be traced to 1962 being one of the prominent distributors of FMCGs in the UAE today. For more than seven decades, Juma Al Majid has been heralded as the leading enterprise for office equipment, home appliances, and quality watches in the UAE. Consequently, the Group's Consumer and Office Solutions division has earned a strong reputation for its revolutionary efforts in these areas (Juma Al Majid Holding Group LLC., n.d.-a).

2.2 Real Estate

To support its real estate activities, Juma Al Majid Group owns three main subsidiaries: Juma Al Majid Holding Group, Al Majid Property CO. LLC, and Al Maarifa Mechanical Electrical and Building Maintenance Company LLC (Juma Al Majid Holding Group LLC, n.d.-c). The Project Development and Management Division of Juma Al Majid Holding Group is responsible for strategic planning, master planning, and feasibility evaluations of investment, private, and Beit Al Khair projects both locally and internationally. Al Majid Property Co. LLC, a wholly owned company of Juma Al Majid Group, is a prominent real estate firm in the UAE, known for its expertise and reputation within the industry.

With its establishment in 1997, Al Maarifa Mechanical, Electrical & Building Maintenance has risen to become a leading company in building maintenance and facilities management in the UAE. The company's dedication to excellence is evident through its strict adherence to meticulously researched and tested Standard Operating Procedures. By consistently meeting high-quality standards, Al Maarifa has fostered a strong track record of delivering utmost customer satisfaction since its inception.

Overall, these subsidiaries contribute to the robust real estate portfolio of Juma Al Majid Group and exemplify their commitment to excellence in project development, property management, and building maintenance services.

2.3 Investment

Juma Al Majid has significantly invested in high-growth industries while considering suitable hedging strategies to manage risk effectively. The group's business under the investment division is the Al Majid Investment CO. LLC. which was established in 1999 with the primary aim of expanding and diversifying the group's investment portfolio in money markets, global equity markets, private equity, direct equity, and fixed income (Juma Al Majid Holding Group LLC., n.d.-d).

2.4 Travel and Tourism

Group businesses in the Travel and Tourism sector have helped meet the leisure travel needs of consumers in the UAE. They include Al Majid Travel LLC and Skyline Travel, Tourism, and Shipping LLC (Juma Al Majid Holding Group LLC., n.d.-e). These businesses offer various leisure travel and business services such as airline ticketing and representation, visas, cargo and shipping, ground transportation, accommodation, and UAE staycations.

2.5 Contracting and Services

The Group's Contracting and Services enterprises collaborate and partner with the preconstruction and design time to warrant the timely execution of projects with utmost quality. The Division has partnered with renowned global brands such as Hindalco, Duro-Dyne, Trane, WISI, Olis, Wefatherm, Edwards, Walker Fire, Angus Fire, and SIGMA elevators, enabling them to bring international construction segment-associated brands and world-class standards to each project undertaken. Businesses or LLCs in the Contracting and Services sector include Al Arabia for Electro-Mechanical, Safety, and Security, Elevators and Moving Systems, Technical Supplies, and Contracts for Operations and Maintenance (Juma Al Majid Holding Group LLC., n.d.-f).

3 Geographic Distribution

The geographic distribution of Juma Al Majid plays a crucial role in its success and ability to serve a wide range of consumers. With a team of talented workers at its core, the company strives to make a difference in the industries it operates in. Juma Al Majid Group has established a strong presence with over 7500 employees working across approximately 35 firms spanning various sectors (Apollo.io, n.d.). Headquartered in Dubai, UAE (Fig. 3), the group benefits from its strategic location, which serves as a gateway to the Middle East and connects it to global markets. The group's geographic distribution enables it to cater to both local and international consumers.

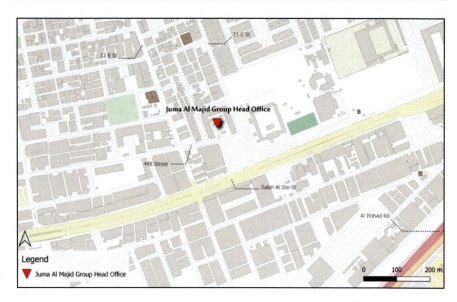

Fig. 3 The geographical location of the Juma AL Majid head office. *Source:* Juma Al Majid Holding Group LLC. (n.d.-b). Published with the company's permission

Through the advancements of the worldwide web, Juma Al Majid has expanded its reach beyond traditional boundaries. Consumers from different parts of the world can access the group's diverse range of products and services by simply visiting their website. This global accessibility allows Juma Al Majid to tap into a broader customer base and engage with consumers from diverse cultural backgrounds. By embracing the digital landscape, the group has overcome geographical constraints and positioned itself as a globally recognized brand.

In summary, the geographic distribution of Juma Al Majid, with its headquarters in Dubai and a wide network of firms, empowers the group to serve consumers locally and internationally. Leveraging the power of the internet, the company has transcended geographical boundaries and offers its products and services to customers worldwide.

4 Work Culture

Work culture denotes a collection of behaviors, beliefs, and attitudes that constitute a typical atmosphere in the workplace. A sound work culture aligns organizational policies and employee behavior with the company goals, objectives, vision, and mission, which is accomplished while considering the employees' well-being (Saad & Abbas, 2018). An organization's work culture influences how employees fit in the working environment and establishes professional relations with coworkers.

The culture established by a family is closely tied to the values of a family business. The work system in a family business is largely shaped by its culture, which serves as a unifying force that integrates ownership, management, and family sub-systems (Anggadwita et al., 2019). The values, norms, and attitudes that prevail within the company are reflected in its culture. Sorenson (2013) suggests that the dominant values of a family business usually reflect the family's identity and values. A family enterprise that can thrive and grow is one that incorporates a positive culture with each change, making it acceptable to all stakeholders. Hence, comprehending the significance of culture in a family business is necessary to gain more knowledge and insights on how to operate and manage such a business.

Juma Al Majid Group highlights the individual competencies of its workers, intending to create a well-rounded and highly functional team. The company is continuously searching for creative personalities with the drive to make a difference in society to join its team. Al Majid Group's work culture is further exemplified through its perspective of developing partnerships with exceptional personalities. To accomplish this, the company leverages the latest work processes and emerging technologies and collaborates with leading firms in its diverse sectors. The conglomerate's work culture is best captioned by its work philosophy, which institutes positive change and improves the community's well-being.

Entrepreneurs leverage creativity and innovation to exploit business opportunities for the primary purpose of profit generation. Legendary entrepreneurs, including Juma Al Majid, realized success by shifting lower productivity resources to higher productivity areas. According to Drucker (2014), identity traits for influential entrepreneurs may include self-image, creativity and innovativeness, risk tolerance, and flexibility. The success realized by Juma Al Majid Group is credited to chairman and visionary founder Juma Al Majid. Due to their quality services, His Highness Sheikh bin Rashid Al Maktoum awarded Majid the Islamic Personality of the Year in 2019.

5 Achievements and Awards

The Juma Al Majid Establishment has become one of the most renowned and well-known companies in the United Arab Emirates. Juma Al Majid Est. has numerous showrooms, workshops, and service locations throughout the United Arab Emirates. Its relationship and journey with Hyundai Motor Company are excellent; therefore, they have received several national awards.

For instance, in appreciation of the Division's remarkable customer engagement efforts and excellent performance for 2017–2018, their Cars Division was named the winner of the highly coveted Hyundai's Best Customer Satisfaction Award. Moreover, Juma Al Majid Est.-Spare Parts & Sales Div. was recognized at the "Safe Driving Stars" ceremony organized by the General Directorate of Transport & Rescue held in Dubai in March 2022.

Gulfco, another Juma Al Majid group subsidiary, received the Best-in-Class Seasonal Execution Award from Goody Middle East for exceeding their goals in 2021 at a recent event held at the Sheraton Grand Dubai hotel to mark its 50th anniversary. Recently, Juma Al Majid Est.-Hyundai UAE has been again named the

Middle East and Africa region's winner of the highly coveted Hyundai's Best Customer Satisfaction Award in honor of its excellent customer engagement initiatives and stellar performance over the past several months during 2022. Moreover, Juma Al Majid Est, the Hyundai After-Sales Division, received an award from Hyundai Motor Company at the global awards ceremony on September 6 and 7, 2022, in Cape Town, South Africa.

6 Financial Operations

Financial statements are essential for stakeholders, including financial analysts, investors, employees, and management, as they accurately depict the firm's financial position and performance. Importantly, they enable stakeholders to evaluate and formulate sound economic decisions while leveraging current and past performance to predict future growth and implementation of the entity (Brazel et al., 2015). The Juma Al Majid's primary operations in the early years were trading related. It became urgently necessary to diversify into other commercial endeavors when the Emirates united into a single nation to support the developing country's economy. Heavy investment was made in the construction industry's core sector to achieve this; in the long term, both the nation and the group profited. Juma Al Majid partnership ventures work in various sectors, including shipping, building, importing food, general business, and travel.

The group is involved in portfolio management and financial investments locally and internationally. The group has established itself as a strong leader in every area of its endeavor. It is prepared for the even bigger challenges and successes that lie ahead of it in the future, thanks to Dubai's development as the region's economic hub.

7 Summary

The journey toward entrepreneurial journey is lengthy, significantly transforming an idea from scratch and making it a profitable venture. Realizing business success necessitates enormous sacrifices and devotion of resources to make the vision a reality. All entrepreneurs, regardless of those whose businesses appear in Forbes or Fortune 500 companies, began from idea recognition in the entrepreneurial life cycle and made their brand successful. The roadmap for all successful entrepreneurs commences from idea recognition, creation and exploitation of opportunity, resource commitment, market entry, business idea or venture launch and growth, expansion and maturation, and exit from the venture to allow incubation and actualization of a new idea. Adopting a positive or appropriate mindset is often termed as one of the critical ingredients of a successful entrepreneur. Although all entrepreneurs make significant efforts to attain financial and business excellence, the successful execution of stages in the entrepreneurial journey ultimately determines excellence.

Juma Al Majid Holding Group is a leading Emirati Family business established in 1950. During its formative years, the company was primarily involved in trading activities. The company began to diversify as the Emirate entrenched itself as a single country. Diversification began in the construction sector but later shifted to other fields such as travel, general trading, food imports, and other industries. The group is involved in several CRS-related activities. For instance, the Juma Al Majid Centre for Culture and Heritage has been instrumental in preserving historic Islamic manuscripts from across the globe. Aside from running charitable establishments, Juma Al Majid is also committed to protecting the environment by inventing clean-energy solutions in different fields to protect the environment. Owing to their excellent services, they have won several achievements and awards, including the best customer satisfaction award, best after-sales services awards, and so on.

8 Questions for Discussion

1. How did Juma Al Majid Holding Group evolve from its trading activities to diversifying into various sectors?
2. How can other businesses learn from the work culture and practices of Juma Al Majid Group in terms of fostering individual competencies, embracing change, and driving positive societal impact?
3. How do the three main subsidiaries of Juma Al Majid Group (Juma Al Majid Holding Group, Al Majid Property CO. LLC, and Al Maarifa Mechanical Electrical and Building Maintenance Company LLC) support the real estate activities of the group?
4. What strategies can family businesses in the UAE employ to stay relevant in today's dynamic business landscape?
5. What are key learning points drawn from Juma Al Majid's entrepreneurial success journey?

References

Al-Ali, J. (2008). Emiratisation: Drawing UAE nationals into their surging economy. *International Journal of Sociology and Social Policy, 28*(9–10), 365–379. https://doi.org/10.1108/01443330810900202

Alkaabi, K., Ramadani, V., & Zeqiri, J. (2023). Universities, entrepreneurial ecosystem and family business performance: Evidence from The United Arab Emirates. *Journal of the Knowledge Economy*. https://doi.org/10.1007/s13132-023-01384-9.

Anggadwita, G., Ramadani, V., Alamanda, D. T., Ratten, V., & Hashani, M. (2017). Entrepreneurial intentions from an Islamic perspective: A study of Muslim entrepreneurs in Indonesia. *International Journal of Entrepreneurship and Small Business, 31*(2), 165–179. https://doi.org/10.1504/IJESB.2017.084086

Anggadwita, G., Profityo, W. B., Alamanda, D. T., & Permatasari, A. (2019). Cultural values and their implications to family business succession: A case study of small Chinese-owned family businesses in Bandung, Indonesia. *Journal of Family Business Management, 10*(4), 281–292. https://doi.org/10.1108/JFBM-03-2019-0017

Apollo.io. (n.d.). *Juma Al Majid holding group L.L.C.* Retrieved June 1, 2023, from https://www.apollo.io/companies/Juma-Al-Majid-Holding-Group-L-L-C/55923b1973696418f633e200?chart=count

Brazel, J. F., Jones, K. L., Thayer, J., & Warne, R. C. (2015). Understanding investor perceptions of financial statement fraud and their use of red flags: Evidence from the field. *Review of Accounting Studies, 20*(4), 1373–1406.

Chabrak, N., Bouhaddioui, C., Thomas, L., & Bascavusoglu-Moreau, E. (2017). *Global entrepreneurship monitor: United Arab Emirates 2016/2017 annual report.* Retrieved from https://www.gemconsortium.org/economy-profiles/uae

Chrisman, J. J., Chua, J. H., & Steier, L. P. (2011). Resilience of family firms: An introduction. *Entrepreneurship Theory and Practice, 35*(6), 1107–1119. https://doi.org/10.1111/j.1540-6520.2011.00493.x

Dana, L. P., & Ramadani, V. (2015). *Family businesses in transition economies.* Springer International Publishing.

Drucker, P. (2014). *Innovation and entrepreneurship.* Routledge. *Gulfco.* (2019). Juma Al Majid Holding Group LLC. Retrieved from https://www.gulfcouae.com/jamgroupc3c6.html?pid=juma-al-majid-holding-group-llc

Forbes Middle East. (2022). *The top 100 Arab family businesses.* Retrieved from https://www.forbesmiddleeast.com/lists/the-top-100-arab-family-businesses/

Juma Al Majid Holding Group LLC. (n.d.-a). *About us.* Retrieved from https://www.al-majid.com/about-us/our-leadership-team/

Juma Al Majid Holding Group LLC. (n.d.-b). *Our group businesses.* Retrieved from https://www.al-majid.com/group_businesses/

Juma Al Majid Holding Group LLC. (n.d.-c). *Real Estate.* Retrieved from https://www.al-majid.com/group_businesses/real-estate/

Juma Al Majid Holding Group LLC. (n.d.-d). *Investment.* Retrieved from https://www.al-majid.com/group_businesses/investment/

Juma Al Majid Holding Group LLC. (n.d.-e). *Travel & Tourism.* Retrieved from https://www.al-majid.com/group_businesses/travel-tourism/

Juma Al Majid Holding Group LLC. (n.d.-f). *Contracting and services.* Retrieved from https://www.al-majid.com/group_businesses/contracting-services/

Koelemaij, J. (2022). The world's number 1 real estate development exporter? Assessing announced transnational projects from The United Arab Emirates between 2003–2014. *Environment and Planning A, 54*(2), 226–246. https://doi.org/10.1177/0308518X211054847

Krarti, M., & Dubey, K. (2018). Review analysis of economic and environmental benefits of improving energy efficiency for UAE building stock. *Renewable and Sustainable Energy Reviews, 82*(April 2016), 14–24. https://doi.org/10.1016/j.rser.2017.09.013

Communication Legal Translation. (2015). *Federal Law No. 2 of 2015 on commercial companies.* Retrieved from *https://ded.ae/ded_files/Files/%D8%A7%D9%84%D9%82%D9%88%D8%A7%D9%86%D9%8A%D9%86%20%D9%88%D8%A7%D9%84%D8%AA%D8%B4%D8%B1%D9%8A%D8%B9%D8%A7%D8%AA%20PDF/Federal_Law_No_(2)_of_2015_AD_On_Commercial_Companies.pdf*

MENAFN. (2022, May 28). *IONIC 5: Juma Al Majid Est unveils Hyundai's fully electric vehicle.* MENAFN. Retrieved from https://menafn.com/1104285581/IONIC-5-Juma-Al-Majid-Est-Unveils-Hyundais-Fully-Electric-Vehicle

Ramadani, V., Hisrich, R. D., & G€erguri-Rashiti, S. (2015). Female entrepreneurs in transition economies: Insights from Albania, Macedonia and Kosovo. *World Review of Entrepreneurship, Management and Sustainable Development, 11*(4), 391–413. https://doi.org/10.1504/WREMSD.2015.072066

Ramadani, V., Hisrich, R. D., Anggadwita, G., & Alamanda, D. T. (2017). Gender and succession planning: Opportunities for females to lead Indonesian family businesses. *International Journal of Gender and Entrepreneurship, 9*(3), 229–251. https://doi.org/10.1108/IJGE-02-2017-0012

Rexhepi, G., Ramadani, V., Rahdari, A., & Anggadwita, G. (2017). Models and strategies of family businesses internationalization: A conceptual framework and future research directions. *Review of International Business and Strategy, 27*(2), 248–260. https://doi.org/10.1108/RIBS-12-2016-0081

RocketReach. (n.d.). *Juma Al Majid group profile*. Retrieved June 1, 2023, from https://rocketreach.co/juma-al-majid-group-profile_b5c78df1f42e0d7e

Saad, G. B., & Abbas, M. (2018). The impact of organizational culture on job performance: A study of Saudi Arabian public sector work culture. *Problems and Perspectives in Management, 16*(3), 207–218. https://doi.org/10.21511/ppm.16(3).2018.17

Sorenson, R. L. (2013). How moral and social values become embedded in family firms. *Journal of Management, Spirituality & Religion, 10*(2), 116–137. https://doi.org/10.1080/14766086.2012.758050

Stevenson, H. H., & Jarillo, J. C. (2007). A paradigm of entrepreneurship: Entrepreneurial management. In Á. Cuervo, D. Ribeiro, & S. Roig (Eds.), *Entrepreneurship* (pp. 155–170). Springer. https://doi.org/10.1007/978-3-540-48543-8_7

Toledo, H. (2013). The political economy of emiratization in the UAE. *Journal of Economic Studies, 40*(1), 39–53. https://doi.org/10.1108/01443581311283493

Esra Qasemi studied Urban Planning at the Geography and Urban Sustainability Department and completed a minor in Geographic Information Systems at UAE University. She worked on a funded research project titled "Impact of Tourism Sector on Economic Growth in the United Arab Emirates: A Case Study of Dibba Al Fujairah City". Esra also volunteered at Takatf and Sand in Expo 2020 and presented her research at the 26th McGill International Entrepreneurship Conference. Additionally, she underwent training at Dubai Municipality and participated in GeoHUB workshops. Her interests lie in GIS urban design, sustainable cities, urban sociology, transportation and mobility, and happiness and well-being.

Hafsah Alderei pursued a bachelor's degree in Urban Planning with a minor in Geographic Information Systems from the Geography and Urban Sustainability Department at the College of Humanities and Social Sciences, United Arab Emirates University. She presented her work at the 26th McGill International Entrepreneurship Conference and has a keen research interest in business, urban planning, and design, as well as transportation design.

Grisna Anggadwita is an Associate Professor at the School of Economics and Business, Telkom University, Indonesia. She teaches courses in Entrepreneurship and Small Business Management. She authored/co-authored more than 100 research articles/book chapters in Indonesian/international journals and conference proceedings. She received the Emerald Literati Award from the Emerald Group Publishing for High Commended Paper (2019 and 2022 in the *Journal of Science and Technology Policy Management*) and Outstanding Reviewer (2021 in the *Journal of Science and Technology Policy Management* and 2022 in the *Journal of Enterprising Communities*). Her research interests include women entrepreneurship, entrepreneurial behavior, small business, and internationalization of businesses.

M Glory Holding: The Aspiration to Establish an Automobile Manufacturing Industry in the United Arab Emirates

Khaula Alkaabi and Majida Alazazi

Abstract

Emirati businesswomen have played an essential role in the economic growth and diversification of the United Arab Emirates (UAE). In recent years, women in the UAE have made remarkable progress in a variety of fields, including finance, technology, and manufacturing. This chapter highlights the accomplishments of Dr. Majida Alazazi, an Emirati businesswoman who founded and managed several factories, including the first gasoline and electric car factories in the UAE. It also discusses the organizational structure and fundamental principles of M Glory Holding Group, which includes sustainable industrial subsidiaries. The chapter concludes with the company's plan to invest in a new assembly and production facility for electric vehicles, aligning with the UAE's national strategy for economic diversification and sustainability.

1 Introduction

M Glory Holding Company includes a variety of subsidiaries that work in different sustainable industries. Through its three businesses, AL Damani Motor Vehicles Manufacturing, which offers various models of electric vehicles; Sandwaves Electric Vehicles Company, which focuses on designing and developing luxury EV, innovative, high-quality, and eco-friendly cars; and EM Company, which is a joint venture

K. Alkaabi (✉)
Geography and Urban Sustainability Department, United Arab Emirates University, Abu Dhabi, United Arab Emirates
e-mail: khaula.alkaabi@uaeu.ac.ae

M. Alazazi
Chairwoman and CEO of M Glory Holding, Dubai, UAE
e-mail: ceo@mglorygroup.com

with the Egyptian Ministry of Military Production. In order to build an Arab-made new CNG pickup vehicle called "EM", M Glory primarily works in the Industrial Automotive Sector. The second industrial division of M Glory is engaged in the production of furniture through the Office Touch Furniture Company, a reputable supplier and manufacturer in the United Arab Emirates that provides a wide selection of office and hotel Furniture to meet the requirements of contemporary office furniture in the GCC market.

With the assistance of Al Qudra International Company, M Glory is also investing in high-tech robotics. Finally, M Glory has expanded to include the field of real estate with distinctiveness through M Glory Zanzibar Investment Company by creating the first smart and sustainable island, which will be the most distinctive and exclusive island in all of Africa ever "The Pearl Island."

1.1 Dr. Majida Alazazi: First Emirati Female Auto Factory Owner in the MENA Region

Dr. Majida Alazazi is an Emirati pioneer in the field of business administration and manufacturing, having achieved the first-ever practical Doctorate in Business Administration (DBA) in Supply Chain Management and Manufacturing from UAE University. Since 2008, she has recognized the importance of industry sector to support economic diversity in the UAE, and driven by her passion to be a leader in the industrial sector, she founded the first Office Furniture Factory in 2009, then established the first gasoline car factory in the United Arab Emirates and Middle East under Arab brand "Sandstorm Motor Vehicles Manufacturing LLC," and on October 2022 launched the first Electric car factory in the United Arab Emirates (UAE) and the Middle East "AL Damani Motor Vehicles Manufacturing LLC," becoming the first woman in the MENA region to establish and run factories of its kind (M Glory Group, n.d.).

As a prominent businesswoman in the UAE, Dr. Majida currently holds several high-ranking positions, including Chairwoman, Board member, and CEO of various companies such as M Glory Holding Group, AL DAMANI Motor Vehicle Manufacturing, Sandstorm Automotive, Office Touch Furniture Factory, and Tiny Dreams Nursery, among others. Her continuous search for new and distinctive fields, as well as her desire to conquer new challenges have led her to pursue applied studies and work in both the private and the public sectors, inspired by the leadership of HH Sheikh Mohammed bin Rashid Al Maktoum and HH Sheikh Mohammed bin Zayed Al Nahyan. Over the last 23 years, Dr. Alazazi has held numerous positions in various sectors, both government and semi-government companies, as a way of giving back to the country. She has carried out numerous research studies on the impacts of the Fourth Industrial Revolution on the national sustainable economy of the UAE, and she is an active member of the Abu Dhabi Businesswomen Council, Emirates Association for Women Entrepreneurs, and the Emirates Volunteer Society.

1.2 Sandstorm Automotive Factory

SANDSTORM Automotive was established on April 29th, 2019, in Dubai with the objective of making a significant impact on the local automotive sector, while also supporting the UAE's long-term goal of creating a robust automotive manufacturing industry that emphasizes innovation and sustainable industrial growth. The factory has the capacity to produce 3800 vehicles annually and includes a 16,000-square foot assembly building, a 7000-square foot testing PDI area, and a 9500-square foot kits building.

Dr. Majida Al Azazi, CEO of SANDSTORM, said "the new car plant offers a great opportunity to attract international manufacturers to the local market, a move that helps support the UAE's strategy for economic diversification." The vehicles were specifically designed to be suitable for the harsh climate and terrain of the Middle East, while also providing customers with vehicle class-leading performance and value.

It is committed to developing a diversified, sustainable, and knowledge-based economy by producing the region's first commercial and retail 4 × 4 vehicles that meet local and international industry standards and customer requirements (Sandstorm Automotive, n.d.).

2 Business Overview

2.1 The Organizational Structure of M Glory Holding Company and Integration of Its Subsidiaries

2.1.1 Damani Motor Vehicles Manufacturing L.L.C.

Al Damani Motor Vehicles Manufacturing L.L.C., the main subsidiary of M Glory Holding, was established by Dr. Majida Al Azazi in 2021 with a primary focus on producing electric cars (Al Damani Motor Vehicles Manufacturing L.L.C., n.d.). The company is based in Dubai and built its first EV factory in the MENA region in October 2022. It started with its flagship model, DMV 300 (Fig. 1), with a plan to introduce several new models. Dr. Majida Al Azazi, the founder of the company, has played a key role in the development of the Electric Vehicle Manufacturing and has contributed to sustainability by founding the first EV factory in the MENA employing a recycling system and green technology.

Advantages of the Electric Car DMV300:

- It is easy to drive due to its simple control.
- It delivers quick acceleration due to the high torque available from the get-go.
- Low maintenance is required, and the service intervals are not as frequent as on petrol vehicles, and it can be done remotely.
- Economic running cost and service cost.
- It produces zero emissions and helps to reduce carbon footprints.
- It can be charged at the home-by-home charger that is provided by Al Damani.

Fig. 1 The "Al Damani—DMV300" Electric Vehicle Model. Source: M Glory Holding. Published with the company's permission

- It is eligible for government incentives.
- The absence of mechanical parts is what ensures a quiet and enjoyable ride without any disturbances.

2.1.2 Sandwaves Electric Vehicles Manufacturing

Sandwaves Auto is also one of the main subsidiaries of M Glory Holding Company, established to develop automotive sector innovation as an (R & D). It was established in Dubai, UAE, in October 2018 and has been integrated with M Glory in 2020. Sandwaves Auto aims to design, develop, and build stylish and innovative luxury EV (eco-friendly car). The brand's focus is on designing and developing electric cars that are practical, stylish, and innovative. Currently, Sandwaves is working with a famous Italian developer to build their first prototype.

2.1.3 EM Company: Arab Manufacturing Partnership to Develop EM Bi-Fuel Pickup Model

The third main company of M Glory Holding in the automotive sector is a collaborative venture to develop the "EM," a bi-fuel pickup vehicle that is Arab-made and under Arab name "Egyptian Emirates Automotive Company." It was established in 2021 and announced in Cairo on August 2022 by the Egyptian Ministry of Military Production and M Glory Holding (Fig. 2). This Egyptian-Emirati automaker uses natural gas as a fuel source for cars to produce more ecologically friendly automobiles.

This Egyptian-Emirati automaker supports Egypt's strategy to localize the sector, take advantage of the nation's vast mineral resources, and utilize natural gas as a fuel source for cars in order to create more ecologically friendly vehicles. The company plans to build 20 plants in Egypt that will manufacture cars with a bi-fuel system (natural gas and gasoline), with a capacity of 12,000 cars yearly (Mikhail, 2022; Mubasher.Info, 2021).

Fig. 2 EM Bi-Fuel Pickup Model (**a**) and related agreement signature (**b**). Source: M Glory Holding. Published with the company's permission

Dr. Majida Alazazi highlighted several advantages the EM automobiles have to offer, such as their strong engine capacity, plush seats, innovative safety systems, and capacity to run on many types of roads at temperatures perfect for the Middle East, the Gulf, and Africa. They are therefore suitable for export to African markets (Mikhail, 2022; Enterprise Press, 2021).

2.1.4 Al Qudra International Companies Representation L.L.C.

Al Qudra International Companies Representation L.L.C. is an Emirati business with headquarters in Dubai and has been operational since November 2007 (Al Qudra International Companies Representation L.L.C., n.d.). The company has a solid reputation for offering world-class solutions to important industries both domestically and internationally. In 2020, Al Qudra International emerged under the umbrella of M Glory Holding Group and started working officially to present "How & How" that produced the "fire fitting robotic" in the UAE and MENA. Besides that, Al Qudra seeks to adopt the newest technology and best practices, with a special emphasis on the Fourth Industrial Revolution, in their business.

2.1.5 Office Touch Furniture L.L.C.

It is the first factory to have been established by Dr. Majida in 2009 and one of her significant companies, with headquarters in Al Sajaa Industrial in Sharjah. In 2020, it emerged under the umbrella of M Glory Holding Group.

Office Touch is a prominent producer and supplier of office furniture in the UAE and GCC, offering a large selection of furniture that meets the demands of contemporary workplaces and hotels (Le Monde Office Furniture, n.d.). In an effort to make sure that the products meet the space and reflect the client's vision, the company offers customized options and provides a wide range of items, including welcome tables, executive tables, workstations, director tables, meeting tables, conference tables, cabinets, and chairs. Today, Office Touch Factory is considered one of the best factories in the UAE and GCC markets, on which all of the major office furniture traders depend, especially for their main and large projects.

2.1.6 M Glory Zanzibar Investment

Dr. Majida Al Azazi established M Glory Zanzibar to invest in different sectors in the Africa region, such as industrial projects, sustainable real estate, and education. In October 2022, it launched the first real estate project in Zanzibar, "The Pearl Island," which introduces Africa's first sustainable and smart city on Mtangani Island, located in Pemba. The project's first phase will include residential villas and two large hotels, with completion scheduled for 2025.

This project will be an eco-friendly, sustainable real estate development that runs on both solar and water-hydrogen energy, as well as using eco-friendly materials during construction.

Moreover, the project will implement a comprehensive recycling system for water and waste management to ensure the preservation of the stunning white sandy beach and crystal-clear waters, ultimately protecting and conserving the environment.

2.2 Ensuring Goal and Value Alignment: M Glory Holding Company's Approach to Divisional Management

M Glory, like any other company, uses a centralized system to control policies for departments such as IT, legal, HR, and finance. This will add value to these subsidiaries while lowering their business costs. Each company has its own goals, but they are part of/inspired by the main goals that M Glory Holding "the parent group" had in mind from the start. It is emphasized that each organization has unique objectives that ensure its continuity, success, and brilliance. It also states that all of its businesses adhere to M Glory's fundamental principles, which include respect for the state's laws and policies, sustainability, resource efficiency, and global aspiration. The government supports and endorses all of these principles.

3 Establishing M Glory Automotive City in Dubai Industrial City: Jabel Ali

M Glory Holding has announced plans to invest Dh1.5 billion in Dubai Industrial City to build a 1 million square foot industrial city, including an assembly and production facility for electric vehicles (EVs) (Nair, 2022; Fig. 3). The plant is anticipated to produce 55,000 EVs yearly, aiming to satisfy the rising demand for environmentally friendly transportation while decreasing global carbon emissions (Dubai Industrial City, 2022).

M Glory intends to build this city using fourth industrial revolution and sustainability technologies such as robotics engineering, artificial intelligence, the Internet of Things, and sustainable raw material and recycling systems. The factory is anticipated to be operational by 2024. The project, which will concentrate on the facility's "transport zone," will be the first EV factory to start building in Industrial City. The new facility will create more than 1000 new jobs, and the manufacturing

M Glory Holding: The Aspiration to Establish an Automobile...

Fig. 3 M Glory Holding lays the groundwork for the UAE's first electric vehicle manufacturing facility. Source: M Glory Holding. Published with the company's permission

process will incorporate cutting-edge Fourth Industrial Revolution technological advances and procedures, such as final assembly lines, welding, dyeing, and robotic systems (Dubai Industrial City, 2022; Vaz, 2022). The manufactured EVs will be exported to a number of GCC and MENA countries.

The opening of M Glory's electric car manufacturing facility is a significant step in promoting the UAE's national strategy, as well as supporting economic diversification. The factory has the potential to significantly contribute to the country's sustainability objectives by implementing cutting-edge technical solutions such as robotics engineering and artificial intelligence, which will be used to create environmentally friendly EVs, reducing carbon emissions and paving the way for a better future (Sadaqat, 2022).

4 Lessons from Dr. Alazazi's Success for Businesswomen and Entrepreneurs in the UAE

Entrepreneurship may seem like an effortless feat to some women, with the belief that anyone can simply innovate and expand with ease. However, it is important to explain that the path toward owning a successful business is not only exciting for its enthusiasts, but it also comes with its challenges and risks and requires significant effort to achieve.

Therefore, having capital or passion alone is not sufficient for success in business. One must first equip themselves with a variety of skills that will aid them in this endeavor. Successful businesswomen can offer valuable leadership lessons that can be learned from their experiences and can benefit new entrepreneurs. In addition, here are some additional leadership lessons that Dr. Majida has learned and applied throughout her journey as a successful businesswoman:

- *Persistence:* Personal businesses require significant effort, and it is important to understand that challenges and setbacks are a common part of the entrepreneurial journey. A determined mindset is needed to push through hardships and stay focused on long-term goals.
- *Vision:* A clear vision of what you wish to accomplish must be established early on and effectively communicated to your team, partners, and customers.
- *Empathy:* An understanding of the significance of empathy is critical in building strong relationships with team members, partners, and customers, as it allows you to comprehend and share the feelings of others, earn their trust and loyalty.
- *Continuous Learning:* Recognizing the significance of continuous learning is paramount in building your knowledge. Keep yourself up-to-date with the latest industry trends, technologies, and best practices.
- *Risk-Taking:* Fearlessly taking calculated risks is critical to achieving success in business.
- *Delegation:* Understanding the importance of delegation is key; delegating tasks to team members based on their strengths and expertise can help achieve goals more effectively.
- *Resilience:* A successful businesswoman must develop resilience, including the ability to rebound from failures and setbacks, learn from mistakes, and leverage knowledge for future decisions.
- *Focus:* Prioritizing time, energy, and resources on significant tasks and activities is essential, as is understanding that focusing on core strengths and values can have the most prominent impact.
- *Communication:* Acting as an excellent communicator is important; being able to articulate a clear and succinct vision, goals, and objectives, while also actively listening to ideas and feedback from others.
- *Collaboration:* Understanding the value of collaboration and being able to work effectively with others to achieve shared goals is crucial. A culture of cooperation and mutual respect must be fostered.
- *Adaptability:* An individual must be adaptable and capable of swift pivoting when circumstances change. They should be open to new ideas and willing to adjust to stay competitive.
- *Integrity:* Leading with integrity in the face of difficult circumstances is a key feature of a successful businesswoman. They must conduct themselves ethically and with principle, even when it is demanding.

5 Summary

Dr. Majida's journey in car manufacturing and her contributions to the UAE economy provide valuable insights into the role of Emirati women in the country's economic development. Her success highlights the opportunities available for women entrepreneurs in the UAE and the government's efforts to promote gender equality and support women's entrepreneurship (Alkaabi et al., 2023). Dr. Majida's success in the automotive industry is an inspiration to Emirati women entrepreneurs, demonstrating that with hard work, dedication, education, and support from the government, they can achieve success and make significant contributions to the country's economic growth. Moreover, Dr. Majida's efforts to promote environmentally sustainable practices in the automotive industry highlight the importance of sustainability in the automobile sector.

6 Question for Discussion

1. What lessons can other aspiring businesswomen and entrepreneurs learn from Dr. Alazazi's success story and leadership journey in the UAE?
2. What are the main subsidiaries of M Glory Holding Company, and in which industries do they operate?
3. How does the establishment of M Glory's EV factory align with the UAE's national net-zero strategy?
4. What are the potential benefits of EM cars, and which markets are they suitable for?

References

Al Damani Motor Vehicles Manufacturing L.L.C. (n.d.). *About us*. Retrieved from https://aldamani-auto.com/

Al Qudra International Companies Representation L.L.C. (n.d.). *Company profile*. Retrieved from https://uploads-ssl.webflow.com/6332c0748128582f18f996e4/6358fd21689ec1887ee8458b_Company-Profile_compressed.pdf

Alkaabi, K., Ramadani, V. & Zeqiri, J. (2023). Universities, entrepreneurial ecosystem, and family business performance: Evidence from The United Arab Emirates. *Journal of Knowledge Economy*. https://doi.org/10.1007/s13132-023-01384-9.

Dubai Industrial City. (2022, March 28). *M Glory set to manufacture 55,000 electric cars annually at Dubai industrial city*. [Press Release]. Retrieved from https://dubaiindustrialcity.ae/en/media/press-releases/m-glory-set-to-manufacture-55000-electric-cars-annually-at-dubai-industrial-city

Enterprise Press. (2021, August 10). *Egypt, UAE to set up JV for manufacturing dual-fuel trucks*. Retrieved from https://enterprise.press/stories/2021/08/10/egypt-uae-to-set-up-jv-for-manufacturing-dual-fuel-trucks-50272/

Le Monde Office Furniture. (n.d.). *About us*. Retrieved April 5, 2023, from http://lemondefurniture.com/about-us

M Glory Group. (n.d.). *About M Glory*. Retrieved from https://www.mglorygroup.com/index.html#header13-1

Mikhail, G. (2022, January 3). *Al-Monitor, LLC*. Egypt aims to localize car industry with Emirati support. Al-Monitor. https://www.al-monitor.com/originals/2022/01/egypt-aims-localize-car-industry-emirati-support

Mubasher.Info. (2021, August 10). *Egypt, UAE's M. Glory partner to produce bi-fuel pickup vehicles*. Retrieved from https://english.mubasher.info/news/3839845/Egypt-UAE-s-M-Glory-partner-to-produce-bi-fuel-pickup-vehicles/

Nair, M. (2022, March 28). M Glory is giving shape to an Emirati electric vehicle at Dubai Industrial City. *Gulf News*. Retrieved from https://gulfnews.com/business/m-glory-is-giving-shape-to-an-emirati-electric-vehicle-at-dubai-industrial-city-1.86792486

Sadaqat, R. (2022, March 28). Dubai welcomes first-ever electric vehicle manufacturing facility. *Khaleej Times*. Retrieved from https://www.khaleejtimes.com/auto/dubai-welcomes-first-ever-electric-vehicle-manufacturing-facility

Sandstorm Automotive. (n.d.). *About us*. Sandstorm automotive. https://sandstorm-auto.com/about.html

Vaz, K. (2022, March 28). M-glory set to manufacture 55,000 electric cars annually at Dubai Industrial City. *Logistics Gulf News*. Retrieved from https://www.logisticsgulfnews.com/free-zones/m-glory-set-to-manufacture-55000-electric-cars-annually-at-dubai-industrial-city/

Khaula Alkaabi is a Professor in the Geography and Urban Sustainability Department at UAEU. She holds a BA degree from UAEU; an MA and a PhD in Geography from UNCG, USA; and a Public Sector Innovation Diploma from the University of Cambridge, UK. Her research interests include transportation, land use planning, spatial analysis and geostatistics, GIS, drone applications, economic geography, smart cities, entrepreneurship, and innovation. She was the Chair of the Geography Department from 2013 to 2017, and the Chief Innovation Officer for UAEU from 2015 to 2022. She has published several academic articles in scientific international journals like the *Journal of Transport Geography*, *Frontiers*, *Journal of Enterprising Communities*, *Geomatics Natural Hazards and Risk*, *Journal of Cleaner Production*, and *Transportation Research Part F*. She has published several book chapters with Ashgate, Routledge, and Springer. She has received several research grants and rewards, including UAEU's "University Excellence Award for Service Excellence" in 2022, "Outstanding Leadership Awards in Education" in 2022, "Feminine Monitoring for Sustainable Environment Award" in 2019, and the "Best Academic Research at Sustainable Transport Competition" by RTA in 2018.

Majida Alazazi has a practical Doctorate in Business Administration (DBA) in Supply Chain Management and Manufacturing in 2018 and a Master of Business Administration (MBA) in 2011 from UAE University. She founded several companies, such as the Office Touch Furniture Factory (2009), Sandstorm Motor Vehicles Manufacturing LLC (2019), Sandwaves Electric Vehicles Manufacturing (2018), M Glory Holding Group (2020), and AL Damani Motor Vehicles Manufacturing LLC (2021). She is the first woman in the MENA region to establish and run automobile factories. Among the pioneers of sustainable business transformation in the UAE is her, as she transformed her business early on.

Printed in the United States
by Baker & Taylor Publisher Services